GERMANY AND THE CAUSES OF THE FIRST WORLD WAR

MARK HEWITSON

Oxford ● New York

First published in 2004 by
Berg
Editorial offices:
1st Floor, Angel Court, 81 St Clements Street, Oxford, OX4 1AW, UK
175 Fifth Avenue, New York, NY 10010, USA

Berg is the imprint of Oxford International Publishers Ltd.

Library of Congress Cataloging-in-Publication Data

A catalogue record for this book is available from the Library of Congress.

British Library Cataloguing-in-Publication Data

A catalogue record for this book is available from the British Library.

ISBN 1 85973 865 6 (Cloth)
1 85973 870 2 (Paper)

Typeset by JS Typesetting Ltd, Wellingborough, Northants.
Printed in the United Kingdom by Biddles Ltd, King's Lynn.

www.bergpublishers.com

To Cécile

Contents

Acknowledgements

In a certain sense, I have been researching and writing this book for the last twenty years, usually with little success or obvious aptitude. As a result, I have acquired a considerable number of debts, from the completion of my first (and unremittingly appalling) essay on the subject to more recent (and perhaps just as ineffectual) published articles. In particular, I would like to thank Neal Rigby, the teacher who first awakened my interest in the topic, and Hartmut Pogge von Strandmann, the supervisor to whom I owe several (although, I am sure he would want to make clear, not all) of the ideas in this volume. I have also been lucky to have had the opportunity to teach many of the themes of the book to students at the University of Exeter and to discuss them at seminars and lectures at the Institute of Historical Research and at the German Historical Institute, London. On different occasions, my colleagues at University College London have been the hapless victims of various ramblings, as have Eckard Michels, who kindly provided advice and information, and Annika Mombauer, who very generously read the manuscript in its entirety. Most of all, I have to apologize, once again, to my family for another series of postponed weekends and another half-neglected Christmas; and both to apologize to, and to thank, Cécile Laborde for putting up with the same (and much more), and for taking an interest in a piece of work which is in many ways far removed from the focus of her own research. For these (and for countless other) reasons, I have dedicated this book to her.

Mark Hewitson,
London, June 2004.

Introduction: Historiography from Fischer to Förster

To Erich von Falkenhayn, speaking on 4 August 1914, the outbreak of the First World War, in which almost 10 million soldiers were to die, was 'beautiful', 'even if we perish because of it'.[1] Theobald von Bethmann Hollweg later condemned the War Minister's opinion as frivolous and irresponsible.[2] In his view, the impending conflagration was a 'crime' and a potential 'disaster'.[3] In an emotional exchange with the British ambassador, which took place on the same day as Falkenhayn's indiscretion, the Chancellor declared that the war had become 'an unlimited world catastrophe'.[4] He went on to contend that Germany had been forced into taking part in the catastrophe by Britain and Russia.[5] A year earlier, he had argued that 'the odds of a war of the future, in which armies of millions will be led into battle against each other, equipped with the most modern weapons, are now even more difficult to predict than before'.[6] Yet he had also admitted, in words redolent of those of his Minister of War, that 'one thing will remain true: the victor, as long as the world has existed, has always been that nation (*Volk*) alone which has put itself in the position of standing there with its last man when the iron dice of its fate are cast, which has faced up to the enemy with the full force of its national character (*des Volkstums*)'.[7] Like many of his contemporaries, the Reich Chancellor was both excited and sickened by the prospect of war.

This study tries to make sense of such confusing testimony in order to discover what caused the First World War. Surprisingly, despite nearly a century of exhaustive research, carried out by governments, survivors and scholars, the question of the war's causes remains a perplexing mixture of consensus, ignorance and contestation. Even the notion that the conflict could have specific and definable 'causes', or antecedent actions which brought it about, is a matter of dispute. Partly, this is the result of a broader poststructuralist assault on the validity of 'causation'.[8] Mainly, though, it derives from arguments of 'inadvertence', first postulated by David Lloyd George, whose memoirs asserted that 'the nations slithered over the brink into the boiling cauldron of war'.[9] Influenced by such arguments, historians have rightly pointed out that protagonists in the run-up to war habitually concealed or failed to understand their own motives. Moreover, their actions often had unintended consequences, produced by particular sets of circumstances and constraints. For this reason, recent scholarship has concentrated on 'unspoken assumptions' about war, armament, empire, diplomacy, national identity and interest, which help to explain the unpredictable formulation, transmission and reception of policy-makers' decisions.[10] At the same time, scholars have investigated the wider context of decision-making, shifting their attention to other groups of intermediaries beyond the confines of the Court, Chancellery and Foreign Office, or looking beyond national borders altogether in order to connect and compare the actions of statesmen – and the conditions shaping their actions – in different countries. Were Austro-Hungarian, Russian, British or, even, Serbian leaders as culpable as their German counterparts, and to what extent were they trapped within the seemingly inescapable logic of a system of alliances, a rush for colonies or an arms race?[11] The proclivity of much of the general historiography on the war in Europe has been to emphasise the constraining effects of circumstance on individual actors and to mitigate individuals' responsibility for causing a world conflagration. Many leaders are held to have acted 'defensively', feeling that their nation, in the words of one study, was 'in decline' or, at least, 'seriously threatened'.[12]

The case about 'national defence' has been made most forcefully in respect of German foreign policy and military strategy before 1914, not least because the Reich's monarch, government and army have historically been allocated the largest share of 'war guilt'.[13] Gradually, and without the furore of Fritz Fischer's original challenge to German revisionism in the 1960s, this new set of arguments, which uncovers a sense of desperation amongst Wilhelmine warplanners and policy-makers, has come to play an important – perhaps a dominant – part in the recent literature on the outbreak of the First World War.[14] 'That the so-called Fischer controversy, which left both the historical discipline and an interested public gasping for their very breath in the sixties and seventies, is fully defeated, comes as no surprise', writes Gregor Schöllgen in a recent summary of studies of pre-war diplomacy. 'The works of Fritz Fischer', he goes on, 'are known today for what they always were: rich, not very readable contributions to the foreign policy of Imperial Germany.'[15] Schöllgen agrees with historians such as Niall Ferguson, the author of the other main review of 'new literature' during the late 1980s and 1990s, that German leaders acted defensively, knowing that 'their military position was deteriorating' and accepting the need for 'a military "first strike", designed to pre-empt a deterioration in Germany's military position'.[16] He also contends, in support of scholars such as Jost Dülffer, Martin Kröger and Rolf-Harald Wippich, that recurrent international crises after the turn of the century did not necessarily betray bellicose intentions on the part of policy-makers or seem likely to escalate into a full-blown conflict.[17] Lastly, in accordance with the conclusions of authors like Klaus Hildebrand and Konrad Canis, he argues that Bethmann Hollweg 'scarcely' had any alternative to risking conflict in 1914 'because the points of German policy and its conduct of war had been set long beforehand' as a result of external pressures and unavoidable circumstances.[18] This book challenges such premises, giving new substance to Fischer's assertions that German leaders were confident that they could win a continental war, that they pursued an offensive policy – at the risk of such a war – at important junctures during the 1900s and 1910s, and that they chose to enter a world war in July 1914.

The point of this study, however, is not to resurrect Fischer's thesis in its entirety, for some of its fundamental propositions are untenable. Most importantly, the Hamburg historian's argument about the primacy of domestic imperatives (*Primat der Innenpolitik*) in the formulation and conduct of foreign policy has been effectively disproved by scholars such as Geoff Eley and David Kaiser, who have successfully challenged the centrality of 'social imperialism' in Wilhelmine policy-making. Notably, they have denied that a coalition (*Sammlung*) of ministers, industrialists and landowners had supported the construction of the fleet in exchange for higher grain tariffs in the late 1890s and early 1900s; they have demonstrated the rarity of official references to naval and imperial expansion as a means of winning votes and deflecting attention from political stalemate at home; and they have questioned the existence of a deepening internal crisis, which was supposedly of such gravity that it drove Germany's ruling elites to contemplate an 'escape into war', or *Flucht nach vorn*.[19] In most areas of domestic policy, critics of a German *Sonderweg*, or special path, have revised the arguments of

3

Fischer, Hans-Ulrich Wehler and their followers about the power of Junkers within the state, the illusory nature of parliamentary democracy, the weakness of German liberalism, the 'feudalization' of the bourgeoisie (*Bürgertum*), the radicalization of public opinion and the growing strength of revolutionary socialism.[20] Once these suppositions are disputed, the important inferences which Fischer draws from them in the realm of foreign policy appear correspondingly precarious. Thus, his assumption in *War of Illusions* that militarism, social Darwinism and xenophobic nationalism, which he frequently equates with majority opinion, became at once more widespread and more extreme as part of a defensive domestic reaction against the rise of the proletariat and the Social Democratic Party (SPD) is, at the very least, open to question.[21] Likewise, his explicit linkage of the allegedly deteriorating position of the German nobility, middle and lower-middle classes, which seemed to have worsened markedly after the SPD became the single largest party in the Reichstag in January 1912, and an increasingly aggressive and unstable foreign policy in the years between 1911 and 1914 is unconvincing. Lastly, his audacious conjecture that Germany's ruling elites planned a war of aggression, proceeding from the Kaiser's so-called 'War Council' of 8 December 1912 to the orchestration of conflict in July 1914, has subsequently, in the absence of supporting evidence, been abandoned by virtually all historians.[22]

The revision of Fischer's arguments has been carried out by very different historians in a number of separate fields, from those like Schöllgen, who are relatively sympathetic to the predicament of Wilhelmine policy-makers and strategists, to those such as Stig Förster, who denounce them as 'absurd' and 'criminal'.[23] Such scholars certainly do not see themselves as belonging to the same camp. Förster and Annika Mombauer, in particular, are scathing about the aggressiveness of German leaders; Schöllgen and Ferguson are more apologetic. Critically, however, such historians agree that decision-makers before 1914 had become more and more pessimistic about the Reich's prospects in a future war. All are referred to as 'revisionists' throughout the course of this study because they argue – or strongly imply – that such pessimism constituted a significant motive of leaders' actions on the eve of the First World War, altering in the process the thrust of the argument put forward by Fischer and the Hamburg School.[24] In this limited but crucial respect, revisionists concur that policy-makers were acting 'defensively', even if only in the sense of averting a putative future defeat.

Much of such revisionist historians' work has concentrated on four overlapping areas and sets of protagonists. The first, which is explored in Chapter 2, concerns the economics of war and the role played by industrialists, financiers and landowners. The topic, which was first investigated by Fischerites such as Volker Berghahn, has been re-examined by Ferguson, who seeks to give a fiscal explanation of why the peacetime strength of the German and Austro-Hungarian armies lagged behind that of France and Russia by 928,000 men in 1914.[25] The Reich had, after all, seen its exports grow faster than those of all its rivals and its population, GNP and steel production increase more rapidly than those of Britain and France, as Ferguson himself points out.[26] What was more, there was 'no shortage of "militarist" sentiment' amongst significant sections of the public, which would have supported a policy of army increases. 'Yet', Ferguson continues, 'the correct measure of military capability is not the rate of economic growth or the degree of popular bellicosity, but the proportion of national product spent on defence in peacetime'.[27] In these terms, the Reich's capability – at 3.5 per cent of GNP spent on the military in 1913 – though slightly greater than that of Britain (3.1 per cent) and Austria–Hungary (2.8 per cent), was less than that of France (3.9 per cent) and Russia (4.6 per cent), even after Erich Ludendorff had begun, in 1912, to push for universal conscription, thus increasing the call-up rate from the existing level of 52 per cent to the French level of 82 per cent.

The reasons were twofold: on the one hand, there was the constraint imposed by the federal basis of the taxation system, which allowed the separate states to control the more lucrative direct levies such as income tax and left the Reich dependent on old consumption taxes and import duties for 90 per cent of its revenues; on the other hand, there was the power exercised by the Reichstag over increases in military spending, with the Centre Party and – especially after its electoral gains in 1912 – the SPD objecting 'to the regressive way taxes were used to finance militarism'.[28] The upshot, according to Ferguson, was that Germany continued to spend less on the military after 1913 than was necessary to keep up with its rivals. Thus, Ludendorff's call in his 'Great Memorandum' of 1912 for 300,000 men, which would have raised German direct taxes to the level of those in Britain and German defence spending as a percentage of GNP to the level of that of Russia, was reduced to 117,000 men, at a cost of 1.9 billion marks over five years instead of the earlier projection of 4.9 billion marks.[29] These figures, and an assessment of their implications, were passed on by industrialists, financiers and officials to the Reich's leaders, Ferguson implies, causing Helmuth von Moltke, the Chief of the General Staff, to lament that the 'enemy is arming more strongly than we are, because money is more tight with us'.[30] It was this sense of financial desperation that led German leaders to contemplate a 'first strike'. 'The paradoxical conclusion', Ferguson writes, 'is that higher German military spending before July 1914 – in other words, a more militaristic Germany – far from causing the First World War, might have averted it.'[31]

The effects of underspending on the military allegedly created frustration and fear amongst Germany's political parties and public opinion, as the Reich failed to acquire territories and consolidate its position abroad. The supposed political ramifications of such fear and frustration – a second area of 'revision' examined by historians such as Stig Förster and Wolfgang Mommsen – are assessed in Chapter 4. To what extent did radicalism amongst Wilhelmine parties and in large parts of the German public constitute one of the principal determinants of government policy?[32] 'In the years immediately before the First World War', asserts Mommsen, 'the German government's relationship with public opinion was reactive rather than active.'[33] Government, particularly under Bülow, had attempted to control the press and orchestrate the nationalist and imperialist sentiments of middle-class and aristocratic sections of society, but it had subsequently become trapped by them. In the opinion of David Kaiser, leaders – particularly Bethmann, who came from the Reich Office of the Interior – were eventually influenced themselves by the assumptions of popular press campaigns.[34] Mommsen, too, especially in his analysis of perceptions of a 'Russian threat' and the 'inevitability' of a European war, shows how official and popular attitudes became interwoven during the decade before the First World War, as newspapers and political parties began to examine and criticize government foreign policy much more extensively.[35] More importantly, from Mommsen's point of view, there was a 'bidding-up' of foreign policy goals, which the government was unable to resist, partly because it 'could not yet point to any positive achievements in foreign affairs'.[36] Bethmann and his Secretary of State at the Foreign Office, Gottlieb von Jagow, 'were well aware that the sort of foreign policy that would have assuaged the febrile demands of large sections of the middle classes – and, now, of Conservatives too – was not a practicable option in the current international situation; but they felt unable to offer an alternative', concludes Mommsen.

'The government was gradually pushed into abandoning the more moderate form of imperialism that would at least have remained compatible with the constraints imposed by the international system.'[37] Thus, even though 'the gulf between public expectations and the real world grew wider by the day', Bethmann's government proved both unwilling and unable – partly because of its weak position within a flawed system of government – to limit the aims and moderate the conduct of foreign policy.[38] In 1914, with the Russian threat 'beginning to be accepted as a reality by the German public as well as by senior government figures and the General Staff', it was 'not surprising' that the Reich government 'decided (contrary to its own real convictions) to make what Bethmann Hollweg himself admitted was tantamount to a "leap in the dark"'.[39] In short, the German government, it is held, was pushed into a policy of 'calculated risk' and, ultimately, war: their psychological state was, to use Konrad Jarausch's formulation, 'defensive', even if the means that they adopted were 'offensive'.[40]

The military – the third object of 'revisionist' scrutiny and the subject of Chapter 6 – did not require popular nationalism to push them towards a policy of 'risk'. Rather, the argument runs, they were motivated by an explosive mixture of bellicosity and an awareness of the Reich's relative military decline. As a result, they wished to act immediately, before it was too late to go to war at all. Even then, Alfred von Schlieffen and Moltke were far from certain that they could win: the latter 'stuck to his predecessor's grand design and did not dare to abandon the Schlieffen plan in spite of its obvious shortcomings', contends Förster. 'Instead, he tried to convince himself and others that there was no alternative to at least trying to go for a rapid campaign against France against all odds.'[41] Annika Mombauer, although she emphasizes the independence of Moltke with respect to the legacy of Schlieffen, agrees with Förster that 'German decision-makers consciously risked war in 1914, in order to improve the country's deteriorating position vis-à-vis her European neighbours. Some of the military went even further in their bellicose designs, and wanted "war for war's sake".' Yet such warmongering was often intermingled with anxiety about the Reich's military position over the medium and longer term, she continues: 'In the not-too-distant future, Germany would no longer be able to wage a war against her neighbours with any real chance of success, their argument ran.'[42] Moltke retained the fundamental premises of Schlieffen's strategy, 'going for broke' in Förster's phrase, because he could not afford to give up the 'cult of the offensive', the illusion of a short war and the idea that war could be used as an instrument of policy-making.

At home, the continuing opposition of conservative militarists to universal conscription, on the grounds that it would alter the social composition of the ranks and officer corps and undermine obedience, meant that the Reich could not keep up with the military increases of its opponents: the Chief of the General Staff 'had failed to press through his demands for a full implementation of conscription, and there was little hope that he would succeed in future'.[43] At the same time, both Moltke and Schlieffen were allegedly convinced that 'there was no alternative to a short, decisive campaign', since they recognised that 'a war could become protracted, ruin the economy, undermine the social and political system, and perhaps lead to revolution'.[44] Abroad, it is held, there seemed to be no alternative to an offensive military strategy, given that the attacker was deemed to have the advantage and that Germany's geographical position was an exposed one. The *Kaiserreich* was, in any event, perceived to be losing the arms race with its neighbours and had to maintain an offensive plan in order to be able to attack sooner rather than later. 'At some point, perhaps in two to three years, the German army would simply no longer be strong enough even to try to put the Schlieffen plan into practice,' writes Förster. 'From then on a defensive war of attrition would be the only option left, entailing certain defeat. Hence, Moltke was determined to go for broke, as long as there was a glimmer of hope.'[45] The need to keep open the possibility of going to war was purportedly necessary for the foreign policy of the Reich and for the very *raison d'être* of the German officer corps: 'The "demigods" inside the General Staff simply could not afford to accept [the Elder] Moltke's verdict that war had ceased to be a viable option.'[46] According to Förster and Mombauer, therefore, the more desperate the General Staff became, the more it pushed for war.

The policies of Germany's civilian government – the fourth topic of 'revision', examined in Chapter 8 – were supposedly based, in part, on pessimistic military estimates. They were also affected, according to diplomatic historians such as Schöllgen, by officials' awareness of 'the exposed geostrategic position of the Reich'.[47] In this account, Germany is depicted as a 'nation-state against history and geography', threatened by a large number of powerful neighbours, which had, in the past, encouraged the fragmentation of the German lands as a buffer zone at the centre of the European pentarchy.[48] According to Andreas Hillgruber, 'because of her position in

Central Europe, rendered increasingly unfavourable by the development of military technology,' the *Kaiserreich* was perhaps best suited to a role of junior partner. 'At that time, however, such an insight would have required an uncommon amount of political acumen and self-restraint, both of which directly contradicted the spirit of the imperialist epoch in general and the Wilhelmine period in Germany in particular.'[49] Thus, although Wilhelmine Germans were especially unlikely to accept – rather than attempting to overcome – such geographical constraints, all contemporary European leaders would probably have acted in a similar way.

The main corollary of these attempts to overcome geography was 'encirclement' (*Einkreisung*), which historians like Hillgruber – notwithstanding their acknowledgement of 'the crude, overbearing style' of German policy – tend to depict as an almost inescapable fact, not the transient product of particular leaders' and journalists' imaginations.[50] In his earlier work, Klaus Hildebrand shows how much significance was given to the notion of *Einkreisung*, which first appeared in the wake of the Anglo-Russian Entente of 1907 and which was preceded by the emergence of a *de facto* 'ring' around the Reich during the first Moroccan crisis in 1905–6. Bülow was too 'superficially' optimistic to think of war as a means of escaping such isolation, but Bethmann, with 'pessimistic conscientiousness', was prepared to countenance 'breaking the circle diplomatically and, in the event of the failure of this strategy, [to take] the risk of war consciously into account'. The need to overcome this exclusion (*Auskreisung*), which was experienced as encirclement (*Einkreisung*), was 'central' to German foreign policy between 1909 and 1914.[51] Although Schöllgen and others are wary of calling such actions 'defensive', in a self-conscious attempt to distance themselves from Gerhard Ritter and German revisionists of the interwar period, they nevertheless eschew the notion of a 'war of aggression' and emphasize the justified anxieties of Wilhelmine policy-makers.[52] Even in his judicious later work, Hildebrand continues to maintain that Bethmann acted 'out of fear' in July 1914.[53] Hillgruber is much more sweeping: 'At stake now [in the period after 1905] was the preservation of the position won in 1866 and 1870–1871, Germany's status as a Great Power, which was, of course, the mainstay of German industry's international role.'[54] From a geopolitical starting point, then, it proved possible for the government to argue that the very foundations of the German nation-state had been threatened in the decade before the First World War.

The four main sets of protagonists – industrialists, financiers and landowners (Chapter 2), parties, press and public (Chapter 4), army and navy (Chapter 6), and the civilian government (Chapter 8) – were all, of course, swayed by a wide variety of arguments and constrained by a significant number of assumptions, in addition to those discussed above. Chapters 3, 5 and 7 examine the most important of these: namely, the extent and impact of nationalist and xenophobic ideas; the incidence of militarism and evaluations of future wars; and the conception of diplomatic relations between states in an age of imperialism and continental alliances. These thematic chapters assess further elements of the revisionist case about 'national defence'. Thus, Chapter 3 reconsiders the work of a large number of historians who have investigated the emergence of radical nationalism and the reshaping of the German right, following the pioneering studies of Geoff Eley and Roger Chickering.[55] Such scholars, in seeking to modify Hans-Ulrich Wehler's assumptions about the relationship between socialization and politics, have usually defined the social constituencies of popular nationalist and right-wing organizations like the Navy and Army Leagues.[56] Their main findings, although pointing to the circumvention of notables and conservative institutions, have done much to establish the idea that a large part of the German public had become infused with nationalist attitudes and assumptions, leading them to call more and more stridently for intervention and expansion abroad. Förster and Mommsen have elucidated the consequences of the alleged radicalization of public opinion for the conduct of Wilhelmine foreign policy and the formulation of military strategy. Their conclusions, from different starting points, identify the rise of independent, popular militarism and nationalism during the later 1900s and early 1910s, which 'took on such proportions', in Förster's view, 'that it seems well-grounded to imagine that the Reichstag would not even have placed obstructions in the way of the complete realization of general conscription'.[57] 'This steadily accelerating process of radicalization', contends Mommsen, has since the Fischer controversy been a focus of historians' attention, but it is now clear 'that the new nationalism cannot be seen merely as the product of a manipulative strategy on the part of the Wilhelmine governing elites, in the sweeping sense in which Wehler, Stegmann, Puhle and others have sometimes been tempted to argue the case'. Rather, he goes on, 'it was the relative powerlessness of the traditional elites, and not any masterful manipulation of public opinion, that led to the escalation in popularity of imperialist sentiment'.[58] The most significant sections of nationalist opinion, it is held, were starting to interfere in military and diplomatic debates – which they had previously accepted as the exclusive preserve of the state – and they were increasingly calling for the aggressive pursuit of German interests in Europe and overseas.

Chapter 5 extends such analysis by investigating popular militarism and expectations of war against the backdrop of a European arms race, which began with naval expansion in the late 1890s and switched during the early 1910s to army increases. In the opinion of David Stevenson, one of the principal exponents of this line of argument, 'the international crises of the pre-war decade, long emphasized in diplomatic accounts of the war, were the essential destabilizing factor. They came unpredictably, in quick succession, and were thought to show the need for permanently higher levels of preparedness.'[59] Competitive armament then took on a momentum of its own, the argument runs, becoming 'a cause as well as a consequence of international tension', not least by permeating a broader public sphere: 'once in motion the spiral intensified public anxiety and instilled both resignation and enthusiasm in the face of impending conflict'.[60] To both Stevenson and David Herrmann, this 'militarization of society and . . . militarization of diplomacy' in themselves destabilized the conduct of foreign policy by creating 'a new attitude to the use of military force in Europe'.[61] Commentators, writes Herrmann, 'routinely compared the strength of armies in public, statesmen explicitly directed military spending bills against the armaments of specific foreign powers, and public movements in favour of military preparedness gained importance'.[62] Unlike nationalism, social Darwinism, alliance systems, offensive military strategies and domestic weaknesses, all of which 'had been constantly present on the European scene for some time by 1914', only the militarization of foreign policy as the result of an arms race was new.[63] In itself, however, it does not explain the transition from international crisis to actual conflict in July 1914. The factor which distinguished the outbreak of war from earlier tension, claims Stevenson, was the fleeting convergence of the two armed blocs, with both sides confident 'that they could win', but within a limited 'window' of opportunity, in Stephen Van Evera's phrase, since 'the balance was unstable, a temporary equivalence between rising and declining elements'.[64] German leaders, realizing that their own bloc was in decline, were pushed into giving to Austria–Hungary a blank cheque, without which it would not have gone to war with Serbia,

Stevenson maintains.[65] Even though Berlin had 'embarked upon an extraordinarily dangerous course', his interpretation emphasizes, like that of Schöllgen, Hillgruber and Hildebrand, 'the opportunist and defensive character of German policy'.[66]

Finally, Chapter 7 explores the precise implications of the arms race, militarism and nationalism on conceptions of diplomatic relations. Here, revisionists have underlined the perceived precariousness of Germany's continental position as a result of imperialism, which is alleged to have created further confusion in the formulation of foreign policy and to have aggravated an already existing and widespread sense of doom. The underlying assumption of this case, articulated by Schöllgen, is that 'Germany felt virtually compelled to take part in the scramble for overseas territories.' According to such a theory, he contends, 'Great Power status *within* Europe could only be maintained by activity and self-assertion *outside* Europe . . . In Berlin, especially after 1890, there was little doubt that a Great Power *had to act* as a world power.' Furthermore, such convictions extended well beyond government to all sections of Wilhelmine society: 'From the 1890s onwards most Germans – whether Conservative, liberal or Social Democratic in allegiance – were convinced that a Great Power such as Germany must also pursue Great Power politics and that, in the age of imperialism, meant *world*-power politics.'[67] The perceived inevitability and later frustration of the Reich's colonial ambitions make it easier to understand Schöllgen's belief that the 'points' of German foreign policy had been set long before the outbreak of the First World War. Consequently, attention shifts, as in Canis's work, to the role of Britain, which – as Paul Schroeder pointed out in the 1970s – is held to be primarily responsible for causing 'movement' within the states system, directing a new constellation of powers against Germany.[68] With the thwarting of German *Weltpolitik*, the defeat of Russia in the Far East and the virtual completion of the division of the rest of the world between the other powers, the focus of foreign policy moved back to Europe. 'The result', according to Schöllgen, 'was a series of grave international crises', as Russia again 'targeted this part of the world'.[69] From this point of view, the outbreak of the First World War can be related to a 'vicious circle' in which the *Kaiserreich* found itself from the 1890s onwards: as it attempted to achieve world-power status overseas and in the Near East, it further undermined its position within the European states system, as the other powers became more and more anxious. The implication is that Germany's aims were not offensive, but rather the product of an almost ineluctable dilemma. 'To a certain extent', Schöllgen concludes, 'the First World War was, among other things, an inevitable consequence of this development.'[70]

This study challenges such controversial revisionist claims. It postulates that there was considerable confidence in many areas of industry and finance about the economic fortunes of the Reich, creating opposition to unpredictable and debilitating conflicts (Chapter 2); there were limits to popular nationalism in the centre and on the left of the Wilhelmine political spectrum, which constituted an increasingly significant obstacle to certain kinds of war, such as a campaign against France, or a European war for the sake of gaining territory overseas (Chapter 4); there was less pessimism in the army and navy than revisionists claim, since the idea of a protracted, two-front war against superior numbers of troops went back to the 1890s and beyond, and it did not rule out the possibility of quick and decisive campaigns against France and Britain in the West (Chapter 6); and there was little doubt in government circles about Germany's military superiority on the European mainland, which allowed the threat of armed force on the Continent to become the cornerstone of German *Weltpolitik* (Chapter 8). Although they are founded on widespread assumptions of military and economic superiority, none of these propositions coincide with those put forward by Fischer and his followers. Thus, the fact that the army and the government pushed for war before 1914, even though significant sections of public opinion opposed the idea, was less the result of desperation at home and the desire for 'an escape into war' – or the slightly different idea of a *Flucht nach vorn* – than the consequence of a belief in the ascendancy of the German nation-state (Chapter 3), in the validity of war as an instrument of policy (Chapter 5), and in the decisiveness of power politics – not law – in international relations (Chapter 7). The thesis of the present study is that the main impediment to war was effectively removed when Russia became Germany's principal enemy during the winter of 1913, in place of France. Because tsarist autocracy and 'Slav' barbarity were traditional bugbears of left liberals, socialists and democratic Catholics, the Reich government was able to undercut public opposition to war by casting Russia as the aggressor in July 1914. This did not mean that German leaders planned war, but rather that they continued a policy of brinkmanship which had been framed against a supposedly weaker French state during the previous decade. The gravamen of such a case is incompatible with the findings of the majority of revisionist historians, which refer to the defensive nature of German foreign policy and military strategy in the years before 1914.

Notes

1. E. v. Falkenhayn, 4 August 1914, cited in H. Afflerbach, *Falkenhayn: Politisches Denken und Handeln im Kaiserreich*, 2nd edn (Munich, 1996), p. 170.
2. Ibid.
3. Bethmann, 4 August 1914, cited in K.H. Jarausch, 'The Illusion of Limited War: Chancellor Bethmann Hollweg's Calculated Risk, July 1914', *Central European History*, 2 (1969), p. 72.
4. Ibid.
5. Ibid., pp. 72–6.
6. Bethmann, 7 April 1913, cited in J. Dülffer, *Im Zeichen der Gewalt. Frieden und Krieg im 19. und 20. Jahrhundert* (Cologne, 2003), p. 139.
7. Ibid.
8. See, for example, D. LaCapra, *History and Criticism* (Ithaca, NY, 1985), and H. White, *The Content of the Form* (Baltimore, 1987).
9. D. Lloyd George, cited in the Introduction of R.F. Hamilton and H.H. Herwig (eds), *The Origins of World War I* (Cambridge, 2003), p. 38.
10. This literature on militarism, imperialism, social Darwinism, and nationalism for each country and for Europe as a whole is vast. The most influential work is J. Joll, '1914: The Unspoken Assumptions', in H.W. Koch (ed.), *The Origins of the First World War: Great Power Rivalry and German War Aims* (London, 1972), pp. 307–28.
11. On Austria–Hungary, see especially S.R. Williamson, *Austria–Hungary and the Origins of the First World War* (London, 1991); S.R. Williamson, 'Vienna and July 1914: The Origins of the Great War Once More', in S.R. Williamson and P. Pastor (eds), *Essays on World War I: Origins and Prisoners of War* (New York, 1983), pp. 8–36; J. Leslie, 'The Antecedents of Austria–Hungary's War Aims: Policies and Policy-Making in Vienna and Budapest before and during 1914', *Wiener Beiträge zur Geschichte der Neuzeit*, 20 (1993), pp. 307–94; F. Kiessling, 'Österreich-Ungarn und die deutsch-englischen Détentebemühungen 1912–1914', *Historisches Jahrbuch*, 116 (1996), pp. 102–25; G. Kronenbitter, 'Bundesgenossen? Zur militärpolitischen Kooperation zwischen Berlin und Wien 1912 bis 1914', in W.L. Bernecker and V. Dotterweich (eds), *Deutschland in den internationalen Beziehungen des 19. und 20. Jahrhunderts* (Munich, 1996), pp.

519–50; G. Kronenbitter, 'Falsch Verbunden? Die Militärallianz zwischen Österreich-Ungarn und Deutschland, 1906–1914', *Österreichische Militärische Zeitschrift*, 38 (2000), pp. 743–54; G. Kronenbitter, '"Nur los lassen": Österreich-Ungarn und der Wille zum Krieg', in J. Burkhardt et al. (eds), *Lange und kurze Wege in den Ersten Weltkrieg* (Munich, 1996), pp. 159–87. On Russia, see D. Geyer, *Russian Imperialism: The Interaction of Domestic and Foreign Policy, 1869–1914* (New Haven, 1987); P.W. Gatrell, *Government, Industry and Rearmament in Russia, 1900–1914* (Cambridge, 1994); W.C. Wohlforth, 'The Perception of Power: Russia in the Pre-1914 Balance', *World Politics*, 39 (1987), pp. 353–81; B. Jelavich, *Russia's Balkan Entanglements, 1806–1914* (Cambridge, 1991); D. MacLaren, *United Government and Foreign Policy in Russia, 1900–1914* (Cambridge, Mass., 1992); C.J. Cimbala, 'Steering through Rapids: Russian Mobilisation and World War I', *Journal of Slavic Military History*, 9 (1996), pp. 376–98. On Britain, see Z. Steiner, *Britain and the Origins of the First World War*, 2nd revised edn (London, 2002); J. Charmley, *Splendid Isolation? Britain and the Balance of Power, 1874–1914* (London, 1999); N. Ferguson, 'The Kaiser's European Union: What if Britain Had Stood Aside in August 1914?', *Virtual History: Alternatives and Counterfactuals* (London, 1997); J.W. Coogan and P.F. Coogan, 'The British Cabinet and the Anglo-French Staff Talks, 1905–1914: Who Knew What and When Did He Know It?', *Journal of British Studies*, 24 (1985), pp. 110–31; K.W. Wilson, *The Policy of the Entente: Essays on the Determinants of British Foreign Policy, 1904–1914* (Cambridge, 1985). On Serbia, see J. Remak, '1914 – The Third Balkan War', in Koch, *Origins of the First World War*, 2nd revised edn (London, 1984), pp. 86–100; M. Cornwall, 'Serbia', in K. Wilson (ed.), *Decisions for War, 1914* (London, 1995), pp. 55–96; R.C. Hall, 'Serbia', in Hamilton and Herwig (eds), *The Origins of World War I*, pp. 92–111.

12. H.H. Herwig, 'Why did it happen?', in Hamilton and Herwig, *The Origins of World War I*, p. 443.

13. A. Mombauer, *The Origins of the First World War: Controversies and Consensus* (London, 2002), p. 2.

14. The Fischer controversy has been so well documented that no reiteration is given here. See J. Langdon, *July 1914: The Long Debate 1918–1990* (Oxford, 1991) and Mombauer, *The Origins of the First World War* for further details.

15. G. Schöllgen, 'Kriegsgefahr und Krisenmanagement vor 1914: Zur Aussenpolitik des Kaiserlichen Deutschlands', *Historische Zeitschrift*, 267 (1998), pp. 399–400.

16. N. Ferguson, 'Germany and the Origins of the First World War: New Perspectives', *Historical Journal*, 35 (1992), p. 734.

17. Schöllgen, 'Kriegsgefahr und Krisenmanagement vor 1914', pp. 403, 413; J. Dülffer, M. Kröger, R.-H. Wippich (eds), *Vermiedene Kriege: Deeskalation von Konflikten der Grossmächte zwischen Krimkrieg und Erstem Weltkrieg 1856–1914* (Munich, 1997), p. 14.

18. K. Hildebrand, *Das vergangene Reich: Deutsche Aussenpolitik von Bismarck bis Hitler 1871–1945* (Stuttgart, 1995), p. 313; K. Canis, *Von Bismarck zur Weltpolitik: Deutsche Aussenpolitik 1890 bis 1902* (Berlin, 1997), p. 396.

19. See, especially, G. Eley, '*Sammlungspolitik*, Social Imperialism and the Navy Law of 1898', 'Social Imperialism in Germany: Reformist Synthesis or Reactionary Sleight of Hand', *From Unification to Nazism: Reinterpreting the German Past* (London, 1986); G. Eley, 'Defining Social Imperialism: Use and Abuse of an Idea', *Social History*, 3 (1976), pp. 265–90; G. Eley, 'Die Kehrites und das Kaiserreich', *Geschichte und Gesellschaft*, 4 (1978), pp. 91–107; D.E. Kaiser, 'Germany and the Origins of the First World War', *Journal of Modern History*, 55 (1983), pp. 442–74.

20. Classic statements of such 'revisionism' can be found in G. Eley and D. Blackbourn, *The Peculiarities of German History* (Oxford, 1984) and R.J. Evans, *Rethinking German History* (London, 1987).

21. Fritz Fischer's *War of Illusions* (London, 1975) was first published in German in 1969. It built on a more cautious statement of his thesis in the first section of *Germany's Aims in the First World War* (London, 1967), published in Germany in 1961 as *Griff nach der Weltmacht*.

22. One exception is J.C.G. Röhl, 'Germany', in Wilson, *Decisions for War*, pp. 27–54.

23. S. Förster, 'Im Reich des Absurden: Die Ursachen des Ersten Welt-krieges', in B. Wegner (ed.), *Wie Kriege entstehen. Zum historischen Hinter-grund von Staatenkonflikten* (Paderborn, 2000), pp. 211–52; S. Förster, 'Der deutsche Generalstab und die Illusion des kurzen Krieges, 1871–1914: Metakritik eines Mythos', *Militärgeschichtliche Mitteilungen*, 54 (1995), pp. 61–98; Schöllgen, 'Kriegsgefahr und Krisenmanagement vor 1914', pp. 399–413.

24. The use of the label 'revisionist' is not intended to imply any connection with the revisionism of the interwar and immediate postwar periods. Rather, it is a convenient shorthand to describe a critical alteration of the Hamburg school case, akin perhaps to the use of the label in respect of historians of Wilhelmine domestic policy, denoting criticism of the Hamburg and Bielefeld school orthodoxy of the 1970s and early 1980s. Interestingly, revisionism here, too, has been carried out by scholars of very different political leanings.

25. N. Ferguson, *The Pity of War* (London, 1998), p. 91.

26. N. Ferguson, 'Public Finance and National Security: The Domestic Origins of the First World War Revisited', *Past and Present*, 142 (1994), p. 148.

27. Ibid.

28. Ibid., pp. 149, 155–9.

29. Ferguson, *The Pity of War*, p. 141.

30. Ferguson, 'Public Finance and National Security', p. 165.

31. Ferguson, *The Pity of War*, p. 142.

Introduction

32. S. Förster, *Der doppelte Militarismus: Die deutsche Heeresrüstungs-politik zwischen Status-quo-Sicherung und Aggression, 1890–1913* (Stuttgart, 1985). For Mommsen, see below.

33. W.J. Mommsen, 'Public Opinion and Foreign Policy in Wilhelmine Germany, 1897–1914', in *Imperial Germany* (London, 1995), p. 202.

34. D. Kaiser, 'Germany and the Origins of the First World War', *Journal of Modern History*, 55 (1983), pp. 442–74.

35. See, especially, W.J. Mommsen, *Grossmachtstellung und Weltpolitik, 1870–1914: Die Aussenpolitik des Deutschen Reiches* (Frankfurt a. M., 1993), pp. 293–321, and W.J. Mommsen, 'The Topos of Inevitable War in Germany in the Decade before 1914', in V.R. Berghahn and M. Kitchen (eds), *Germany in the Age of Total War* (London, 1981), pp. 23–45.

36. W.J. Mommsen, 'The Causes and Objectives of German Imperialism before 1914', in *Imperial Germany*, p. 94.

37. Ibid., p. 99.

38. Ibid., p.98.

39. Mommsen, 'Public Opinion and Foreign Policy', p. 203; Mommsen, 'Causes and Objectives of German Imperialism', p. 99.

40. Jarausch, 'The Illusion of Limited War', p. 75. Also, K.H. Jarausch, *The Enigmatic Chancellor: Bethmann Hollweg and the Hubris of Imperial Germany* (New Haven, 1973).

41. S. Förster, 'Dreams and Nightmares: German Military Leadership and the Images of Future Warfare, 1871–1914', in M.F. Boemeke, R. Chickering and S. Förster (eds.), *Anticipating Total War: The German and American Experiences, 1871–1914* (Cambridge, 1999), p. 362.

42. A. Mombauer, *Helmuth von Moltke and the Origins of the First World War* (Cambridge, 2001), p. 1. Also, A. Mombauer, 'A Reluctant Military Leader? Helmuth von Moltke and the July Crisis of 1914', *War in History*, 6 (1999), pp. 417–46.

43. Förster, 'Dreams and Nightmares', p. 374. On the extent of conservative militarism, see S. Förster, 'Alter und neuer Militarismus im Kaiserreich: Heeresrüstungspolitik und Dispositionen zum Krieg zwischen Status-quo-Sicherung und imperialistischer Expansion, 1890–1913', in J. Dülffer and K. Holl (eds), *Bereit zum Krieg: Kriegsmentalität im wilhelminischen Deutschland, 1890–1914* (Göttingen, 1986), pp. 122–45.

44. S. Förster, 'The Armed Forces and Military Planning', in R. Chickering (ed.), *Imperial Germany: A Historiographical Companion* (Westport, 1996), p. 468. Also, L. Burchardt, *Friedenswirtschaft und Kriegsvorsorge: Deutschlands wirtschaftliche Rüstungsbestrebungen vor 1914* (Boppard, 1968).

45. Förster, 'Dreams and Nightmares', p. 374.

46. Ibid., p. 360.

47. G. Schöllgen (ed.), *Escape into War? The Foreign Policy of Imperial Germany* (Oxford, 1990), p. 13.

48. M. Stürmer, 'A Nation-State against History and Geography: The German Dilemma', ibid, pp. 63-72; D. Calleo, *The German Problem Reconsidered: Germany and the World Order, 1870 to the Present* (Cambridge, 1978), on the nature of the German dilemma after unification.

49. A. Hillgruber, *Germany and the Two World Wars* (Cambridge, Mass., 1981), pp. 11-12.

50. Ibid., p. 9.

51. K. Hildebrand, *Deutsche Aussenpolitik 1871-1918* (Munich, 1989), pp. 35-6, 41. See also G. Schöllgen, *Das Zeitalter des Imperialismus*, 2nd edn (Munich, 1991), p. 66; M. Rauh, 'Die "Deutsche Frage" vor 1914: Weltmachtstreben und Obrigkeitsstaat?', in J. Becker and A. Hillgruber (eds), *Die Deutsche Frage im 19. und 20. Jahrhundert* (Munich, 1983), pp. 155-6, 160-1, 166.

52. Schöllgen, *Escape into War?*, pp. 3-4; Ferguson, *The Pity of War*, p. xxxviii.

53. Hildebrand, *Das vergangene Reich*, p. 358.

54. Hillgruber, *Germany and the Two World Wars*, p. 18.

55. G. Eley, *Reshaping the German Right: Radical Nationalism and Political Change after Bismarck* (New Haven, 1980); G. Eley, 'Army, State and Civil Society: Revisiting the Problem of German Militarism', in *From Unification to Nazism*, pp. 85-109; R. Chickering, *'We Men Who Feel Most German': A Cultural Study of the Pan-German League, 1886-1914* (London, 1984); R. Chickering, 'Die Alldeutschen erwarten den Krieg', in Dülffer and Holl, *Bereit zum Krieg*, pp. 20-32; M.S. Coetzee, *The German Army League: Popular Nationalism in Wilhelmine Germany* (Oxford, 1990); T. Rohrkrämer, *Der Militarismus der 'kleinen Leute': Die Kriegervereine im Deutschen Kaiserreich, 1871-1914* (Munich, 1990); S. Goltermann, *Körper der Nation: Habitusformierung und die Politik des Turnens, 1860-1890* (Göttingen, 1998); O. Dann, *Nation und Nationalismus in Deutschland, 1770-1990*, 3rd revised edn (Munich, 1996); D. Langewiesche, *Nation, Nationalismus, Nationalstaat in Deutschland und Europa* (Munich, 2000).

56. H.-U. Wehler's, *The German Empire, 1871-1918* (Oxford, 1985), originally published in German in 1973, perhaps did most to define the research agenda of historians in this field.

57. Förster, *Der doppelte Militarismus*, p. 299.

58. Mommsen, 'The Causes and Objectives of German Imperialism before 1914', p. 95.

59. D. Stevenson, *Armaments and the Coming of War: Europe, 1904-1914* (Oxford, 1996), p. 13.

60. Ibid., p. 417.

61. Ibid., p. 414; D.G. Herrmann, *The Arming of Europe and the Making of the First World War* (Princeton, 1996), p. 226.

62. Herrmann, *The Arming of Europe*, p. 226.

63. Ibid., p. 230.

64. Stevenson, *Armaments and the Coming of War*, pp. 417–18; S. Van Evera, 'The Cult of the Offensive and the Origins of the First World War', in S.E. Miller et al. (eds), *Military Strategy and the Origins of the First World War* (Princeton, 1991), pp. 59–108.

65. D. Stevenson, *The Outbreak of the First World War: 1914 in Perspective* (London, 1997), p. 8.

66. Ibid., p. 19.

67. Schöllgen, 'Germany's Foreign Policy in the Age of Imperialism: A Vicious Circle?', in *Escape into War?*, p. 123.

68. Canis, *Von Bismarck zur Weltpolitik*, p. 395; Schöllgen, 'Kriegsgefahr und Krisenmanagement', p. 410; P.W. Schroeder, 'World War I as Galloping Gertie: A Reply to Joachim Remak', in Koch, *The Origins of the First World War*, 2nd edn, pp. 105–17, 125–6.

69. Schöllgen, 'Kriegsgefahr und Krisenmanagement vor 1914', p. 405.

70. Schöllgen, 'Germany's Foreign Policy in the Age of Imperialism', pp. 132–3.

2

The Economics of War: Industrialists, Financiers and Landowners

Fritz Fischer devoted about a third of *War of Illusions*, his main work on the causes of the First World War, to an examination of the relationship between economic interest groups and policy-makers. Although eschewing a Marxist interpretation of the conflict, the Hamburg and Bielefeld schools have subsequently tended to place economics, together with its social and political ramifications, close to the centre of their explanation of the outbreak of war. Foreign policy was largely determined, the general argument runs, by an explosive mixture of rapid industrial growth, resultant social and economic transformations, authoritarian traditions, late unification 'from above', a malfunctioning system of government, and the continuing political power and social status of the nobility, all of which supposedly underpinned the primacy of domestic policy (*Primat der Innenpolitik*). The role of industrialists and landowners is held to have been of critical importance, shoring up the conservative or reactionary policies of the government. Accordingly, Fischer begins *War of Illusions*, in a section investigating the foundations of Wilhelmine Germany, with chapters on the transition 'From the Agrarian to the Industrial State' and on 'The Supremacy of the Junkers and Industry'.

Fischer's case, and that of followers such as Hans-Jürgen Puhle and Dirk Stegmann, turns on the decision of ruling, industrial and agrarian elites to create a defensive domestic alliance (*Sammlung*) against 'the socialist threat'.[1] 'The development of a policy designed to rally big business and large-scale agriculture behind it', writes Hans-Ulrich Wehler, 'was to form the basis of government policy right up until 1918.'[2] The most significant component of the policy was arguably the manipulation of foreign affairs in order to rally working-class voters to the existing social and political order, and to divert the attention of all voters away from domestic conflicts and crisis. Such 'social imperialism' was certainly an aim of policy-makers like Secretary of State at the Navy Office Alfred von Tirpitz and Chancellor Bernhard von Bülow, who thought that it would offer 'a strong palliative against educated and uneducated Social Democrats'.[3] The policy is also held, following the testimony of contemporaries such as the historian Friedrich Meinecke, to have been 'much too narrowly interwoven with particular social and internal political special interests', particularly those of entrepreneurs.[4]

Volker Berghahn has gone as far as to suggest that a 'military–industrial complex' came into existence before 1914, with closer and closer links between large firms and government bodies.[5] 'Besides the familiar enthusiasts, all sorts of influential people here are against any limit on armament', recorded the courtier Robert von Zedlitz-Trütschler. 'The power of the steel kings weighs heavily, and concern about their business and the wish for a good mood on the stock-exchange have already often been served up for us as matters of national concern.'[6] Industrialists, financiers, agrarians and ministers, it is postulated, had begun to collaborate, against the backdrop of a growing 'socialist threat', in the formulation of an expansionist and bellicose foreign policy and, once war had broken out, a radical programme of annexations.[7] Fischer's allegation that industrialists, right-wing publicists, nationalist organizations, the military and the government had cooperated before and after July 1914 to draw up an extensive series of war aims, culminating in Bethmann Hollweg's September Programme, constituted the kernel of his thesis in *Griff nach der Weltmacht*.[8] It was the contention that a reactionary coalition of officials, Junkers and businessmen had led Germany to war for their own aggressive ends which started the 'Fischer controversy' in 1961.

Since the 1980s, historians influenced by Fischer have played down the significance of industrialists and financiers in the making of German foreign policy, pointing out amongst other things that economic self-interest and a shortage of capital predisposed much of big business towards international joint ventures and the avoidance of conflict.[9] Such arguments have been endorsed by Niall Ferguson, who writes that 'there is scarcely any evidence that these interests [in armaments industries] made businessmen want a major European war'.[10] Nevertheless, he goes on, economics remained central to the outbreak of the First World War because of financial weakness, not because of industrial strength: 'By comparing the political economy of German security with that of her principal ally and principal antagonists, I suggest that Germany could and should have spent more on defence before 1914, but that domestic political factors prevented it, and in that sense can be seen as a root cause of the war.'[11] Despite the expansion of the German economy, maintains Ferguson, in opposition to the arguments of Fischerites such as Imanuel Geiss and Paul Kennedy, 'the most important economic factor in early twentieth-century world politics was not the growth of German economic power at all. Rather, it was the immense extent of British *financial* power'.[12] In this respect, as a result of a shortage of capital and an inability to raise adequate direct taxes at the level of the Reich, which was a corollary of Germany's federal structure, both Bülow and Bethmann Hollweg found that they were unable to fund – or encourage business to participate in – expensive colonial projects and increased spending on arms. By contrast, enemy states like Britain and France had unitary systems of government and a surplus of private capital, which allowed large-scale foreign investment – with the two countries accounting for more than 60 per cent of the world total in 1913 – and greater expenditure on armaments, guaranteed by centralized fiscal regimes and higher direct taxation. Financiers, industrialists, officials and, eventually, generals all became aware of this critical German weakness, Ferguson contends, to the point where 'domestically determined financial constraint was a – perhaps *the* – crucial factor in the calculations of the German General Staff in 1914', pushing the Reich 'from fiscal impasse to strategic despair'.[13]

There are several flaws in Ferguson's argument. Even with reference to his own figures, some of the economic historian's conclusions about financial desperation in the Reich seem misplaced. Germany and Austria–Hungary had begun to catch up with France and Russia, their main continental enemies, in terms of defence spending, which increased from £45.8 million in 1894 to £118.4 million in 1913, compared with an increase from £123.4 million to £173.7 million for the two Entente powers over the same period. Moreover, German military expenditure, which was related to rapid mobilization and was targeted almost entirely at the Reich's immediate neighbours, increased almost threefold, rising from £36.3 million in 1894 to £93.4 million in 1913. Much of Russian and British military spending, which rose more slowly, was channelled towards areas beyond Europe. An examination of other financial indices reveals that Germany's position was still better than that of its principal continental rivals: its national debt by 1913 was £1,061 million or 44.4 per cent of net national product, whereas that of France was £1,308 million or 86.5 per cent, and that of Russia £937 million or 47.3 per cent; the burden of taxation was 47.77 marks per head in Germany in 1914, 75.18 marks in Britain and 83.25 marks in France; public spending had risen gradually since 1890, but remained similar to that of France, at between 16 and 17 per cent of gross national product, and less than that of Russia; and German bond yields, at 4.06 per cent in 1914, were still close to those of France, at 3.81 per cent, and markedly lower than those of Russia, at 4.66 per cent, despite the fact that most purchasers were either British or French, and therefore might have been deterred from buying the bonds of an enemy state. In other words, the statistics on which Ferguson bases much of his case show that the Reich's position was better than that of either France or Russia. Although, by the same financial indices, Germany was weaker than Britain, there was little evidence that the latter could or would intervene in a significant way on the European mainland, where any major war involving the former was likely to take place. As a consequence, the link between financial discomfiture and military preparedness appears more tenuous than Ferguson implies, since Britain alone was stronger in a fiscal sense, but was a largely maritime power and was seeking a rapprochement with Germany by the 1910s, whilst France and Russia, notwithstanding the threat that they posed to German national security, were themselves severely weakened by constraints on taxation, budget deficits and indebtedness.

A more important shortcoming of Ferguson's argument is the scant attention which it pays to contemporary perceptions of economic strength and weakness. Many Wilhelmine Germans, including most industrialists and financiers, saw the years after the turn of the century as a 'boom' era. Karl Helfferich, a director of the Deutsche Bank, a professor of economics and a former functionary of the Colonial Division of the Foreign Office, published the best known assessment of the German economy during this period, entitled *Deutschlands Volkswohlstand 1888–1913*. The main thrust of the book was that Germany under Wilhelm II had reached an historical high point, comparable with the Renaissance and characterized by an 'onrushing victorious boom' with 'hardly a precedent in world history'.[14] 'Germany had the most to make up in the way of economic development', he went on. 'Since the German people have entered world history, they have stood second to none in moral fibre and strength . . . , have taken a leading part in science . . . [and] won a place in the first ranks of literature and the arts.'[15] The Reich, he pointed out, had surpassed Britain in the production of iron and steel, and it had overtaken France in the generation of national income. Of course, Helfferich's volume was written, in part, to celebrate Wilhelm II's silver jubilee and was criticized at the time by the liberal journalist Theodor Wolff as 'courtierly economics'.[16] Yet it voiced, in exaggerated form, the commonplace opinions of virtually all industrialists, merchants and financiers, and many landowners. The Hamburg banker Max Warburg, for instance, advised the Kaiser one week before the Sarajevo assassination that 'Germany will grow stronger with every year of peace' and that 'waiting can only benefit us', since France was in a financial crisis, Britain was threatened by Home Rule and Russia was unreliable. The Berlin electricity magnate Walther Rathenau considered it obvious that Germany was the 'leading economic power in Europe', and the Ruhr coal and iron producer Hugo Stinnes reassured the Pan-German leader Heinrich Class in 1912 that 'the French have been left behind us', as 'a people of small rentiers', and that 'the English are not industrious enough and are without the courage for new undertakings'.[17] 'Otherwise, there is no one in Europe who could dispute our place', concluded the latter. 'So, three or four years of peace and, calmly, secure German predominance in Europe.'[18]

Such confidence in Germany's economic growth, prosperity and power was almost universal. Even prominent Prussian Conservatives and landowners like Wolfgang Gans zu Putlitz were, on occasion, happy to remind audiences 'that progress has been registered in all areas in an economic sense, including in those areas of manufacture and commerce which regularly complain that they are being trampled underfoot'.[19] Public well-being had increased 'as in no other country of the world', he declared.[20] The point about such belief in Germany's growing prosperity and economic strength, the existence of which Ferguson himself accepts, is that it either offset or obscured contemporary views of taxation, debt, and capital markets. There is little evidence that Wilhelmine businessmen, landowners or officials placed financial weakness, if they were conscious of it at all, above economic strength in their assessment of the Reich's strategic position, as Ferguson assumes. To Helfferich and many others, France – sometimes together with Britain – was discounted as 'the land of the annuity', whereas Germany was exalted as 'the land of work'.[21]

The Reich's financial difficulties, which were mainly the concern of bankers, officials in the various finance ministries and a limited number of other experts, were frequently perceived to be the necessary concomitant of industrial growth. The scarcity and expensiveness of credit, as well as the loss of value of government bonds, were the other side of 'strong, healthy economic expansion', asserted Warburg.[22] The National Liberal Gustav Stresemann, a member of the board of the Bund der Industriellen, made the same point at greater length in 1913:

> I am . . . of the opinion that it would be quite wrong to deduce any kind of financial weakness . . . from this interest rate . . . If we have so few purchasers of loans, then this rests, in my opinion, on the fact that we are precisely not a saturated state of rentiers, but that we are advancing so wildly in our economic development, as the rising export figures of the last years demonstrate, that precisely in this country what is actually put aside in millions and billions of an expanded German national wealth is not put into loans . . . but goes into new investments in German industry, into great new factory buildings, into everything which we have seen in this almost catapulting development of the last decades in Germany. Therefore, this interest rate is certainly not a sign of weakness, but of economic strength.[23]

The SPD's economic expert, Max Schippel, went even further, suggesting that 'the much regretted constraint, which for years affected the entire economic system . . . above all through the shortages of the money markets', had in fact prevented overproduction and a cyclical economic crisis such as had occurred in the past. Although the economy had slowed down in 1913, he claimed, the money markets had already begun to recover.[24] Bankers agreed, continuing to defend the free play of markets, the necessity of 'exporting' capital and of avoiding greater government regulation. The report of the Disconto Gesellschaft for 1913 argued that 'the momentary position of the money market', which could easily – it was implied – become more favourable, had not been 'the decisive factor' in the bank's strategy.[25] In particular, capital was tied up in foreign loans 'of a political and economic nature', relating to 'the importance of a nation in the council of nations'.[26] Within government, ministers adopted a similar line of argument, despite misgivings about the cost of public loans raised on German capital markets. Thus, in response to Conservative calls for increased state control of banks and the stock exchange, the Reich Secretary of State for the Interior, Clemens von Delbrück, told the Reichstag that the export of capital resulted from Germany's high savings quota. Moreover, it helped the country's balance of trade and encouraged further export of industrial goods.[27] In short, although capital was scarce, the government was not prepared to intervene, as Conservative landowners desired, in order to control its movement and supply.

It is debatable whether those who knew the true state of the Reich's finances were driven to a state of despair, not to mention those, such as members of the General Staff or Navy Office, who were relatively ignorant. There were, of course, major problems, as Ferguson indicates. The navy building programme of the 1900s had been funded largely by borrowing, which had helped to double the size of the Reich's debt. Rebalancing the income and outgoings of the Reich proved to be difficult because of the spiralling costs of military armament, with navy spending almost trebling between 1895 and 1905 and with the army increases of 1913 amounting to 1.9 billion marks over five years. Furthermore, the opposition of state governments, Conservatives and the Centre Party, which provoked Bülow's resignation in 1909 by blocking the direct inheritance tax component of his finance reform bill and which hampered Bethmann's attempts to introduce a new finance bill in 1913, made it difficult for the Reich to find new sources of revenue. It is often forgotten, however, that the 1909 finance reform, though iniquitous, provided the government with an extra 500 million marks per annum, so that the budget, which had been 238 million marks in deficit in 1908, was in surplus by 249 million marks by 1911. This, as the stringent Treasury Secretary, Adolf Wermuth, made clear in a memorandum, did not mean that the Reich's long-term debt had been cleared nor that its finances were sound, but they were on the way to recovery.[28] At the same time, the Treasury Secretary produced a much more positive picture to the Reichstag in December 1911, asserting 'that we have the prospect of returning the Reich finances to a healthy state several years earlier than had been assumed on all sides in 1909'.[29] Such public statements, despite being aimed at left-wing critics of the government prior to the 1912 elections, reinforced the claim of Secretary of State at the Navy Office Alfred von Tirpitz and War Minister Josias von Heeringen that 'the financial situation is as favourable as possible for the bringing in of a defence bill'.[30] By February 1912, Bethmann himself was voicing the suspicion that Wermuth had unjustifiably created a reserve of 80–100 million marks.[31]

Shortly afterwards, the Treasury Secretary was allowed to resign, bringing rumours in government circles of financial ruin to an end. His successor, Hermann Kühn, gave up Wermuth's attempt to make additional spending dependent on finding suitable sources of funding in advance, but nevertheless promised the Reichstag in April 1912 'not to allow the debts of the Reich to accumulate'.[32] What is remarkable about the following two years, if Rudolf Kroboth's exhaustive account is to be believed, is how little dispute there was within the Reich and Prussian governments about whether and how the largest army increases in modern German history to that point could be funded. The debate in 1913, therefore, was not whether the German tax regime could cope, but whether the existing alignment of forces would permit the passage of a suitable bill through the Bundesrat and Reichstag: namely, the individual states, which opposed a Reich capital gains tax as an infringement of their right to direct taxation; the Conservative Party, which continued to reject an inheritance tax; and the SPD, which warned against further indirect taxation. Eventually, of course, the increases – a massive 996-million-mark, one-off 'defence contribution' and an addition of 512 million marks to the yearly budget – were passed, albeit against the wishes of the DKP. Accordingly, Kühn felt a sense of achievement, besides frustration at the opposition of Conservatives, even as he handed in his resignation, which was refused, in February 1914: 'I have committed the crime, by creating the finances, of making possible the most comprehensive armaments legislation in our history.'[33] Bethmann's mood, characterized by his complaint in June 1913 that he had had 'quite enough of war and calls for war and of huge armaments programmes', seems to have been similar.[34] The Reich's position does not appear to have been sufficiently desperate to have ruled out further army increases, if and when they became necessary, nor to have pushed the Chancellor towards a pre-emptive war.

Lothar Burchardt's analysis of German economic preparations for war before 1914 corroborates such testimony. There is little indication that civilian planners, on the basis of their knowledge of the Reich's financial predicament, were preparing for an imminent conflict. Clemens von Delbrück, who was charged with coordinating the various agencies of state, consistently rejected plans to set up an 'Economic General Staff'. Thus, when the Lübeck entrepreneur Emil Possehl came forward with ideas for financial and other forms of economic preparation for war, the Secretary of State for the Interior discounted them as having no practical worth.[35] The latter also insisted that conditions for food supply were 'relatively favourable', despite convincing evidence to the contrary.[36] In a similar vein, the Prussian Ministries of Commerce and Agriculture complacently maintained in March 1914 that the division of labour within agriculture could 'quietly be left until times of emergency'.[37] The implication was that such an emergency might never occur. This was apparently the assumption of the minister responsible for the Reich's finances, the Treasury Secretary, who, in Burchardt's words, remained 'completely uninterested' in preparing economically for a conflict.[38] Accordingly, when Delbrück returned from a ten-day holiday on 24 July 1914, having ordered minimal purchases of grain on 14 July, he found that Kühn had refused to grant the money, since the latter was confident that there was little risk of war.[39] It is notable that, of all the state agencies, the General Staff seems to have insisted most on 'a thorough enquiry into how food supply and monetary transactions would fare in a war', as Moltke put it in 1907.[40] With the exception of the Foreign Office, most other civilian agencies neglected such questions and left the military in ignorance. Notwithstanding occasional calls for public intervention, the leaders of industry, finance and agriculture were generally lulled by a lack of government action into believing that the outbreak of hostilities was unlikely.[41] The correspondence in July 1914 between Stinnes and his son, who was visiting family businesses in Britain, was not unusual: until war was actually declared, both were exclusively preoccupied with industrial relations and the possibility of an international mining strike.[42] Likewise, according to his publisher, Rathenau 'spoke thoroughly optimistically of the situation' on the Wednesday before the outbreak of war.[43] All such evidence from those closest to the Reich's finances and economy – that is, the potential heralds of Ferguson's 'fiscal impasse' – suggests that they did not anticipate conflict, certainly not as a result of an impending financial crisis. 'We were, at bottom, prepared for nothing', recorded Warburg in his memoirs. 'It was really difficult to understand just how little one had thought in Germany about what should be undertaken in a financial sense, were the misfortune of a war to occur.'[44]

The arguments against Ferguson's thesis of financial despair, outlined above, do not validate the Fischerite case about a widespread overestimation of Germany's economic performance and the existence of a 'military–industrial' complex. It is well established that most industrialists and many financiers supported aggressive forms of imperial expansion and navalism. Albert Ballin, the head of the

Hamburg–America Shipping Line, is a good example of the lengths to which even a moderate, anglophile businessman could go during the first phase of naval enthusiasm in the early 1900s. Not only did he join the Hamburg section of the Navy League, backing their call for a fleet 'strong enough to protect Germany's growing overseas trade and its fledgling colonies with force and might', he also wrote supportive articles in the press, such as 'War Fleet and World Trade', which appeared in the *Hamburger Nachrichten* in February 1900:

> We are not thinking about a war between any particular powers, although a cosmopolitan statesman will not hide from himself that in any future war the fleet will play an entirely different role than before because now the whole world instead of continental Europe has become the arena of politics. Without a strong fleet, Germany will be very much reduced as a power, for friend and foe alike, in a future war; with a strong fleet, the German Empire will hold the balance in its hand, perhaps for a long time. But in time of peace as well, Germany needs a powerful war fleet. If England, France, Russia, and the United States of America make greater efforts from year to year to strengthen and increase their navies, so the German Empire, as a competitor in world markets, dares not content itself with a modest instrument and should put an end to its miserable make-shift fleet of the last fifteen years. In the brutal struggle of nations for light and air, strength alone counts in the final analysis. Diplomatic dexterity and clever political moves, alliances and declarations of neutrality – in the long run all these have value and effectiveness only if real power stands behind them. Germany has an incomparable land army, but beyond the seas only its warships can create respect for it.[45]

Comparable statements were made by the representatives of industry, commerce and banking.[46] In general, however, business became less aggressive in its support for imperialism as it became accustomed to Germany's shortage of capital, to the relatively small returns and high risks of imperial ventures, and to stubborn British resistance to fleet-building and unilateral colonial expansion. Leading German firms preferred to involve themselves, if at all, in joint ventures with their French and British counterparts. This was even the case in Morocco, where the Mannesmann brothers' demands for concessions of mineral deposits, which went on to provoke the Agadir crisis in 1911, were opposed by a French-led consortium that included Krupp. Ballin, who had come to oppose Tirpitz's programme of 'naval expansionism at any price' by 1908, dismissed the crisis as the 'Morocco comedy'.[47] He later wrote that Tirpitz had lacked the statesmanship to come to an agreement with Britain once Germany 'had fortunately got through the danger zone' by 1908–9, having acquired a navy large enough to defend German interests abroad and deter attack.[48] For Ballin and others like him, 'limitless construction' – like unlimited imperialism – simply made no business sense.[49]

Imperialism and navalism had never, for the majority of businessmen, been closely linked to the eventuality of war. Helfferich, who handled the Reich's major financial and industrial imperial project – the Baghdad railway – on behalf of the Deutsche Bank, appeared to believe that such endeavours served to defuse international tensions:

> If Germany devotes a part of its excess strength . . . to this task, it will remove a good part of the mistrust with which people all over the world follow and interpret our every movement . . . . Other nations see our burgeoning power, our rapidly growing population, the expansion of trade and industry, and a spirit of economic enterprise for which no task appears too great; these nations have the distinct feeling that every force requires adequate occupation if it is not to have destructive effects; these nations also have the feeling that Germany so far has found no . . . peaceful occupation for these forces.[50]

Others were perhaps less naïve, but they, too, widely eschewed the idea of war. Indeed, this was one of the reasons, in addition to a distaste for unbridled imperialism on its own account, for the lack of popularity of the Pan-German League amongst industrialists. Alfred Hugenberg, who had become chair of the Krupp board in 1909, was therefore adamant that his own Pan-German affiliations be kept secret, even at the heart of the Ruhr arms industry: 'It is better to represent Pan-German points of view without it being too externally visible.'[51] Rathenau, the most prominent advocate of the high-technology, export-led industries, was more forthright, dismissing the Alldeutscher Verband as isolated 'screachers' (*Schreihälse*).[52] War, he argued, was not something to be treated lightly. 'Don't believe, if Germany loses a war, that it will receive any favours', he warned colleagues from the chemical industry in 1912. 'On the contrary, it will have to pay what it can. And which circles in Germany are capable of paying? Agriculture won't pay much, nor the middle class very much; only industry will have to pay; that is, the victors will become the purchasers of our industry and we shall become wage slaves.'[53] The strength of such feeling was so great that, even after war had broken out in July 1914, financiers such as Arthur Gwinner, the most influential director of the Deutsche Bank in the 1900s, continued to blame the government, notwithstanding the changed atmosphere of the 'August days' at the start of Germany's great patriotic war:

> I was, at the time, of the opinion that certain persons in the Foreign Office had wanted the outbreak of war. In the meantime, I have become convinced that those in question merely played a dangerous game, with the intention of restoring Austrian prestige, which had been severely shaken through the murder of the heir to the throne; similar to what happened in the Bosnian crisis of 1908/9, when Germany stood behind Austria in 'shining armour' and diverted the menacing danger of war. The whole way in which the highly serious incident in Sarajevo was handled by Germany was a blunder, which in statecraft is a crime or, as a well-known phrase has it: 'worse than a crime – an error.'[54]

Contrary to Fischer's and Berghahn's contentions, most industrialists and bankers seem to have assumed that the increasing inter-linking of economic interests, frequently across national borders, served to prevent conflict rather than leading to military struggles for scarce resources. Rathenau, once again, was the most articulate exponent of this point of view, admitting the possibility of conflict but emphasizing that 'wars are only seldom decisive' in a world of machines and technicians, transactions and economists: 'Peoples are no longer good enemies, but rather evil competitors, and the game of foreign policy strives for strength of position, not for catastrophes.'[55] Many businessmen concurred, even those within the Centralverband Deutscher Industrieller (CVDI), which represented, above all, heavy industry. Max Roetger, the organization's chair and a director of Krupp, was keen, like Rathenau, to stress that 'the world stands under the sign of communication and exchange (*Verkehr*)': 'Germany has, in the rational shaping of free exchange and free movement, achieved extraordinary successes and has brought about a colossal economic boom.'[56] Yet he also rejected the military realization of industrial ends.[57] With significant exceptions, the CVDI defended peaceful international competition, which, it believed, had benefited German industry so spectacularly in the past. Correspondingly, most members, including the later annexationist Emil Kirdorf, concentrated, until 1910 at the earliest, on keeping open export markets rather than taking control of territory.[58] Stinnes, busily buying up companies in France, Russia, Britain and elsewhere, gave an indication, as he sought to dissuade Heinrich Class from agitating for war in 1912, of how such industrialists thought:

> And look what that means when I slowly but surely acquire the majority of shares from this or that firm, when I gradually get hold of more and more of the provision of coal to Italy, when I get a foothold, unnoticed, in Sweden and Spain because of necessary ores, or when I establish myself in Normandy – allow another 3–4 years of quiet development, and Germany will become the undisputed economic master of Europe.[59]

The influential chairmen and owners of the Reich's biggest companies – Krupp, Thyssen, Stinnes, AEG, Siemens, HAPAG, Lloyd and the Deutsche Bank – all stood to lose affiliated firms abroad, their principal markets, sources of raw materials and employees, as well as suffering from a more general disruption of trade, as a consequence of war. It is perhaps not surprising, then, after a period of unprecedented growth in the two decades before 1914 that the majority of them sought to avoid an international conflict.

Such a reassessment of the foreign-policy goals of German industry and finance brings into question the very basis of Fischer's thesis about the causes of the war – the alleged existence of a *Sammlung* of industrialists and landowners, or of 'iron and rye'. Since the 1980s, revisionist historians of Wilhelmine politics and society have questioned the strength and significance of this coalition, which was supposedly underpinned by a *quid pro quo* of high grain tariffs, passed in 1902 at the instigation of agrarians, and the Navy Laws of 1898 and 1900, supported by heavy industry and the CVDI. Geoff Eley, in particular, has demonstrated the fragility of agrarian, industrial and ministerial protagonists' commitments to each other and the contradictory nature of their various understandings of *Sammlungspolitik*, most notably those of the Prussian Finance Minister and Frankfurt banker Johannes von Miquel and of the Navy Secretary, Tirpitz.[60] Some historians have pointed to a lack of correspondence between a putative coalition of economic interests and the shifting alliances of political parties, which supposedly represented them. Others have revealed the social and cultural disparity between agrarian and industrial or commercial milieux.[61] With regard to foreign affairs and the prospect of war, conflicts of interest between large landowners, on the one hand, and industrialists and financiers, on the other, were equally marked, overlaying divisions within such groups.

Conservative agrarians had, throughout the Wilhelmine era, stressed their willingness to go to war in the name of king and country. 'We Conservatives can and will not leave the Reich government in the lurch in its task of defending and realising the honour, power and national worth of the fatherland, whether for the protection of the German Reich itself or for that of its colonies, which have been acquired at great cost and courageously defended with the blood of numerous sons of our country', declared the DKP's manifesto in 1907.[62] Under the chancellorship of Bethmann Hollweg, especially after Heydebrand's criticism of the government during the second Moroccan crisis in 1911, the majority of large landowners, who were closely tied to the Conservative Party, were increasingly reconciled with the expansionist rhetoric of nationalist organizations such as the Army and Navy Leagues.[63] In 1913, the Pan-German League began to formulate the foreign-policy platform of the DKP's sister organization, the Bund der Landwirte (BDL).

Although not ruling out tactical cooperation, such as that of the CVDI and the BDL within the Cartel of Productive Estates during the year before the First World War, there is evidence that many industrialists and financiers were alienated by the landowners' drift towards the bellicose nationalism of the leagues. Since the late 1890s, when manufacturing had come to account for a larger sector of the workforce than agriculture, a debate had raged in Germany about the relative merits of industrial and agrarian states (*Industriestaat* and *Agrarstaat*). In this debate, even the CVDI, which on occasion was prepared to contemplate the necessity of war, strongly opposed the arguments and aims of landowners, since it was sure that 'only after Germany . . . had become an industrial state in the full sense of the word' had it been able 'to take up its place in the group of great world powers'.[64] 'Thus, in complete contrast to earlier times, the whole of so-called high politics turns on economic questions, on the expansion and development of economic exchange', continued the CVDI's leadership in 1905. 'Does the Secretary of State believe that he will arm the state more effectively for such struggles through a return to the agrarian state?'[65] Later, as large landowners began to move further to the right, the association's chair, Roetger, became increasingly convinced that 'the Conservative Party today is not what industry needs'.[66] Neither in their domestic nor in their foreign-policy platforms were industry and commerce, taken as a whole, close enough to East Elbian agriculture to form the basis of an effective *Sammlungspolitik*.

The claim of Fischer and his followers that an alliance of 'iron and rye', which informed state policy and was predicated on tariffs, armament and opposition to socialism, pushed the Reich towards war in 1914 no longer stands up to historical scrutiny. Most industrialists and financiers – and many officials – were impressed by Germany's recent economic growth and the possibility of becoming a world power, but they did not want war, since they feared the disruption that it would cause. Both of these facts – economic leaders' confidence in the Reich's economy and their rejection of war on commercial grounds – militate against Ferguson's thesis about financial weakness and strategic despair. As the following chapters demonstrate, there is little reason to believe that the formulation and conduct of foreign policy was dominated by a sense of despair in the decades before 1914. The next two chapters examine how optimism amongst broad sections of the public, similar to that of industrialists and financiers, helped to guard against a descent into war.

Notes

1. F. Fischer, *War of Illusions* (London, 1975), pp. 13–25. D. Stegmann, *Die Erben Bismarcks. Parteien und Verbände in der Spätphase des Wilhelminischen Deutschlands* (Cologne, 1970); H.-J. Puhle, *Agrarische Interessenpolitik und preussischer Konservatismus im wilhelminischen Reich, 1893–1914* (Bonn, 1975).

2. H.-U. Wehler, *The German Empire, 1871–1918* (Oxford, 1985), pp. 94–5.

3. Tirpitz, cited in V.R. Berghahn, *Germany and the Approach of War in 1914* (London, 1973), p. 29.

4. Meinecke, in Stegmann, *Die Erben Bismarcks*, p. 282.

5. V.R. Berghahn, *Rüstung und Machtpolitik. Zur Anatomie des 'Kalten Krieges' vor 1914* (Düsseldorf, 1973), pp. 47–69.

6. Ibid., p. 62.

7. Fischer's initial innovation in *Germany's Aims in the First World War* (London, 1967) was to link the war aims of the 'September Memorandum' to the aspirations of industrial and ruling elites before August 1914.

8. Fischer, *Germany's Aims in the First World War*, is the translated version of *Griff nach der Weltmacht*, published in 1961.

9. See, most notably, W.J. Mommsen, 'The Causes and Objectives of German Imperialism before 1914', in *Imperial Germany* (London, 1995), pp. 75–100.

10. N. Ferguson, *The Pity of War* (London, 1998), p. 32. Also, Ferguson, *Paper and Iron: Hamburg Business and German Politics in the Era of Inflation, 1897–1927* (Cambridge, 1995), pp. 31–92.

11. N. Ferguson, 'Public Finance and National Security: The Domestic Origins of the First World War Revisited', *Past and Present*, 142 (1994) p. 143.

12. Ferguson, *The Pity of War*, pp. 34–5.

13. Ibid., pp. 135, 140. See also N. Ferguson, 'Germany and the Origins of the First World War: New Perspectives', *Historical Journal*, 35 (1992), pp. 742–52.

14. J.G. Williamson, *Karl Helfferich, 1872–1924* (Princeton, 1971), p. 112.

15. Ibid.

16. Ibid., p. 111.

17. M.M. Warburg, *Aus meinen Aufzeichnungen* (Glückstadt, 1952), p. 29, and Ferguson, *The Pity of War*, p. 33; G. Hecker, *Walther Rathenau und sein Verhältnis zu Militär und Krieg* (Boppard 1983), p. 82; G.D. Feldman, *Hugo Stinnes. Biographie eines Industriellen, 1870–1924* (Munich, 1999), p. 350.

18. Feldman, *Hugo Stinnes*, p. 350

19. *Verhandlungen des Reichstages*, 19 February 1912, vol. 283, p. 120.

20. Ibid.

21. Williamson, *Karl Helfferich*, p. 112.

22. R. Kroboth, *Die Finanzpolitik des Deutschen Reiches während der Reichskanzlerschaft Bethmann Hollwegs und die Geld- und Kapitalmarkt-verhältnisse 1909–1913/1914* (Frankfurt a. M., 1986), p. 102.

23. Ibid., pp. 102–3.

24. Ibid., p. 106.

25. Fischer, *War of Illusions*, p. 356.

26. Ibid.

27. Kroboth, *Finanzpolitik*, p. 94.

28. Ibid., p. 129.

29. Ibid., p. 132.

30. Ibid., pp. 134–5.

31. Ibid., p. 149.

32. Ibid., p. 177.

33. P.-C. Witt, *Die Finanzpolitik des Deutschen Reiches von 1903 bis 1913* (Lübeck, 1970), p. 376.

34. Kroboth, *Finanzpolitik*, p. 312.

35. L. Burchardt, *Friedenswirtschaft und Kriegsvorsorge. Deutschlands wirtschaftliche Rüstungsbestrebungen vor 1914* (Boppard, 1968), pp. 138–40.

36. Ibid., p. 189.

37. Ibid., p. 228.

38. Ibid., p. 76.

39. Ibid., p. 238.

40. Ibid., p. 164.

41. Ibid., pp. 88-93.

42. Feldman, *Hugo Stinnes*, pp. 371-3.

43. E. Schulin, *Gespräche mit Rathenau* (Munich, 1980), p. 139.

44. Warburg, *Aus meinen Aufzeichnungen*, p. 23.

45. L. Cecil, *Albert Ballin: Business and Politics in Imperial Germany, 1888-1918* (Princeton, 1967), pp. 151, 155-6.

46. See, for instance, Fischer, *War of Illusions*, pp. 3-12, 26-43, 230-58; L. Gall et al., *Die Deutsche Bank, 1870-1995* (Munich, 1995), p. 91; H. Kaelble, *Industrielle Interessenpolitik in der Wilhelminischen Gesellschaft. Centralverband Deutscher Industrieller 1895-1914* (Berlin, 1967), pp. 147-55.

47. Cecil, *Albert Ballin*, pp. 179-80.

48. Ibid., p. 159.

49. Ibid.

50. Williamson, *Karl Helfferich*, p. 55.

51. J.A. Leopold, *Alfred Hugenberg: The Radical Nationalist Campaign against the Weimar Republic* (New Haven, 1977), p. 171.

52. Schulin, *Gespräche mit Rathenau*, p. 134.

53. Ibid., pp. 126-7.

54. Gall et al., *Die Deutsche Bank*, pp. 106-7.

55. Hecker, *Walther Rathenau*, p. 71.

56. Kaelble, *Industrielle Interessenpolitik*, pp. 148-9.

57. Ibid., p. 150.

58. Ibid., p. 151. On similar views in the Hansabund, see Fischer, *War of Illusions*, p. 236.

59. Feldman, *Hugo Stinnes*, p. 350.

60. G. Eley, '*Sammlungspolitik*, Social Imperialism and the Navy Law of 1898', in *From Unification to Nazism: Reinterpreting the German Past* (London, 1986), pp. 110-53.

61. David Blackbourn's essay in *The Peculiarities of German History: Bourgeois Society and Politics in Nineteenth-Century Germany* (Oxford, 1984), pp. 159-292, remains the classic exploration of such political and social divisions, on which much of the last decades' revisionism has been based.

62. A. Schildt, *Konservatismus in Deutschland* (Munich, 1998), pp. 123-4.

63. See J. Retallack, *Notables of the Right: The Conservative Party and Political Mobilization in Germany, 1876-1918* (London, 1988), pp. 208-15.

64. Henry Axel Bueck in 1905, cited in Kaelble, *Industrielle Interessen-politik*, p. 152.

65. Ibid., p. 153.

66. Stegmann, *Die Erben Bismarcks*, p. 191.

3

Nationalism and Images of the Enemy

Nationalism plays an important part in the accounts of the Hamburg school and those of a number of prominent revisionists. The *Kaiserreich*, contend Fischer, Berghahn and others, was an incoherent, aristocratic and anachronistic system of government, increasingly out of kilter with the economic foundations and class composition of an industrializing society; the continuing power of this state, propped up by an expanding, independent and Junker-dominated army, had the double-edged effect of 'feudalizing' significant sections of the German middle classes and of prompting Bülow and Bethmann Hollweg to pursue a diversionary and expansionist policy of 'social imperialism'. German nationalism, it is held, became a means of escape – a *Flucht nach vorn* – from the conflicts and fragmentation of Wilhelmine society.[1] Historians such as Otto Dann and Hans-Ulrich Wehler, who have recently turned their attention to nationalism in its own right, agree with Fischer's claim that there was a radicalization of the national debate after unification – and especially after the 1890s – which gave an unprecedented influence to the far right.[2] In the words of Harold James, who has combined the state-centred explanation of the Fischerites with Hans Kohn's and George Mosse's thesis about popular racism and ethnic nationalism, 'Germany alone played Great Power politics with all the unfulfilled ambitions and romantic expectations of a movement for national awakening.'[3]

Revisionists such as Förster – and those who have modified the Fischerite case 'from within' such as Mommsen – have tended to stress the independence of popular right-wing nationalism. Drawing on the work of Geoff Eley and Roger Chickering, they have argued that public opinion had become too diverse and self-confident to be controlled by government press offices and ministerial interventions, as the Hamburg school had initially claimed. Rather, having been convinced by radical nationalist arguments about 'encirclement', the necessity of a strong navy and the Reich's right to a 'place in the sun' overseas, the extra-parliamentary leagues began to dictate the tone and content of foreign policy.[4] This was the period, it is argued, when an emancipatory national movement of the left, which had dictated concepts of the nation in the mid-nineteenth century, was eclipsed by the xenophobic, integral nationalism of the right. The first anti-Semitic organization was founded in 1879, the Society for Germandom Abroad in 1881, the German Language Association in 1886, the Colonial Society in 1887, the Pan-German League in 1891, the German Society for the Eastern Marches in 1894, the Navy League in 1898, the Kyffhäuser Association in 1899, the Imperial League to Combat Social Democracy in 1904, the Patriotic Book League in 1908 and the Army League in 1912. Many of these mass-membership organizations were based on the notion of political, linguistic or racial defence and expansion. Observing the leagues' success in recruiting new members, it is contended, many of the German parties moved to the right, calling into question the existing borders of the *Kaiserreich*, traditional levels of military expenditure and conscription, and the government's naval, colonial and foreign policies. The resonance of such ideas was allegedly so great that significant sections of the left-liberal parties and the SPD repudiated their anti-imperial past and began to call for the expansion of the Reich. This new, cross-party emphasis on foreign policy was supposedly motivated partly by a justified sense that Germany's interests abroad were being ignored, and partly by a national-minded or politically self-interested desire to deflect attention from the domestic failings of the German Empire, with its contradictory institutions, stalemated parties and class conflict. Förster and Mommsen both suggest that the Reich government, buffeted from all sides, gradually gave way to the demands of the radical right and adopted an aggressive foreign policy of prestige and brinkmanship.

There are many indications that 'German-nationals' on the far right became more radical in the pre-war period, detecting what one correspondent of the *Alldeutsche Blätter* termed 'a broadly based conspiracy . . . with the aim of harming Germandom'.[5] This plot or war against the Germans was conducted both at home – by Jews, ultramontanes, Freemasons, socialists – and abroad – by the same groups and by other 'enemy' nationalities or 'races' such as the French, the 'Slavs', and the 'Anglo-Saxons'. 'Everything that relates to the preservation, promotion, future, and greatness of our people is national', wrote another correspondent of the Pan-German League's mouthpiece. 'That means that national questions of the first order are: the army, the navy, colonies, Germanization of the Prussian eastern provinces and North Schleswig, de-Latinization (*Entwelschung*) of Alsace-Lorraine, honourable representation of the German Empire, protection of Germans, preservation of the citizenship and civil rights of Germans abroad, combating the treacherous (*vaterlandslose*) Social Democrats, *und so weiter*.'[6] In such a world of increasing enmity and threats to the very existence of a German state, it seemed to the leader of the Pan-German League, Ernst Hasse, that 'the only thing that possesses stability in the flux of a thousand years of development is the *Volk*'.[7] 'States, as conglomerations of ethnic groups, come and go; and even more transitory are political constitutions and social conditions', he went on.[8] Defence of a German *Volk* was therefore justified in virtually all circumstances, with radical nationalist commentators, confident of the existence of a Darwinian 'struggle for survival', making little distinction between offensive, pre-emptive, preventive and defensive conflicts. 'Enemies all around us (*Feinde ringsum*): that has always been our position. And we have suffered from this like no other people (*Volk*)', wrote Hasse in his 1907 treatise on *Die Zukunft des deutschen Volkstums*: 'Enemies all around us, this also remains our position forever in the future. And that is our good fortune.'[9] Hasse's successor as president of the league, Heinrich Class, continued to assure his members and warn the Reich government of 'the great seriousness of the position of the whole of Germandom in *Mitteleuropa*' in the years before 1914, becoming more and more shrill after each 'national humiliation'.[10]

Revisionist historians like Richard Evans, David Blackbourn and Geoff Eley have challenged the notion that such extreme opinions were representative of the majority of a Wilhelmine 'public'. Their works, however, despite altering common perceptions of many aspects of domestic policy and social history, have had less impact on analyses of German nationalism, xenophobia and belligerence. Although research has been redirected away from the state and the instrumentalization of national sentiment towards the realignments of the German right and the democratization of politics, historians rarely distinguish banal from radical nationalism and, as a result, they still assume that extreme nationalism was widespread or even preponderant between 1890 and 1914.[11] Such assumptions mean that they have attempted to trace the infusion of anti-Semitic, racist, xenophobic and integral nationalist ideas into different sections of Wilhelmine society, including working-class *milieux*, rather than starting with an investigation of everyday concepts of the nation and asking at what point banal nationalism, which was characteristic of almost all European countries, became radical or dangerous, tending towards persecution at home or aggression abroad. From this latter perspective, it appears that the majority of Wilhelmine Germans were more, not less, wary and sceptical of strong expressions of national belonging and national interest than in previous decades. Thus, whilst it is true that national identity in Germany had been defined, to a greater extent than in Britain or France, in terms of culture and ethnicity, not political affiliation or history, and that national affairs, which comprised matters of state, military security and foreign policy, had enjoyed an unusual degree of exemption from political scrutiny and debate, it was movement *away* from these definitions of identity and this type of exemption which created the false impression that mainstream German nationalism had become more extreme. In fact, what had changed was the extent to which Wilhelmine parties, press and public were prepared openly to discuss questions of national identity and national interest. Such discussion, though it alienated and radicalized part of the German right and unsettled much of the centre, helped to demonstrate the particularity of Germany's system of government, making the political components of German identity more salient, just as it helped to clarify what was central to German culture and what was peculiar about the Reich's international position. That the discussion occurred at all was an indication of increased confidence – on the part of the government and majority public opinion – about the stability and solidity of the German nation-state.

By the turn of the twentieth century, most German commentators treated the Reich as a normal nation-state, comparable to Britain, the Netherlands, Sweden or France. Even critics of the structure of the German Empire like Friedrich Meinecke, who drew attention to the continuing duality or 'schizophrenia' between 'old Prussia' and the 'new Reich', remained certain that 'the goal to which everything is directed is an all-inclusive community of the German nation-state, a community so strong that it is able to tolerate, utilize and overcome all the separate nationalities of its individual members'.[12] In spite of the popularity of the 'grossdeutsch' idea in 1848, the waging of a German 'civil war' in 1866, the existence of German-speaking populations outside the borders of the Reich, and Polish, French and Danish-speaking nationalities within them, as well as the persistence or exacerbation of regional, confessional and class divisions, the

Reich had quickly been accepted as a *Nationalstaat*, in contrast to other recently unified nation-states such as Italy. Advocates of a parliamentary regime like the left liberal Friedrich Naumann admitted that the German polity had stood the test of time, becoming 'a solid political body'. 'The danger that we shall again sink back into a confusion of small states (*Kleinstaaterei*) can be regarded as having been removed', he went on. 'The fear that this constitution would only be an interlude has not been borne out by events.'[13]

Supposed supporters of *Grossdeutschland* in the Centre Party, anxious to overcome their reputation during the *Kulturkampf* as enemies of the Reich, generally refrained from calling for a revision of the borders of 1871. Indeed, the assertion of the influential Catholic publicist Carl Bachem that the founder of the *kleindeutsch* German Empire, Bismarck, was the 'greatest German statesman of the modern age' was closer to the party line in the Wilhelmine period, as German Catholics severed their links with their Polish counterparts in eastern Prussia, than were demands for a redrawing of the Reich's borders.[14]

Social Democrats were less charitable to Bismarck, but they, too, habitually acknowledged the validity of the nation-state and its borders, even if SPD politicians took care, in the words of the Bavarian reformist Georg von Vollmar, 'not to mistake the fatherland for its present rulers'.[15] In this respect, the view of the revisionist Eduard Bernstein that 'great differences exist in different lands' probably reflected majority opinion in the party: 'Peculiarities of geographical situation, rooted customs of national life, inherited institutions, and traditions of all kinds create a difference of mind which only slowly submits to the influence of [industrial] development.'[16] Even though German workers did not yet have the full rights and entitlements of citizenship, Bernstein continued, it could not be 'a matter of indifference to German Social Democracy whether the German nation, which has indeed carried out, and is carrying out, its honourable share in the civilizing work of the world, should be repressed in the council of the nations.'[17] During the main debate about the nation in the SPD, at the time of the Stuttgart conference of the Second International in 1907, the party's leader August Bebel, along with most other Social Democratic deputies, applauded Gustav Noske's call in the Reichstag for the defence of an independent German nation-state. Despite their support for a revolutionary general strike at the outbreak of any war, the left wing of the SPD, likewise, claimed that 'their nationality was worthy and their fatherland dear'.[18]

As the German nation-state began to seem self-evident and secure from both internal and external enemies, it gradually became an object of political discussion. By the 1900s, as the Berlin historian Friedrich Meinecke noted, virtually all groups claimed the right to reinterpret the nation and to debate national affairs, including foreign policy and declarations of war. 'In older nation-states, there was, as a rule, no doubt about who was the head and who constituted the limbs which responded to it', he wrote in *Weltbürgertum und Nationalstaat* in 1908: 'Yet, in younger nation-states, where the most diverse individualities and social groups seize the idea of the nation and project themselves onto it, there is no end to the doubt and struggle over the issue.'[19] Because of the novelty of this type of debate, many Wilhelmine onlookers expressed concern about the instability and insufficiency of German patriotism, and about the possible disintegration of the German nation-state. 'In Germany, even the love of country has not found a valid form of expression', lamented Walther Rathenau, who was also a left-liberal publicist as well as the chairman of AEG. 'Servile devotion and the noisy patriotism of business societies are not balanced by a secure national consciousness.'[20]

Previously, national sentiment had constituted an unspoken assumption of German politics, not a topic for party disputation: the label 'vaterlandslos' was used to exclude groupings like the Centre Party and the SPD from the political nation. Now, public controversy about national affairs helped to produce a multitude of different readings of national interest and identity, and to consolidate and radicalize a minority movement of right-wing nationalists, which found a focus in the extra-parliamentary leagues and parts of the National Liberal and Conservative parties. To August Keim, later leader of the Army League, this 'fragmentation' showed the necessity of 'a crusade of national education' so that the 'development of our inner unity and thereby the completion of the work of our national unification', which was derived from 'the blood-brotherhood of the German tribes', could at last occur; to his colleague and leader of the Pan-German League, Heinrich Class, it evinced that German politics had been subverted by Jews, who had exploited popular disaffection over the diplomatic failures of the Reich government and created an alliance amongst socialist, liberal, Catholic, Polish, Danish, Alsatian and Hanoverian enemies of the state.[21] Keim, Class and other radical nationalists claimed to exercise a monopoly over the expression and meaning of German patriotism, extending the tradition of the 'national' or 'state-supporting' parties of the 1870s and 1880s, which had successfully ostracized Catholics and socialists by pointing to their supposed lack of patriotic feeling. Such a strategy failed during the 1900s and 1910s because Catholics and socialists resisted attempts to build a national consensus against them, putting forward their own patriotic credentials and their own vision of the nation. At the same time, the state-supporting parties themselves were prepared to discuss national affairs, revealing in the process an unsuspected diversity of opinions.

Strident and unprecedented disputes about the identity, interest and policy of the German nation, together with the repeated assertions of league members that they alone were truly national, convinced observers like Rathenau that a 'secure national consciousness' did not exist. In other words, such manifestations failed to persuade him that the 'noisy patriotism of business societies' was to be equated with the views of the majority. Many Germans agreed with the moderate right-wing publicist and historian Hans Delbrück 'that the Pan-Germans were a small, almost comical sect with no significance' in the 1890s and 1900s, even if the *Alldeutscher Verband* appeared to have become more influential in the 1910s.[22] Most Germans, including a significant number on the right, did not hold radical nationalist views and did not harbour dreams of aggressive expansionism abroad. Excluding affiliates, only the Navy League amongst the so-called 'national associations' (*nationale Verbände*) had a membership of more than 100,000, and even its highest figure of 330,000 was less than a third of the SPD's pre-war total. Allowing for overlapping membership between leagues, it has been estimated that the 'German-national' public numbered between several hundred thousand and 3 million people from an electorate of 14.5 million in 1912. Of the 12.2 million who voted in the same year, 8.25 million supported the Social Democratic, Centre, left-liberal and minority-nationality parties, which had few, if any, connections with national associations. In addition, many Conservative and National Liberal Party voters had little sympathy for radical nationalism. Instead, a significant number of Germans preferred what Meinecke called an 'active, free idea of the nation'.[23] It was for this reason that members of leagues were frequently ridiculed in the press as 'Teutschen' and 'Teutsch-Nationale', depicted as top-hatted, over-weight, bearded and credulous old men indulging in frivolous 'Deutschtümelei'. Even the language of radical nationalism was challenged and mocked. One cartoon in *Simplicissimus* translated distorted 'patriotic' words into pictures: the 'people' (*das Volk*) was represented as a motley, pompous procession of decorated, black-suited septuagenarians. The caricaturist assumed, without further commentary, that his readers would understand the emancipatory, inclusive, heroic connotations of the term 'Volk'.[24] By the 1900s, it was evident that national feeling, which had been seen during the 1880s as a uniform qualification for full political participation, had taken a variety of forms, all of which were open to party discussion and political satire. The novelty of this debate about the German nation in itself caused considerable anxiety and precipitated the radicalization of the far right, which, in turn, created the illusion that the Wilhelmine period was an age of extreme and aggressive nationalism. Yet the fact that the debate took place was a sign that the old division in Germany between politics and the nation had begun to disappear.

Political discussion of national affairs was particularly pronounced in the area of international relations. Yet contemporaries' fears of national disintegration and later historians' condemnations of radical and popular nationalism prove, on closer inspection, to be exaggerated. Party scrutiny and criticism of foreign policy became obvious during the first Moroccan crisis in 1905–6, as the German government was forced to give way to France, which was backed by most of the international community, at the conference of Algeciras. To the left, Bülow and Wilhelm II had acted too aggressively, failing to cajole the Quai d'Orsay into making concessions over the 'Tunisification' of Morocco; to the right, the Chancellor and the Kaiser had lost their nerve, missing the opportunity of inflicting a humiliating defeat on the 'hereditary enemy' and of destroying the Entente Cordiale. The leader of the National Liberals, Ernst Bassermann, marked the change in public attitude in 1906:

> So long as a great statesman like Bismarck guided our foreign policy we could submit to his guidance. But now we will take the liberty of criticising . . . and it will be well in the future if the people of Germany will show more interest in foreign affairs . . . The times are past when we remained silent before such a state of things, and, moreover, we will take the liberty of discussing it in the Reichstag.[25]

Outside observers like the British ambassador in Berlin, Sir Frank Lascelles, concurred that 'the change' which had 'come over public opinion' during the 1890s and 1900s, becoming 'apparent' only in the course of the Moroccan crisis, was 'remarkable'. 'This, and similar questions,' he went on, 'were symptomatic of a general feeling that the foreign affairs of Germany were not skilfully dealt with.'[26] Britain's envoy in Munich made similar observations a year later: 'A generation ago, the German public took but little interest in general foreign affairs . . . Things have changed since then.'[27] During the second Moroccan crisis in 1911–12, as the government again stopped short of armed conflict with few tangible gains, after sending a German gunboat to Agadir, criticism of official policy-making increased. It continued unabated until the outbreak of the First World War, obscuring substantial points of agreement between parties and encouraging an overestimation of the importance of nationalist leagues. Although hysterical censure of the government and eye-catching predictions of national collapse came from 'German-national' circles, the majority of Wilhelmine Germans shared a less threatening set of images of the Reich's western European rivals than had their predecessors. Unlike extreme nationalists, most were opposed to the notion of an offensive or preventive war.

Proximity and familiarity, of course, did not mean that Wilhelmine observers saw their own culture as interchangeable with those of other Western European countries, however much they agreed with Treitschke that 'the Germans are always in danger of losing their nationality' because they were too open to the ideas of their neigh-bours.[28] Rather, the Reich's rivals were treated, despite their distinct historical traditions and geographical locations, as a single foil for the definition of German values and practices: Germany, it was implied, offered the sole modern alternative system of thought and institutions to the dominant and overlapping systems of France, Britain and the United States. Such national difference and opposition could – and did – foster stereotypes, on which the enmities of the First World War were later based. These images of the enemy had been constructed during the eighteenth and nineteenth centuries, when German culture had been defined primarily through a reaction against French administration, etiquette, learning and art, as these were manifested in the occupied territories of the Napoleonic wars, in the princely courts of the German states and in the monarchical, Bonapartist and republican regimes of the 'hereditary foe' (*Erbfeind*) of the Confederation and the Reich. France, whose role as Germany's 'mentor and teacher' had – according to the liberal politician Friedrich Naumann in 1900 – only recently been challenged, appeared to have maintained a similar set of values throughout the preceding century. The French were, in the words of one widely read book, charming, polite, witty, flexible, boastful, superficial, tasteful, artificial, civilized, classical, sociable, conventional, individualist, egalitarian, centralized, nationalistic and morally relativist. The neighbouring state's Roman heritage and its rejection of Protestantism were seen to have produced a rationalist culture which had fostered social conventionality, centralized administration and unhistorical political dogmatism: 'Rationalism', wrote the historian Karl Hillebrand, 'is the essential feature of the French mind (*Geist*).'[29]

From the mid nineteenth century onwards, Britain, which had earlier been depicted as a 'Germanic' self-governing society, and the United States, which had been portrayed as a romantic, wild and free-spirited antithesis to Europe, were both gradually transformed, if German accounts were to be believed, into calculating, capitalist, industrial powers and oppressive, Puritan, empirical and materialist cultures, which more closely resembled the strict social form, rational science and commercialism of France. There were, of course, still thought to be marked differences between 'Romanism' and 'Germanism', and between the 'Old' and 'New World', as Karl Lamprecht spelled out in his popular diary of *Americana* in 1906: 'If the present American civilization disappeared: what would remain for posterity? Practically nothing . . . It has to be expressed in no uncertain terms: vis-à-vis the old culture of the European population, both the Germanic and the Romance, the Americans are still behind.' Yet, with the democratization of British politics, the growth of French financial capitalism and the emergence of French, British and American positivism, few Germans questioned the political and cultural propinquity of France, the United Kingdom and the United States, for it seemed that the populations of all three countries were preoccupied with external form, observation, numbers, utility and, increasingly, equality. The majority of Wilhelmine commentators assumed that Germany was different.[30]

A sense of national particularity, which had in some respects been reinforced by a series of international comparisons, was not, as some historians claim, an explosive and unpredictable cause or effect of Germans' anxieties about the Reich's position in the world, however. As could be expected in an age of *Weltpolitik* and of photographs in newspapers, magazines and encyclopedias, which presented New York skyscrapers and Japanese warships to an unaccustomed public, there was considerable discussion and uncertainty about Germany's transformation into a 'world empire' or 'world state'.[31] The popular prediction that the future belonged to vast trading areas and blocs of territory such as Greater Britain, Russia and the United States compounded existing convictions about a national struggle for survival. The idea that the Reich had to expand or decline was widely believed. It was not seen by most Germans, though, as a sufficient reason for war, nor was it perceived to be a constant or overriding aim of Germany's foreign policy. The fact that neither the United States, which had not come into conflict with the Reich until the late 1880s over Samoa, nor Russia, which had been weakened by defeat in the Russo-Japanese war and revolution in 1905, constituted direct threats to German national security over the short term, meant that attention remained fixed on Europe. During the 1900s and 1910s, as in the nineteenth century, France remained the principal military threat to the Reich, and Britain the main economic threat. Accordingly, Wilhelmine newspapers and magazines, although devoting more attention to extra-European powers than in previous decades, continued to concentrate on the Reich's western neighbours. In a comparative survey of the four major party publications, 35.5 per cent of articles for the years 1900, 1906 and 1912 were on France, 30.4 per cent on Britain, 23.85 per cent on Russia and 10.35 per cent on the United States. In the leading political journals, 30.65 per cent of articles for the years between 1898 and 1914 were on Britain, 29.15 per cent on France, 27.25 per cent on Russia and 12.95 per cent on the United States. Since much of this reporting went into considerable detail and included uninterpreted information from news agencies, it is not surprising that changes in the European balance of power in favour of Germany rapidly, if still distortedly, found their way into print.[32]

Western Europe was probably seen by the majority of turn-of-the-century readers in Germany to constitute less of a threat to the Reich than at any point since the mid seventeenth century, in part because of the perceived decline of France and in part because of a more visible cultural proximity, which had been reinforced by the advent of a mass press, photographic journalism, increased foreign reportage, most of which was on Europe, and, by 1907, newsreels. In contrast to exotic territories overseas, countries like France, the Netherlands and Britain appeared to be nearer to Germany than ever, belonging to a shared European culture which extended to British dominions and former colonies in North America and the Antipodes. This culture, which was characterized by Graeco-Roman philosophy, Christian morality, the science of the Enlightenment, industrial capitalism and imperialism, was divided into individual nation-states competing for supremacy and survival. A failure to compete success-fully, as the historian Heinrich von Treitschke reminded his readers, would lead to eclipse, as in the case of Holland, or to annexation, as in Poland.[33] By the early twentieth century, Germany was believed to be in competition with France, Britain and the United States for the intellectual and political leadership of a modern 'European' world of *Kulturländer*. 'Germany', wrote Bülow, reflecting on Treitschke's *Deutsche Geschichte im 19. Jahrhundert*, 'is the youngest of the Great Powers in Europe, the *homo novus* who, having sprung up very recently, has forced his way by his superior capacity into the circle of the older nations.'[34] Towards the other end of the political spectrum and on the other side of the state–society divide, Theodor Wolff, the editor of the left-liberal *Berliner Tageblatt*, concurred that the Reich had 'taken up a primary position' amongst the European nations.[35] German leaders had to be extremely careful, therefore, to take the sensibilities of the traditionally dominant powers of Europe into account, given that the *Kaiserreich* had only recently begun to challenge their tacit predominance.[36] Even the less orthodox and more nationalist left-liberal publicist Paul Rohrbach, who was convinced that the concert of Europe had been eclipsed by 'world empires', nevertheless accepted that 'the German idea' (*der deutsche Gedanke*), in the title of his 1912 book, *Der deutsche Gedanke in der Welt*, had to match the 'moral conquests' of Britain and France, from which, in addition to the exercise of brute strength, 'powerful and thankfully received cultural influences have gone out into the world'. Such moral conquests had given 'many peoples a strong sense of what Englishness and Frenchness means for world culture'.[37] By 1912, the publicist continued, 'only the German nation had, besides the Anglo-Saxons, developed to such an extent that it appeared numerous and internally strong enough to claim for its national ideas a decisive right to shape the coming world epoch'.[38] In other words, the coming age of world empires was seen to have emerged – and to be derived – from an enduring modern era of European cultural and political hegemony.

When Wilhelmine commentators measured the progress of the Reich against a French yardstick, they had every reason to feel confident, not defensive. German depictions of France's decadence can be traced back to criticisms during the revolutionary and Napoleonic wars of the atheism and artificiality of French society. They became more common during the second half of the nineteenth century, as national-minded German historians and journalists revealed the 'frivolity' and 'hollowness' of the Second Empire, the 'hypocrisy' of France's claim to represent 'civilization' in 1870, and the 'instability' and 'corruption' of the Third Republic. Yet, such representations were juxtaposed with the historical accounts of the early nineteenth century by authors like Karl von Rotteck and Karl Theodor Welcker, which were overwhelmingly laudatory, and with justifiedly positive appraisals of French power even after 1870, which rested on increasingly voluminous and precise reports in German newspapers.[39] According to such reportage, Germany had only surpassed France militarily during the late 1890s when 'republicani-zation' – which became a cross-party label during the Dreyfus Affair for unwarranted political interference – was widely believed to have destroyed military discipline, strategy and armament. By the 1900s, most correspondents shared Bülow's belief that the French army had been undermined, despite the government's efforts to maintain forces – with almost 5 million conscripts and reserves in 1914 – as large as those of Germany: 'One must ask oneself if an army which contains so many contradictory elements and such a spirit of revolt will be united enough to succeed against an external enemy', wrote the Chancellor.[40] With a demographic deficit of 23 million by 1910, compared with 5 million in 1880, France simply could not keep up with Germany. This was the meaning of the *Simplicissimus* cartoon '30-Year Military Service: A Picture of the Future', which appeared in 1913 at the time of the French law increasing the length of conscription from two to three years: it envisaged a couple of tired, quinquagenarian French soldiers telling each other they should not complain, for 'who knows how long the next generation will have to serve!'[41] When such prophecies were combined with the realiza-tion, around 1900, that Germany's economy had outgrown that of France, making the Reich the largest and most powerful economic bloc on the European mainland, many Wilhelmine Germans began to feel, like the economist Adolph Wagner, that 'The German is again emerging as the major people.'[42]

Such judgments were based on comparisons with Britain as well as France, as Wagner's addendum made clear: 'If anyone is to be first among equals, then it will be he [the German] and not the Frenchman or the Briton.'[43] This perceived reversal of British and German for-tunes was just as important as the Reich's alleged ascendancy vis-à-vis France, for the British Empire not only constituted Germany's principal economic rival, but was also a 'world state' and the main obstacle to German maritime and colonial ambitions. For much of the nineteenth century, Britain had been admired by liberals for its balanced, constitutional system of government, its robust parliamentary style of politics, its defence of basic freedoms of association, assembly and expression, and its pursuit of free trade and unencumbered industrial growth. It had also been praised by many conservatives – and a significant number of liberals – for its aristocratic parties, its incremental, historical approach to policy-making, its tradition of common law, its deferential, Protestant and patriotic society, and its 'Germanic' and dynastic ties to the states of the Confederation. These images of Britain altered decisively between 1871 and 1914, as German academics and journalists began to emphasize the self-interest of British foreign policy, the geopolitical implications of British imperialism and the wider ramifications of Britain's relative economic decline. Conservatives, Catholics and National Liberals, who were already suspicious of what Ludwig von Gerlach termed the 'advancing democracy' of 'old England' after the 1867 Reform Bill, led the way in revising German attitudes.[44]

Treitschke, a National Liberal deputy who came to vote with the Free Conservatives, marked the transition. In the 1850s and early 1860s, he had been convinced that 'admiration is the first feeling which the study of English history calls forth in everyone'. During the late 1860s, he had gradually given up the idea of transferring British political institutions to Germany, since the monarchical and state traditions of the *Kaiserreich* were better suited to German conditions. Finally, from the mid 1870s onwards, he came to contrast the two countries, making a distinction between 'Anglo-Saxon' and 'Teutonic' cultures, and concentrated on unmasking the arrogance, inhumanity, hypocrisy and selfish materialism of British foreign policy: 'In the halls of parliament', he declared, 'one heard only shameless British commercial morality, which, with the Bible in the right hand and the opium pipe in the left, spreads the benefits of civilization around the world.'[45] In the 1900s, a long line of liberal and conservative successors to Treitschke, including historians and economists like Dietrich Schäfer, Hermann Oncken, Friedrich Meinecke and Gerhard von Schulze-Gävernitz, went on to show how the expansion of the British Empire had been the fortuitous consequence of Britain's advantageous trading position as an island and of its duplicitous policy of divide and rule on the European mainland, which allowed it to acquire colonies in the eighteenth and nineteenth centuries with little opposition from other powers. Thus, historians often overlooked the industrial and administrative foundations of

British imperialism. Many concurred with Otto Hintze that Britain had, by the early twentieth century, become a cautious, uncompetitive 'pensioners' state' (*Rentnerstaat*), attaining 'a satisfied, stationary condition' which was 'not favourable to the needs of a national and political extension of power, to the striving for Anglo-Saxon domination of the world'.[46] Revisionist social imperialists in the SPD and left-liberal imperialists around Friedrich Naumann expressed similar points of view. Compared with Britain and France, Germany seemed to have grown stronger since unification in 1871.

The Reich's position vis-à-vis Russia was much less certain, not least because contemporaries' knowledge of the country was haphazard and sporadic. 'The two great neighbouring nations understand each other very little', wrote the sociologist Max Weber, who felt the need to learn Russian after the revolution of 1905 in order to comprehend the significance of the event.[47] On the one hand, Russia was treated as a culturally – and sometimes racially – inferior power, with the left-liberal satirical journal *Simplicissimus*, for example, portraying Russians variously as primitive subhumans, lice and rats. As Troy Paddock has shown, such views seemed to have been confirmed by defeat in the Russo-Japanese war and by the onset of revolution in 1905.[48] They continued to permeate most press reportage until the Balkan wars in 1912–13.[49] Russia was, in the words of a contemporary cliché, a 'colossus with feet of clay'; an Asiatic power with a corrupt administration, despotic rule and a backward church, which had attempted to implement policies of 'Westernization' under Peter and Catherine the Great, but which had failed. On this reading of Russian history, put forward by the Baltic German and holder of the first chair in the field, Theodor Schiemann, the tsarist state posed no threat to the Reich:

> For us the Russian drive for expansion, which in the last fifty years has occurred with surprising tenacity and has met with even more surprising success, means only a temporary political relief because the political situation dictates more and more the further expansion of Russian rule, or at least of Russian influence, to the South and East. While to the West every territorial enlargement means a predicament and every war policy is a serious danger for Russia. These very simple, but often overlooked truths are to be reckoned with in every judgement on German–Russian relations. Therefore, we do not get very upset over the snarling in the Russian press, because we know that it is basically impotent rage.[50]

On the other hand, Russia was depicted as a barbaric and potentially powerful enemy, criticized and feared at different times by most German parties. The neighbouring state, which had already been described as barbaric in the eighteenth century, came to represent 'Asia', menacing the borders of Germany and Europe.

To the German left, such perceptions went back to the Karlsbad Decrees in 1819 and the revolutions of 1848 and 1849, when Russian armies had supported the reactionary policies of Austria–Hungary. By the mid-nineteenth century, it was common, as Friedrich Engels demonstrated, to slip from criticism of a despotic, centralized Russian state to denigration and subordination of entire Slavic cultures: 'Peoples, which have never had a history, which, from the very moment when they reached the first, rawest levels of civilization, fell under foreign domination or which were first forced up to the first stage of civilization, have no capacity for life, will never be able to attain any degree of independence.'[51] Such hierarchies of culture persisted in socialist circles until the Russian Revolution in 1917. Thus, Bebel's declaration to the Reichstag in 1896 that 'the East' was characterized by 'a lack of culture and a piece of barbarism', whereas 'true culture' found 'its home in Central, Southern and Western Europe', was echoed in 1914 by an unofficial SPD press release justifying the party's decision to go to war:

Defeat would be something unthinkable, something frightful. If war is the most horrible of all horrors, the frightfulness of this war will be intensified by the fact that it will not only be waged by civilized nations. We are sure that our comrades in uniform of all sorts and conditions will abstain from all unnecessary cruelty, but we cannot have this trust in the motley hordes of the Tsar, and we will not have our women and children sacrificed to the bestiality of Cossacks.[52]

On the German right, the picture was more complicated, with reactionaries like August von Haxthausen, who was one of the most well-known mid-nineteenth-century foreign observers of Russian culture, interpreting the peasant commune or 'mir' as a pre-revolutionary, pre-industrial barrier against European decadence.[53] Most conservative commentators, however, saw Russia as a culture which had barely been touched by Greek thought, Western Christianity, Roman law or the Enlightenment. By the 1900s, Russia's defeat in the Crimean (1856) and Russo-Japanese wars (1905), sporadic Russo-German hostility after St Petersburg had signed the Dual Alliance with France in 1894, and the collapse and partial restoration of tsarism in the bloody revolutions of 1905 and 1906 all allowed *émigré* Baltic Germans like Friedrich von Bernhardi and Theodor Schiemann, who dominated the academic study and newspaper reporting of Russian affairs, to discredit both state and society as the products of a foreign-dominated, backward and violent 'Unkultur'. This remained the dominant image of Russia until the outbreak of the First World War, despite the efforts of the historian Otto Hoetzsch and a number of reform-minded conservatives to represent the Russian regime as an imitation of the German Empire in the early 1910s. Most commentators saw themselves as fundamentally different from their 'Asiatic' Russian or Slav neighbours, on many occasions disregarding, but occasionally fearing, turns of events in the tsarist state.[54]

In the decades before the First World War, images of a Russian enemy were less consistent and realistic than corresponding depictions of Britain, France and other 'European' states. Given the double-edged nature of Wilhelmine stereotypes of Russia – backward and barbaric, rural, illiterate and demographically fertile, lacking industry yet abounding in raw materials, defeated but expansionist, corrupt and despotic, Asiatic but with elements of European 'civilization' – cross-party ignorance of the Reich's eastern neighbour during the 1900s and early 1910s was always liable to turn quickly to fear, once Russian foreign policy began to collide with that of Berlin and Vienna. In particular, the German left had long harboured both contempt for and fear of Russian 'autocracy' and 'barbarism', which allowed the Reich government – in contrast to earlier crises concerning Britain and France in Morocco – greater freedom of manoeuvre in 1914 by uniting political parties behind a 'war of defence'. As is shown in the next two chapters, support for war on the part of the SPD, left liberals, the Centre Party and, even, moderate Conservatives and National Liberals was by no means automatic after the turn of the century, as the parties had begun to discuss Germany's national interest and foreign policy much more openly, challenging government interventions and justifications for the first time. Simultaneously, commentators on the left and in the centre had reassessed and downgraded the threat posed by the main 'European' powers and the Reich's principal rivals during the 1900s and early 1910s – Britain and France – because they felt closer to such countries and because they were convinced, like Conservatives, that the countries were in decline. It was therefore essential during the July crisis for Bethmann Hollweg to put Russia, in the words of the Head of the Naval Cabinet, 'in the wrong'.[55] Failure to portray the tsarist state as a credible aggressor threatened to encourage the growing rift in German politics between radical nationalists and loyalist Conservatives, on the one hand, and a political majority of socialists, liberals and Catholics, on the other. The former, which had been radicalized by 'national' debates about foreign policy, the role of the Kaiser and the nature of the German Empire itself, were increasingly prepared by 1911 to back any conflict, whether colonial or continental, offensive or defensive. The latter, however, whose backing – as a vocal political majority – was vital for the commencement of a genuinely 'national' military campaign, seemed more and more willing to criticize and oppose the wrong kind of war against implausible enemies. As has been seen, this national-minded but moderate majority was increasingly prepared to defend its views and to criticize both the government and radical nationalists on the German right. The next chapter shows how the interference of such moderate parties and newspapers in the realm of foreign policy developed during the decade or so before 1914.

Notes

1. F. Fischer, *War of Illusions* (London, 1975); V.R. Berghahn, *Imperial Germany, 1871–1918* (Oxford, 1994).

2. O. Dann, *Nation und Nationalismus in Deutschland, 1770–1990*, 3rd revised edn (Munich, 1996), pp. 16, 20; H.-U. Wehler, *Nationalismus* (Munich, 2001), pp. 77–83.

3. H. James, *A German Identity, 1770–1990* (London, 1989), p. 33.

4. S. Förster, *Der doppelte Militarismus: Die deutsche Heerestüstungspolitik zwischen Status-quo-Sicherung und Aggression, 1890–1913* (Stuttgart, 1985), especially pp. 144–300; W.J. Mommsen, *Imperial Germany* (London, 1995), pp. 75–100, 163–204. G. Eley, *Reshaping the German Right: Radical Nationalism and Political Change after Bismarck* (New Haven, 1980); R. Chickering, *'We Men Who Feel Most German': A Cultural Study of the Pan-German League, 1886–1914* (London, 1984).

5. *Alldeutsche Blätter* (1908), cited in Chickering, *'We Men Who Feel Most German'* (London, 1984), p. 123.

6. *Alldeutsche Blätter* (1907), cited in Chickering, *'We Men Who Feel Most German'* p. 79.

7. Chickering, *'We Men Who Feel Most German'* p. 77.
8. Ibid.
9. R. Chickering, 'Die Alldeutschen erwarten den Krieg', in J. Dülffer and K. Holl (eds), *Bereit zum Krieg: Kriegsmentalität im wilhelminischen Deutschland, 1890–1914* (Göttingen, 1986), p. 24.
10. H. Class, *Wider den Strom. Vom Werden und Wachsen der nationalen Opposition im alten Reich* (Leipzig, 1932), p. 257.
11. See, for example, D. Blackbourn, *Germany, 1780–1918* (London, 1997), pp. 424–40.
12. F. Meinecke, *Cosmopolitanism and the Nation-State* (Princeton, 1970), pp. 368, 374.
13. F. Naumann, 'Die Umwandlung der deutschen Reichsverfassung', *Patria* (1908), p. 95.
14. C. Bachem, cited in H.W. Smith, *German Nationalism and Religious Conflict* (Princeton, 1995), pp. 61–78, 138–40, 185–205.
15. G. v. Vollmar and other references to the SPD, in D. Groh and P. Brandt, *'Vaterlandslose Gesellen': Sozialdemokratie und Nation, 1860–1990* (Munich, 1992), pp. 112–57.
16. E. Bernstein, *Evolutionary Socialism* (New York, 1952), pp. 165–6.
17. Ibid., p. 170.
18. Groh and Brandt, *'Vaterlandslose Gesellen'*, pp. 112–57.
19. F. Meinecke, *Weltbürgertum und Nationalstaat*, 7th edn (Berlin, 1927), p. 13.
20. Rathenau, cited in W.T. Allen, *Satire and Society in Wilhelmine Germany* (Kentucky, 1984), p. 76.
21. Keim, cited in Eley, *Reshaping the German Right*, pp. 265–6; H. Class cited in Chickering, *'We Men Who Feel Most German'*, p. 285.
22. Chickering, *'We Men Who Feel Most German'*, p. 283.
23. Meinecke, cited ibid., p. 296.
24. *Simplicissimus* (1897), shown in N. Stargardt, *The German Idea of Militarism: Radical and Socialist Critics, 1866–1914* (Cambridge, 1994), p. 37.
25. E. Bassermann, F. Lascelles and F. Cartwright, cited in P.G. Lauren, *Diplomats and Bureaucrats* (Stanford, 1976), p. 57.
26. Ibid., p. 55.
27. Ibid., p. 59.
28. Treitschke, *Selections from Treitschke's Lectures on Politics* (London, 1914), p. 10.
29. F. Naumann, in *Hilfe*, 28 (1900); O.A.H. Schmitz, *Das Land der Wirklichkeit*, 5th edn (Munich, 1914), pp. 22–3, 38, 56–7, 61, 67–8, 73, 111, 114–15, 142, 146; K. Hillebrand, *Frankreich und die Franzosen*, 4th edn (Strasbourg, 1898), p. 9.
30. Lamprecht, cited in F. Trommler, 'Inventing the Enemy: German-American Cultural Relations, 1900–1917', in H.-J. Schröder (ed.), *Confrontation and Cooperation: Germany and the United States in the Era of World*

War I (Oxford, 1993), p. 113; D.E. Barclay and E. Glaser-Schmidt (eds), *Transatlantic Images and Perceptions: Germany and America since 1776* (Cambridge, 1997), pp. 65–86, 109–30; D. Diner, *America in the Eyes of the Germans* (Princeton, 1996), pp. 3–51; C.E. McClelland, *The German Historians and England* (Cambridge, 1971); P. M. Kennedy, *The Rise of the Anglo-German Antagonism, 1860–1914* (London, 1980), pp. 59–145, 306–437.

31. See Chapter 7.

32. Reportage is examined more fully in M. Hewitson, *National Identity and Political Thought in Germany: Wilhelmine Depictions of the French Third Republic, 1890–1914* (Oxford, 2000); see also M. Hewitson, 'Germany and France before the First World War', *English Historical Review*, 115 (2000), pp. 570–606, on the question of enmity and threats to national security.

33. Treitschke, *Selections from Treitschke's Lectures on Politics*, p.20.

34. B. v. Bülow, *Imperial Germany* 6th edn (London, 1914), p. 1.

35. T. Wolff, *Das Vorspiel* (Munich, 1924), vol. 1, p. 41. Here, he equates 'the circle of nations (*Völker*)' and the 'peace of Europe'.

36. Ibid.

37. P. Rohrbach, *Der deutsche Gedanke in der Welt* (Düsseldorf, 1912), pp. 217–18.

38. Ibid., p. 7.

39. H.-O. Sieburg, *Deutschland und Frankreich in der Geschichtsschreibung des neunzehnten Jahrhunderts*, 2 vols (Wiesbaden, 1954–8); M. Jeismann, *Das Vaterland der Feinde* (Stuttgart, 1992), pp. 27–102, 241–95.

40. B. v. Bülow memorandum, 15 May 1909, *Auswärtiges Amt Bonn*, R6605, A8510.

41. *Simplicissimus*, 17 March 1913, no. 51.

42. A. Wagner, cited in Kennedy, *The Rise of the Anglo-German Antagonism*, p. 310. Also, G. Krumeich, 'La puissance militaire française vue de l'Allemagne autour de 1900', in P. Milza and R. Poidevin (eds), *La Puissance française à la belle époque* (Brussels, 1992), pp. 199–210; H. Kaelble, 'Wahrnehmung der Industrialisierung: Die französische Gesellschaft im Bild der Deutschen zwischen 1891 und 1914', in W. Süß (ed.), *Übergänge: Zeitgeschichte zwischen Utopie und Machbarkeit* (Berlin, 1989), pp. 123–38. The arguments here are made in more detail in M. Hewitson, 'German Public Opinion and the Question of Industrial Modernity: Wilhelmine Depictions of the French Economy' *European Review of History*, 7 (2000), and M. Hewitson, 'Images of the Enemy: German Depictions of the French Military, 1890–1914' *War in History*, 11 (2004).

43. Wagner, cited in Kennedy, *The Rise of the Anglo-German Antagonism*, p. 310.

44. Gerlach, cited in Kennedy, *The Rise of the Anglo-German Antagonism*, p.73.

45. Treitschke, cited in McLelland, *The German Historians and England*, pp. 168, 184.

46. Hintze, cited in W. Schenk, *Die deutsch–englische Rivalität vor dem Ersten Weltkrieg in der Sicht deutscher Historiker* (Aarau, 1967), p. 77.

47. M. Weber, 'Russlands Übergang zum Scheinkonstitutionalismus' (1906), cited in T.R.E. Paddock, 'German Perceptions of Russia before the First World War' (Diss., Berkeley, 1994), p. 341.

48. Paddock, 'German Perceptions of Russia before the First World War', pp. 156–241.

49. Ibid., p. 242.

50. Schiemann, article for the *Kreuz-Zeitung* in 1902, cited ibid., p. 289.

51. Engels, cited in L. Kopolew, 'Zunächst war Waffenbrüderschaft', in M. Keller (ed.), *Russen und Russland aus deutscher Sicht*, vol. 3 (Munich, 1992), p. 51.

52. Bebel, cited in Stargardt, *The German Idea of Militarism*, p. 59; Stampfer, cited in P. Scheidemann, *Memoirs of a Social Democrat*, vol. 1 (London, 1929), p. 189.

53. C. Schmidt, 'Ein deutscher Slawophil? August von Haxthausen und die Wiederentdeckung der russischen Bauerngemeinde 1843/44', in Keller, *Russen und Russland*, vol. 3, pp. 196–216.

54. G. Voigt, *Russland in der deutschen Geschichtsschreibung, 1843–1945* (Berlin, 1994), pp. 66–114; D. Groh, *Russland im Blick Europas*, 2nd edn (Frankfurt a. M., 1988), pp. 97–412; T.R.E. Paddock, 'Still Stuck at Sevastopol: The Depiction of Russia during the Russo-Japanese War and the Beginning of the First World War in the German Press', *German History*, 16 (1998), pp. 358–76.

55. G.A. v. Müller, cited in N. Ferguson, 'Public Finance and National Security: The Domestic Origins of the First World War Revisited', *Past and Present*, 142 (1994), p. 18.

4

The Politics of War: Parties, the Press and Public Opinion

'Public opinion', as contemporaries were all too aware, had come to play an important role in the formulation and conduct of foreign policy by the mid-1900s. Deference and unquestioning support for the state in the diplomatic sphere had diminished, overturning the practices of the Bismarckian era. Although in many respects vociferously nationalist, significant sections of an expanded German public were prepared to criticize the conduct and limit the scope of the Reich government's external policy. By the mid-1900s, as outside observers noted, public opinion had been transformed, partly as a consequence of a feeling that foreign affairs had been mishandled by the Kaiser, Chancellor and Foreign Office.[1] Thus, during the first Moroccan crisis, Ernst Bassermann, leader of the National Liberals and a long-standing supporter of the administration, had warned the government of his intention to discuss foreign policy in the Reichstag on future occasions.[2] By November 1911, during the alleged fiasco of the second Moroccan crisis, the liberal leader was even more forthright, arguing that 'we have just seen that foreign policy cannot be pursued with complete disregard for popular feeling. That is what those in charge of our foreign policy have failed to understand, and that is the reason for the justifiable discord in the country'.[3] Public opinion, then, as Mommsen, Förster and Eley acknowledge, had not merely become more vocal; it had also become more independent, to the point where Bethmann believed that it was almost impossible to influence.[4] Much of the discord between the government and the public derived from differing images of the Reich's neighbours and from divergent understandings of Germany's international position.

Contrary to Mommsen's claims, however, the growing prominence and independence of public opinion (öffentliche Meinung) were not largely the result of radical nationalist and imperialist critiques of government amongst Germany's middle and upper

61

classes, and within the Conservative and National Liberal parties and extra-parliamentary leagues. Rather, they derived from a rapid expansion and diversification of the public sphere (*Öffentlichkeit*), which at once extended the discussion of foreign policy to new groups beyond the boundaries of educated elites within an old 'political nation' of notables (*Honoratioren*), and blurred the loyalties and attitudes of formerly 'state-supporting' (*staatstragend*) parties and presses. Two overlapping processes were discernible, both of which increased the voice of the centre and left.

On the one hand, the emergence of a mass press in the 1890s and 1900s – with an eightfold increase in the number of newspapers and magazines sent by post between 1868 and 1900 – had been based on the increasing circulation of liberal newspapers like the *Berliner Tageblatt*, with almost a quarter of a million copies sold daily by the 1900s, socialist publications such as *Vorwärts* and *Der Wahre Jakob*, with 100,000 and 450,000 respectively, and unaffiliated papers like the *Berliner Morgenpost*, *Berliner Illustrierte Zeitung* and *Die Woche*, which had between 400,000 and 1 million subscribers each during the 1900s and 1910s, alongside smaller nationalist publications like the *Leipziger Neueste Nachrichten*, *Berliner Neueste Nachrichten* and the *Rheinisch-Westfälische Zeitung*. With the socialist newspapers alone counting 1.5 million subscribers – and perhaps between three and five times as many readers – by 1914 and the 445 Catholic newspapers boasting a similar circulation, leaders and public alike felt that they were facing a leviathan-like 'Great Power', in the words of one academic, bewildered by its novelty and variety.[5] Certainly, ministers and other officials, all of whom were anxious to gauge the mood of a German 'public' (*Publikum*), were presented by the press bureaus of the Foreign and Navy Offices with a wide range of newspaper clippings, including those from major left-liberal, Catholic and socialist publications, not just from nationalist and right-wing newspapers and magazines, as Mommsen implies.

On the other hand, the political parties of the centre and left had become stronger by the turn of the century, so that governments could no longer rely largely or exclusively on the 'state-supporting' Conservatives, Free Conservatives and National Liberals in order to enact legislation. Thus, Bülow depended first on the Centre Party and then on the left liberals, and Bethmann was obliged to call on the cooperation, on various occasions, of Catholics, left liberals and, even, Social Democrats. The finance bill which funded army increases in 1913, for instance, had required the tacit support of the SPD.

Unlike extra-parliamentary nationalist associations such as the Navy and Army Leagues, these parties had regular direct access to government ministers via the Reichstag and its various committees and they figured prominently in Bethmann's calculations during the second Morocco crisis, the drafting of the Army Bill and the July crisis. As early as 1911, the Chancellor had not only come to terms with left liberals, who constituted his most reliable base of support in the Reichstag, and with the Centre Party, which he declared alone 'had political sense', but also – for the first time since the party's founding – with the SPD, arguing that 'we must cooperate with the Social Democrats from issue to issue'.[6] Although it is true that Bethmann still yearned for the support of 'Conservatives and moderates' and that he sometimes referred to nationalists as 'the German people' in its entirety, at other times he used the labels 'people' and 'nation' in a much broader sense and, throughout his period of office, he pursued policies which were intended to gain the backing of centrist and left-wing parties.[7] This redefinition of the political nation and public opinion had important consequences for the conduct of foreign policy, creating a counterpoint to the nationalist leagues and organizations of Eley's and Chickering's 'reshaped right', as parties of all types began to articulate views about international affairs during the 1900s and early 1910s.

Some historians, including – despite their disagreements – Fischer and Geiss as well as Schöllgen, have argued that this expanded public, like the government, had become preoccupied with attaining the status of a world power, effectively obscuring older Great Power rivalries in continental Europe.[8] Even some socialists, writes Schöllgen, conceded in the *Sozialistische Monatshefte* that a 'great empire, which our exporters entertain . . . [is] in itself very legitimate'.[9] Widespread popular frustration, as the *Kaiserreich* failed to make expected imperial gains, pushed many Wilhelmine Germans to contemplate the necessity of war, frequently believing that decline and collapse were the alternative to expansion overseas. Thus, whether pushing for colonies, for the consolidation of a German-dominated, Central European trading bloc, or for a land bridge to the Near and Middle East, contemporaries acted out of fear, to the point where they risked war, despite suspicions that they would be vanquished in such a conflict – or, at least, these are the implications of the case made by Schöllgen and others. The most important consequence appeared to be the elevation of Britain to the role of principal bugbear, in accordance with the arguments outlined by Paul

Kennedy and Volker Berghahn.[10] 'The German people', recorded the *Schlesische Zeitung* in a review of the 1890s, 'is gradually coming to recognise that England is Germany's worst enemy.'[11]

The weaknesses of such overlapping contentions are manifold, although difficult to prove with certainty, in the absence of a systematic study of press and party attitudes to *Weltpolitik*. What is certain, however, is that the majority of parties were extremely reluctant to accept the first Navy Bills and the imperialist premises on which they were founded. Notably, the agrarian-minded Centre and Conservative parties were never unreservedly convinced that the commercial and global aims of *Weltpolitik* were worth pursuing, especially the building of what one leading functionary of the Farmers' League called the 'ugly and dreadful navy' (*hässliche und grässliche Flotte*).[12] Other parties such as the left-liberal *Freisinnige Volkspartei* and the SPD were respectively persuaded to support state-sponsored imperialism only belatedly – by 1906 – or not at all. Even many, if not most, National Liberals seem to have favoured a policy of imperialism based on pragmatism rather than on aggression.[13] This conditional and measured backing of the Reich's colonial and naval policies on the part of most deputies makes their readiness to re-evaluate and criticize *Weltpolitik* easier to understand, after it appeared to have failed to improve Germany's international position. In correspondence with the Centre Party leader Georg Hertling, Bethmann attempted to use such readiness in order to effect a shift from naval to army increases in 1912: 'Because of the navy we have neglected the army and our "naval policy" has created enemies around us. We did not need that and could have built ships anyway.'[14] In other words, the Chancellor thought that he could count on the agreement of party leaders like Hertling – at least in private – that navalism and imperialism had been pursued with too much vigour and fanfare, and that they could now be compromised for the sake of Germany's continental policy. Accordingly, Bethmann seemed to believe that contemporary views of the principal imperial power, Britain, had fluctuated enough to justify a policy of rapprochement between 1912 and 1914. On the other side of the political spectrum, left-wing newspapers like the *Frankfurter Zeitung* and *Vorwärts* likewise indicated the fickleness of popular attitudes to Britain, rapidly shifting the main focus of their enmity. 'For many years,' noted the latter, 'one declared a war between Germany and England to be inevitable and demanded, year after year, a strengthening of the fleet. Now Russia is turned into the aggressive enemy.'[15]

Imperialism, it appeared, was not sufficiently important to most of the Wilhelmine public, notwithstanding continued anglophobia on the far right, to maintain Britain's position as Germany's 'arch enemy' or to rule out the possibility of Anglo-German cooperation.

The most telling measure of the public's evaluation of imperialism was its unwillingness, in the event, to go to war over Morocco in 1905 and 1911. On both occasions, German chancellors recognized such unwillingness and refrained from provoking conflict. Thus, during the first Moroccan crisis, Bülow became convinced that 'neither public opinion, parliament, princes or even the army will have anything to do with a war over Morocco'.[16] Similarly, after the second crisis, Bethmann was not only sure that 'war for the Sultan of Morocco, for a piece of the Sus or Congo or for the Brothers Mannesmann would have been a crime', but also that 'the entire nation would ask me, why this?', if he 'had driven towards war' for such a cause. 'And it would rightly string me up on the nearest tree', concluded the Chancellor, anticipating that most sections of Wilhelmine society would not countenance a continental conflict in order to make territorial gains or keep open markets overseas.[17] Rather, they were closer to the injunction of the journalist Hans Plehn's pamphlet, 'German World Policy and No War' (*Deutsche Weltpolitik und kein Krieg*), published anonymously in 1913 with the help of a counsellor at the German embassy in London as a direct response to Friedrich von Bernhardi's book, *Deutschland und der nächste Krieg*. It was symptomatic that the Pan-German League initially saw the tract as an attempt by the government to gain popular support for its foreign policy.[18] Although the charge was later repudiated by the Wilhelmstrasse, Bethmann and other officials were certainly aware that the majority of parties and, possibly, electors did not believe that the frustration of the Reich's colonial ambitions constituted an immediate threat to national security or economic prosperity. The latter had been regaled for more than a decade after all with stories of German growth and power, from those of the left-liberal journalist and reformer Friedrich Naumann, who exalted in the fact that 'the German race . . . brings army, navy, money and power', to those of the right-wing, 'agrarian' economist and publicist Adolph Wagner, who asserted that the Germans were 'again emerging as the major people'.[19] The predicted export losses as a result of foreign imperialism – and gains from German colonies – had not been borne out by the German Empire's economic record. Consequently, it is debatable whether Wilhelmine leaders were under more or less pressure to acquire colonies in the period immediately before the First World War than at the turn of the century.

Much of the public still looked to the European mainland for the main actual threat to Germany, even if Britain was frequently depicted in the press as the instigator of anti-German campaigns. Accordingly, in 1905 and 1911, newspapers – particularly but far from exclusively those on the right – repeatedly blamed the 'malicious agitators on the Thames' and 'London puppeteers' for the Moroccan crises, yet they tacitly acknowledged that Britain had no chance of defeating the Reich on its own, since it lacked continental land forces. The French had correctly noted 'that England risked almost nothing in the case of war, which meant that France risked all the more when the German army was mobilized', reported the left-liberal *Freisinnige Zeitung* during the first crisis.[20] The like-minded *Berliner Tageblatt* pointed out that Britain had the prospect of making 50,000 million francs during a continental conflict, with possible losses of 13,000 million, whereas a war would cost France and Germany 51,000 million francs each, because they would do most of the fighting.[21] This picture of a future war fitted in with Wilhelmine Germans' historical understanding of conflict, including the myth of German fragmentation enforced by the Great Powers after the Treaty of Westphalia, the defeat of Prussia by France at Jena in 1806, the 'wars of independence' between 1813 and 1815, and the 'wars of unification' during the 1860s. In all such instances, the principal threat to Germany appeared to come from the European continent, usually from France. These memories were overlaid, rather than replaced, by turn-of-the-century debates about imperialism, the navy and world powers like Britain, Japan and the United States, with continuing press interest throughout the 1900s in both France and Russia as continental states. As has been seen, as many articles were written about Germany's western neighbour as about Britain during this period, and two to three times as many were devoted to France or to Russia as to the United States.[22] Despite alarums in the late 1890s and early 1900s about British protectionism in its empire and American expansionism in the Pacific, West Indies and South America, reports continued to concentrate for the most part on European affairs and the rivalries of European states. As a result, right-wing supporters of the fleet such as Delbrück, the editor of the *Preussische Jahrbücher*, continued to point to the need for 'very strong armament on land as well as on sea'.[23]

The main question is to what extent Germany's continental enemies were assessed by the public as a single bloc or as separate states. Historians like Hillgruber and Hildebrand have tended to assume the former, emphasizing the rigidification of alliance structures and the consolidation of fears of encirclement. However, they overlook the fact that the notion of 'Einkreisung' or 'Isolierung', which became common during the first Moroccan crisis, had been replaced in most of the press by a sense of confidence by 1908 and the Austro-Hungarian annexation of Bosnia–Herzegovina.[24] This point was made explicitly by the socialist mouthpiece *Vorwärts* in June of that year, and by the conservative *Preussische Jahrbücher* in February of the following year: 'The epoch in which Germany had to be afraid of becoming "encircled" is clearly over, and all the powers are competing again for our friendship.'[25] Confidence in the Reich's position was such that the *Reichsbote* had put forward a similar argument during the latter part of the first Moroccan crisis itself: 'One doesn't paint frightening visions of coalitions and terrible dangers on the wall in Germany; at present, we have nothing at all to fear. One doesn't speak well of us abroad and wishes a plague and pestilence on all our houses; but the gentlemen have every reason to leave us in peace in the future.'[26]

Throughout much of the decade or so before the First World War, the majority of journalists seemed to believe, like the German government, that rapprochements or even agreements were possible with rival states like Russia and Britain.[27] France, too, in spite of Alsace-Lorraine constituting an insuperable obstacle to any alliance, remained the object of what the French correspondent of *Der Tag* referred to, in December 1912, as German 'seduction'.[28] Until the Agadir crisis in 1911, most newspapers, including those of the right, had foreseen the possibility of better relations between the *Kaiserreich* and the Third Republic. The behaviour of the French nation during the first Moroccan crisis itself, the Conservative Party *porte-parole*, the *Neue Preussische Zeitung*, declared, had demonstrated that 'hopeless pessimism' was no longer a necessary component of Franco-German relations'.[29] Such movement in public opinion, as newspapers oscillated between foreign friends and foes, encouraged the separate evaluation of neighbouring states, since commentators were rarely certain about the future alignment of forces. This, of course, was reinforced by the intrinsic proclivity of virtually all publications to report on states in separate columns of their foreign affairs pages.

The largest single threat to the *Kaiserreich* for most of the decade and a half before the First World War was France. Calling France to account and removing French enmity 'through the violence of weapons', was therefore 'the first and most essential demand of a healthy German policy', according to the publicist and former member of the General Staff, Friedrich von Bernhardi in 1912.[30] Yet the neighbouring state had also been diagnosed in presses from across the political spectrum to be in a state of political, economic and demographic decline since the Dreyfus Affair in the late 1890s. Such decline was widely perceived to be relative rather than absolute, not least because the French army remained the most immediate menace to German national security. Consequently, even critical publications such as the Catholic journal *Stimmen aus Maria Laach* conceded that the development of France's economy under the Third Republic 'has not been an unfavourable one', when considered in isolation. The question, though, was 'not whether the French economy has made progress but whether it has progressed at the same speed as its rivals or whether it has lagged behind'.[31] It was evident from a reading of the German press that France had fallen behind, militarily as well as economically, notwithstanding journalists' regular caveats that 'France is certainly not an opponent of inferior quality'.[32] The overall verdict, which was reached by newspapers of almost all political leanings, was echoed by the *Post* in October 1911: 'We do not mistake the fact that work in France's army has been carried out with extraordinary effort . . . What is awry in the French army, however, where it is ill, is *the pernicious state of its officer corps* and *too little discipline*, although this should not be measured according to Prussian criteria.'[33] Political interference, nepotism, a divided officer corps, disobedience, mutinies, antimilitarism, defective equipment, and demographic stagnation were all believed to have weakened the French army for the foreseeable future, giving the Reich an unprecedented military superiority. When a rump of nationalist newspapers challenged such an orthodoxy in 1912–13, contending that the French Three Year Law had given the neighbouring state a military advantage over the Reich, most journalists, including many Conservative ones, disagreed, arguing that France's extension of conscription had overstretched the country's resources.[34] These public perceptions of the decline of the main military threat to Germany until 1913 at the earliest are difficult to reconcile with Hildebrand's, Schöllgen's and Ferguson's description of widespread anxiety in Wilhelmine Germany about the Reich's deteriorating position abroad.

Newspapers' confidence in German power as a consequence of French 'decline' was demonstrated during the two Moroccan crises. In 1905, there was broad agreement, in accordance with the so-called 'hostage' theory, that France would be the Reich's principal military opponent in a future war. 'Germany', wrote Schiemann in the *Kreuz-Zeitung*, 'can only conduct a war with England . . . in France.'[35] The assurance of the Conservative *Post* that 'the bill would be presented in Paris, if the German fleet succumbed to the British', was matched by that of the left-leaning Catholic publication the *Kölnische Volkszeitung* that 'France must serve us as a hostage for the good conduct of her Foreign Office'.[36] Implicit in the notion of a hostage was the idea that the neighbouring state was a potential victim, not a genuine threat. Correspondingly, both left-wing and right-wing journalists discounted the possibility of a French attack in the first Moroccan crisis, since Paris had supposedly accepted German ascendancy. No further pressure would be needed, wrote the left-liberal journalist Theodor Wolff in June 1905, to deter the Quai d'Orsay from going to war.[37] 'If Germany will only remain firm and self-confident, success must be ours, for Paris has neither the leader nor the courage to fight us', concurred the *Rheinisch-Westfälische Zeitung* in the same month.[38] This sense that Germany had managed to 'convince France that she was powerless', in the triumphant words of the Pan-German leader Ernst Hasse, was perceived to constitute a reversal of the two states' historical positions; 'an event of almost world significance', as the Catholic *Historisch-Politische Blätter* put it, 'for French statesmen had been wont to overthrow German princes'.[39] Although the German right occasionally regretted that 'the stage setting' in Morocco was 'all wrong', preventing an act of force, most parties sought to use the Reich's military superiority as a means of effecting a rapprochement with France, rather than waging a war against it.[40] The mouthpiece of the Conservative Party was typical of most political opinion during the crisis:

> If one follows . . . the declarations of opinion in public life [in France], one can see that the Morocco incident has proved useful, not damaging. Certainly, the 'Alsace-Lorraine question' will not disappear in the foreseeable future, and we will not be able to lay down our arms. But the behaviour of the French nation in the last months has shown that hopeless pessimism is no longer appropriate when one observes our relations with our western neighbour.[41]

After Delcassé's forced resignation in June 1905, even the Pan-Germans were moved to call for a continental alliance with France.[42] Later, when Germany had been outmanoeuvred at the conference of Algeciras by the Entente powers, those on the far right were much more hostile towards the neighbouring state. Most other politicians and journalists would probably have accepted Delbrück's verdict, however, that the Entente had been reinforced against Germany as a result of fear, not aggression.[43]

By the time of the second Moroccan crisis in 1911, although the majority of right-wing commentators – and some in the centre – had given up the hope of a Franco-German rapprochement, their assessment of French power – and that of the Entente – remained the same. If France did not back down, 'then the Panther [may] have the effect of the Ems dispatch', wrote the *Rheinisch-Westfälische Zeitung* in July 1911, threatening a repeat of 1870.[44] The Reich, it was believed, as in 1905 and 1908, was too powerful to encounter resistance in continental Europe. 'Again it is seen', asserted the organ of the Pan-German League, 'that the foreign policy of a great nation, of a powerful state, cannot exhaust itself in patient inaction: it must will and act.'[45] It was for this reason that most of the German right breathed 'a sigh of relief' at the prospect of action, in the phrase of the Conservative *Kreuz-Zeitung*, even though such action might have led to war.[46] Many nationalist publications welcomed the idea of military conflict, contending that there had never been so unanimous a demand for a strong policy.[47] Germany's position was so advantageous, they implied, that Britain, too, in addition to the continental powers France and Russia, would be destroyed. '*There is not the shadow of a doubt*', predicted the *Deutsche Tageszeitung*, '*that a war would endanger Great Britain's existence as a world and commercial power.*'[48] Both National Liberals and moderate Conservatives talked, at times, of the inevitability and desirability of such a conflict.[49] If French chauvinists, urged on by British jingoists, succeeded in 'rekindling the idea of *revanche*' and pushing France into a conflict, it was said, 'the current general situation is by no means unfavourable for us'.[50] War would show the hollowness of French culture.[51] Accordingly, even the official publication of the Conservative Party was prepared to advocate the use of military force, albeit as one of three possible outcomes of the Agadir crisis, together with full diplomatic recognition of Germany's equal status or the withdrawal of all French and Spanish troops from Morocco. 'There should not be a particle of doubt that we are ready for any of these contingencies', the DKP mouthpiece concluded.[52] When the Reich government stopped short of war and accepted French 'compensation' in the form of territory in the Congo, the right-wing press and parties united in their condemnation of what the *Berliner Neueste Nachrichten* termed 'a policy of concessions and of retreat'.[53] The Reichstag, the newspaper urged, 'should declare with the greatest emphasis that it *disapproves* the present *policy of peace at any price* ... and that it is *ready to undertake every sacrifice necessary for a strong, manly, and honest policy*'.[54] A day later, the leader of the Conservatives, Ernst von Heydebrand, delivered his speech to the chamber, criticizing Bethmann's foreign policy for the first time and signalling his party's participation in a 'national opposition'. 'We Germans will be ready ... for the necessary sacrifices', he warned, to cheers from the right.[55]

The fact that Bethmann's address to the Reichstag, justifying the supposed caution of official policy, was greeted with a silence which 'was like that of a grave', in the opinion of the *Berliner Tageblatt*, might suggest that the majority of parties favoured war or, at least, a policy of brinkmanship.[56] However, such a supposition would not be warranted, in spite of almost universal opposition in Germany to France's 'Tunisification' of Morocco and Britain's 'agitation' on its own behalf.[57] As in 1905, many on the left and in the centre did not consider, in Theodor Wolff's words, that 'the worth of the *pursued aims*' justified the violence of the government's preferred diplomatic means.[58] More importantly, most left-wing and centrist newspapers and politicians continued to assume that France and the Entente were too weak to constitute an offensive military threat.[59] Thus, the immediate response of publications such as the *Frankfurter Zeitung* and the *Vossische Zeitung* to the dispatch of the 'Panther' to Agadir was to treat it as a mere bargaining chip and to discount the possibility of war.[60] 'We demand', called *Germania* on 4 July 1911, 'that the government do everything in its power to prevent a serious international conflict from arising on account of Morocco'.[61] Following the lead of the *Kölnische Zeitung*, which often inserted articles by the Foreign Office, the presses which were closest to the political centre-ground in Germany expressed the hope that 'the affair would be dealt with calmly and in a business-like way'.[62] They stressed that France had exceeded the provisions of the Algeciras agreement, sometimes without due cause, and that, as a result, the treaty needed to be renegotiated in order to safeguard German economic interests.[63] Only extreme chauvinists, it was implied, wanted to use the threat of war to achieve such ends. The Pan-Germans were the instruments of industrial interests, wrote the Conservative journal the *Grenzboten*, and the 'Mannesmann' press – the *Rheinisch-Westfälische Zeitung, Tägliche Rundschau* and the *Post* – had deliberately exaggerated the bellicosity of the German government's policy.[64] Faced with this menace of war for the sake of Morocco, remarked the right-wing *Deutsche Tageszeitung*, the support of the German public could not be counted upon.[65] The 'German nationalists', proclaimed the most prominent left-leaning Catholic paper, did not speak for the nation: 'Their press does not reflect real public opinion any more than Berlin is Germany. It is well that this is so, for otherwise we would have to conclude that we have become a nation of neurasthenics!'[66] The British ambassador, from a very different point of view, concurred: the majority of Germans in 1911 did not want war.[67] France, as the Reich's principal continental opponent, was simply not threatening enough and Morocco not sufficiently significant to warrant the use of military force.

France remained the main threat to the Reich until a year or so before the First World War partly because Russia had been discredited or overlooked. Wilhelmine publicists, although they were still conscious of Russia's 'resources' and 'barbarity', provided reasons to take a 'Russian menace' less seriously than in the past.[68] 'Russia is, on the whole, weak in times of war because its military leadership is corrupt and the soldiers, from the most highly placed officer to the new recruit, can be corrupted', wrote the Baltic German historian and foreign-policy expert of the *Neue Preussische Zeitung*, Theodor Schiemann, in 1913, agreeing with the analysis of a British colleague: 'It is weak because it possesses no navy worth the name and must import all its munitions and guns; weak also because there is a lack of national traditions in the army.'[69] Like other academic publicists such as Max Lenz, Schiemann emphasized the internal flaws of the Russian state and Russian society, including backwardness, a superficial assimilation of Western traditions and a mixture of nationalities, which looked set to undermine Russian expansionism in the future. Revolutions in such a country, contrary to those in France, threatened to tear it apart rather than leading to the imposition of a strong centralized state.[70] The result was 'that Russia is, for the foreseeable future, to be completely struck off the list of those powers which are in a position to wage a great, modern war', as the publicist Paul Rohrbach spelled out in the second edition of *Deutschland unter den Weltvölkern*, which came out after Russia's defeat in the Russo-

Japanese war in 1904-5 and subsequent revolution in 1905-6. He made the same points again four years later in his popular work *Der deutsche Gedanke in der Welt*, echoing the arguments of fellow Baltic German Friedrich von Bernhardi: 'a nation, which is so spiritually undeveloped and is so saddled with the pronounced ethical defects of its upper stratum as the Russians are . . . would no longer be able to wage a war with a European Great Power of the first rank, and least of all would its army be able to measure itself against ours'.[71] Other publicists and academics like Friedrich Mein-ecke and Otto Hoetzsch, who distanced themselves from caricatures of Russian 'backwardness' and 'barbarity', pointed out that 'Russia has never been an hereditary arch enemy [*Erz- und Erbfeind*] for us'.[72] Present circumstances and the history of Russo-German relations suggested that enmity between the countries was temporary.

The transient and conditional nature of Russo-German enmity seemed clear from a reading of the press during the Bosnian crisis of 1908-9, after Vienna had annexed territory which had been under Austrian occupation since 1878. When Serbia refused to recognize the annexation and Russia prevaricated, Bülow warned St Petersburg that he would allow 'developments to take their course' - a veiled reference to a German-backed Austrian declaration of war against Serbia - unless the Russian government unequivocally sanctioned Vienna's action through an exchange of diplomatic notes.[73] Confronted with such threats of war, few German newspapers were enthusiastic. Thus, although there were injunctions after Algeciras to 'remember how Friedrich II had suddenly foiled the plans of a circle of enemies', most journalists had accepted the Anglo-Russian Entente of 1907 without raising the spectre of a military conflict.[74] 'The island empire can make as many agreements as it desires', declared the *Vossische Zeitung*; 'no one believes any more that it is organising an aggressive coalition against us'.[75] Russia, it was implied, was even less likely to be organizing such a coalition. Consequently, when Austria and Germany were ranged against Russia in 1908-9, many leader-writers were cautious, avoiding bellicose outbursts. The *Berliner Tageblatt*, notwithstanding its sympathy for Austria–Hungary, was characteristic of the liberal press, asking 'is it one of Germany's obligations to agree cheerfully every time Herr von Aehrenthal wishes to hitch the German Empire to Austria's wagon?'[76]

On the right, few newspapers objected to Austria's use of force, but a significant number, including the *Hamburger Nachrichten*, the *Deutsche Zeitung*, the *Leipziger Neueste Nachrichten* and the

Alldeutsche Blätter balked at what the *Rheinisch-Westfälische Zeitung* described as Germany pulling Austria's chestnuts out of the Balkan fire.[77] Such publications generally argued for a narrow interpretation of the terms of the Dual Alliance in order to obviate the need for German intervention, since Vienna was not acting defensively. Some journalists on the far right even called for a rapprochement with Russia rather than continuing loyalty to Austria–Hungary. Others, such as those from the *Tägliche Rundschau, Berliner Neueste Nachrichten* and the *Deutsche Tageszeitung*, backed Vienna, as did the Catholic journalists of the *Kölnische Volkszeitung*, but few actively counselled war.[78] Likewise, after Russia had given way to German pressure and acknowledged the annexation of Bosnia–Herzegovina, certain right-wing commentators persisted, amidst broad jubilation that a war had been won 'without firing a shot', in criticizing Bülow's support for Austria. In this respect, the contention of the new editor of the *Alldeutsche Blätter*, Ernst von Reventlow, that 'Germany has no reason for enthusiasm' was not unusual.[79] On the left, the *Frankfurter Zeitung* was more forthright than most other newspapers, yet it did express broader disquiet amongst liberals, Catholics and Social Democrats that 'such a success may be highly prized in professional diplomatic circles, but politics is not a game; when it is a question not only of the driver but also of the fate of the carriage and that of millions, it is permissible to ask for greater caution and conscientiousness'.[80] The Bosnian affair, although it had shown those on the right – and in government – that an act of force against Russia and the Entente could be successful, had not convinced the majority of journalists and politicians that such conduct was either wise or justifiable.

The Balkan wars between 1912 and 1913, in which Austria and Russia seemed prepared to intervene, revived similar doubts, despite the warnings of newspapers such as the *Münchener Neueste Nachrichten* that Germany could not be counted on to accept peace at any price.[81] 'We all know that blood will flow the more, the longer we wait', wrote one correspondent in the chauvinist publication the *Post*.[82] Nevertheless, when they were confronted by a genuine possibility of military intervention, many right-wing commentators shied away from the idea. 'So far as we are concerned', recorded the *Berliner Neueste Nachrichten*, 'we cannot possibly desire a European war for the sake of the Balkans.'[83] Such a conflict would be 'unnatural', since Germany had not gone to war to protect its own interests in Morocco in 1911. Austria was, therefore, to be restrained.[84]

The *Post* was wrong, contended the *Deutsche Tageszeitung*, to support an Austrian offensive against Serbia, since such an action would precipitate a general conflagration.[85] The government should 'do everything in [its] power to prevent the *casus foederis* from arising', wrote the *Hamburger Nachrichten*, anticipating the relief of the *Rheinisch-Westfälische Zeitung* in October 1912 at Bethmann's cautious policy of mediation between the Great Powers.[86] After Germany had helped to keep Austria out of both Balkan wars, the verdict of the left and much of the right remained the same: the Reich's interests had been best served by peace. Reason, rather than sentimental notions of 'the loyalty of the Nibelungen' (*Nibelungentreue*), should inform German foreign policy, declared the organ of the Bund der Landwirte. Most observers concurred with the judgement of the nationalist *Leipziger Neueste Nachrichten* that the Reich government had been justified in refusing to give unconditional promises to Vienna and would continue to be circumspect in the future.[87] Unsurprisingly, the centre and the left backed such a prudent and peaceable policy, with the *Berliner Tageblatt* noting that even the mention by Bethmann of the eventuality of joining Austria in a defensive war had been unenthusiastically received by most deputies in the Reichstag.[88] Instead, a policy of caution and mediation, which the government appeared to favour, was carried out 'in agreement with the entire nation, from the extreme right to the Social Democrats', in the words of the progressive *Freisinnige Zeitung*.[89] As most newspapers and parties refused to take up the Pan-German call for annexations in Asia Minor, to the delight of the left-liberal *Frankfurter Zeitung* and moderate liberal *Vossische Zeitung*, the SPD's press could be unusually confident of support for its proposition that the 'German people' should not 'consent to act as [Austria's] hired soldier (*Landesknecht*)'.[90] Few onlookers desired war in 1912 or 1913, despite remaining sure, in the words of one nationalist correspondent, that Germany had nothing to fear from Russia and its allies, whatever the outcome of the Balkan war might be.[91]

Some far-right-wing newspapers had persisted throughout the 1900s and early 1910s in issuing warnings about the 'Russian menace'.[92] By the spring of 1914, they had been joined by many publications of the centre and centre-right, after the St Petersburg correspondent of the *Kölnische Zeitung* had prophesied that Russia was arming in order to go to war against Germany in three years' time. Yet, even the far right acknowledged that the weakening of

Russia during the mid-1900s left the Reich in a strong international position. 'If we strive for nothing more than to have the reassurance from one day to the next that no one will attack us, then we can sleep more assuredly in the coming years than hitherto', admitted the mouthpiece of the Pan-German League, the *Alldeutsche Blätter*, before adding a characteristically Darwinian qualification: 'But those are the political ideals of a dying nation [*Volk*], and hopefully we have not yet gone so far.'[93] Some far-right-wing newspapers such as the *Rheinisch-Westfälische Zeitung* and the *Post* continued to call for a distancing of Berlin from Vienna and closer cooperation with St Petersburg during the 1910s.[94] Arguably, most other publications either refuted the very idea of a Russian menace, as repeatedly occurred on the left and centre-left, or they wavered between scare stories and moderation, particularly on the centre-right, but also in Conservative newspapers like the *Neue Preussische Zeitung*, which relied on the pro-Russian Hoetzsch for its foreign-affairs commentaries on the eve of the First World War. As a consequence, at the low-points of Russo-German relations – the meeting of the King of England and the Tsar in 1908, the Bosnian crisis in 1908–9 and the Balkan wars in 1912–13 – there was always a significant number of papers to oppose the extreme claims of the 'German-national' (*deutsch-national*) press. During the war scare of spring 1914, for instance, as Russia became the principal enemy of the Reich in the minds of many German onlookers, the left-liberal *Frankfurter Zeitung* questioned whether Russian troops were directed against Germany at all and dismissed any predictions about the state of alliances and enmities in 1917. The *Berliner Tageblatt* went further to underline the unreliability of Russia's soldiers, the dubious quality of its armament and the corruption of its army. This and other arguments, such as the likelihood of revolution in Russia and the peaceful intentions of ruling elites, were cited by liberal publications like the *Vossische Zeitung* and the *Münchner Neueste Nachrichten*, which were further to the right. The Conservative *Kreuz-Zeitung* stated that Russia had improved its military but refused to say whether this signified bellicose intentions, repeating the commonly cited slogan 'we Germans fear God, but otherwise nothing on earth'.[95] Other crises involving Russia and Germany witnessed similarly measured or confident statements, sometimes interspersed with anxiety about what *Germania* termed the 'threatening future of Pan-Slavism', from an even wider range of newspapers.[96] Despite the stridency of the nationalist press, then, the Reich government could also call on more moderate sections of 'public opinion', which it could use to counterbalance the bellicosity of the right.

Contrary to some historians' depictions of a sense of doom amongst broad sections of Wilhelmine society, the majority of German parties and newspapers appear to have been relatively optimistic about the Reich's military position during the decade and a half before the First World War, agreeing with Maximilian Harden's assertion in 1909 that Germany was 'again seen as the strong military power, which was not to be tamed through scares, not to be shackled by chains of roses'.[97] The debate about the Army Bill in 1913, with its unprecedented increase in the scope of conscription, constituted the main test of public opinion on this question, not least because it coincided with the Balkan wars and with French and Russian armaments programmes. The discussion was introduced by Bethmann with a scare-mongering speech to the Reichstag on 7 April 1913, in which he warned of a possible struggle for survival in a future war, and it was reinforced by the Chancellor's and the War Minister's more extreme descriptions of French chauvinism and an imbalance of military power to private sittings of the Reichstag committee on the Army Bill on 24 and 25 April. Viewed cursorily, it appears that most shared the opinions expressed by the government: after the first speech, the Conservatives, National Liberals and Centre Party backed the Chancellor, whilst the left-liberal spokesman called his justification of army increases a 'scandal' and the SPD speaker rejected it outright; after the second set of speeches, the left liberals professed that they, too, had been convinced that Germany's external predicament was potentially precarious, leaving the Social Democrats alone to reject the government's explanation of its proposals.[98] The army increases, of course, were subsequently passed with little party opposition. However, such acceptance of the bill, although it undoubtedly reflected politicians' concern that the concentration and alignment of forces in Europe had altered, does not prove the existence of a widespread panic or of overbearing aggressiveness. Thus, in commentaries about the Balkan wars, the *Frankfurter Zeitung* argued that Russia's recovery after defeat against Japan was expected and hardly justified large-scale German counter-measures; the *Vossische Zeitung* admitted that Pan-Slavism had become stronger, but was still much weaker than at the time of the Berlin Congress in 1878; and the *Berliner Tageblatt* asked 'where is the enemy of Europe hiding which imperils peace so seriously that Germany must mobilise?'[99] Many more publications agreed with the National Liberal

Münchner Neueste Nachrichten's injunction that 'only strength is secure'. The implication was that the Reich was secure and could remain so, with appropriate military increases. Certainly, most newspapers' assessments of a parallel Army Bill in France, whose status as Germany's principal enemy was revealed by the war scare of spring 1913, argued that the neighbouring state had been over-stretched, pushed by competitive armament beyond its economic, demographic and military capacity. Only a rump of nationalist publications suggested that France threatened to gain ascendancy.[100]

After the turn of the century, significant sections of German public opinion – and probably the majority of large-circulation newspapers and magazines – continued to spurn the politics of radical nationalism and to oppose armed conflict. Of course, there were many nationalist and Conservative, and some National Liberal and Catholic, journalists and politicians who were prepared – especially by 1911, after France had 'proved' that it was not interested in an alliance – to accept war as an instrument of foreign policy.[101] The fact that France was perceived to be in decline, Britain a negligible continental force and Russia a weakened and backward 'Asiatic' power encouraged many papers to contemplate war.[102] By the same token, however, such 'facts' also convinced other National Liberal and Catholic publications, together with virtually all left-liberal and socialist newspapers, that an armed conflict – except perhaps a 'defensive' war against Russia – was at once less likely to take place and more difficult to justify. Thus, during the Agadir crisis, even though journalists of the *Frankfurter Zeitung* and the *Berliner Tageblatt* were angered by France's attempt to dominate Moroccan politics and protect its markets, they remained confident that 'no reasonable person holds it to be possible that a question of national honour between Germany and France can be derived from this affair'.[103] Would the French be so foolish, asked the *Vossische Zeitung*, 'to allow themselves to be pushed into a war, in which their entire future, not just the fate of their "Tunisified" sherifian empire, but that of all their colonies and of the motherland, is in play?'[104] The Conservative *Neue Preussische Zeitung*, the Catholic *Kölnische Volkszeitung* and the liberal and semi-official *Kölnische Zeitung* all concurred that France – either in the form of 'the people' or 'government' – was peaceable and that there were no grounds for war.[105] Such newspapers, even at moments of international tension, constituted an alternative public and a base of support, beyond the SPD, which appears to have influenced the Reich administration and countered the effect of nationalist outrage in the right-wing press. It is, therefore, misleading to portray government largely as the victim of radical nationalists during the late 1900s and early 1910s. In fact, as is demonstrated below, predominant groups in both the army and state pushed for war earlier and more consistently than most sections of public opinion.

Notes

1. See, for instance, P.G. Lauren, *Diplomats and Bureaucrats* (Stanford, 1976), p. 55.

2. Ibid., p. 57.

3. Bassermann, cited in W.J. Mommsen, 'Public Opinion and Foreign Policy in Wilhelmine Germany, 1897–1914', in *Imperial Germany* (London, 1995), p. 197.

4. Ibid., p. 198.

5. H. Dietz, *Das Zeitungswesen* (Leipzig, 1910), p. 2. The figures here are taken from K. Koszyk, *Deutsche Presse im 19. Jahrhundert* (Berlin, 1966); P. Winzen, *Bülows Weltmachtkonzept: Untersuchungen zur Frühphase seiner Aussenpolitik, 1897–1901* (Boppard, 1977), Appendix; T. Nipperdey, *Deutsche Geschichte, 1866–1918*, vol. 2 (Munich, 1990), pp. 797–811.

6. Bethmann cited in K. Jarausch, *The Enigmatic Chancellor: Bethmann Hollwegg and the Hubris of Imperial Germany* (New Haven, 1973), pp. 87–9.

7. Ibid., pp. 125–6.

8. F. Fischer, *World Power or Decline* (New York, 1974); I. Geiss, 'The German Version of Imperialism, 1898–1914: *Weltpolitik*', in G. Schöllgen (ed.), *Escape into War? The Foreign Policy of Imperial Germany* (Oxford, 1990), pp. 105–19.

9. Cited in G. Schöllgen, 'Germany's Foreign Policy in the Age of Imperialism: A Vicious Circle', in *Escape into War?*, p. 123, f. 6.

10. V.R. Berghahn, *Germany and the Approach of War in 1914* (London, 1973), pp. 1–124; P.M. Kennedy, *The Rise of the Anglo-German Antagonism, 1860–1914* (London, 1980).

11. Cited in Kennedy, *The Rise of the Anglo-German Antagonism*, p. 312.

12. S. Förster, *Der doppelte Militarismus: Die deutsche Heerestüstungspolitik zwischen Status-quo-Sicherung und Aggression, 1890–1913* (Stuttgart, 1985), pp. 81–6.

13. D. Langewiesche, *Liberalism in Germany* (London, 2000), p. 237.
14. Cited in Jarausch, *The Enigmatic Chancellor*, p. 96.
15. Cited in Berghahn, *Germany and the Approach of War*, p. 181.
16. Cited in K.A. Lerman, *The Chancellor as Courtier: Bernhard von Bülow and the Governance of Germany, 1900–1909* (Cambridge, 1990), p. 142.
17. Cited in Jarausch, *The Enigmatic Chancellor*, pp. 125–6.
18. F. Fischer, *War of Illusions* (London, 1975), p. 267.
19. Cited in Kennedy, *Rise of the Anglo-German Antagonism*, p. 310.
20. *Freisinnige Zeitung*, 29 September 1905. For more on the extent of German inculpation of Britain in 1905 and 1911, see M. Hewitson, 'Germany and France before the First World War: A Reassessment of Wilhelmine Foreign Policy', *English Historical Review*, 115 (2000), pp. 588–9, 592–3.
21. *Berliner Tageblatt*, 8 November 1905.
22. For more details, see M. Hewitson, *National Identity and Political Thought in Germany: Wilhelmine Depictions of the French Third Republic, 1890–1914* (Oxford, 2000), pp. 7–11.
23. Delbrück in the *Post*, 20 April 1904, cited in E.M. Carroll, *Germany and the Great Powers, 1860–1914: A Study in Public Opinion and Foreign Policy* (New York, 1938), p. 497.
24. Carroll, *Germany and the Great Powers* (New York, 1938), pp. 573–642.
25. *Preussische Jahrbücher*, 1909, p. 169. *Vorwärts*, 16 June 1908.
26. *Reichsbote*, 10 April 1906, cited in Carroll, *Germany and the Great Powers*, p. 485.
27. R. Ropponen, *Die russische Gefahr* (Helsinki, 1976), pp. 52–95. Carroll, *Germany and the Great Powers*, on Britain.
28. *Tag*, 25 December 1912. See also, H.C. Löhr, 'Für den König von Preussen arbeiten? Die deutsch-französischen Beziehungen am Vorabend des Ersten Weltkriegs', *Francia*, 23 (1996), pp. 141–54.
29. *Neue Preussische Zeitung*, 4 July 1905.
30. F. v. Bernhardi, *Deutschland und der nächste Krieg* (Stuttgart, 1912), p. 97.
31. *Stimmen aus Maria Laach*, 71 (1906), p. 285. Also, H. Kaelble, 'Wahrnehmung der Industrialisierung: Die französische Gesellschaft im Bild der Deutschen zwischen 1891 und 1914', in W. Süß (ed.), *Übergänge: Zeitgeschichte zwischen Utopie und Machbarkeit* (Berlin, 1989), pp. 123–38; M. Hewitson, 'German Public Opinion and the Question of Industrial Modernity: Wilhelmine Depictions of the French Economy', *European Review of History*, 7 (2000), pp. 45–61.
32. *Deutsche Tageszeitung*, 16 September 1911. Also, *Berliner Tageblatt*, 28 April and 17 November 1906; *Reichsbote*, 2 March 1906 and 27 September 1911; *Leipziger Neueste Nachrichten*, 7 November 1906; *Berliner Neueste Nachrichten*, 14 May 1906 and 26 June 1912; *Berliner Morgenpost*, 8 December 1911; *Vossische Zeitung*, 11 December 1911; *Schlesische Zeitung*,

29 December 1911; *Deutsche Zeitung*, 9 July 1912; *Vorwärts*, 14 September 1911.

33. *Post*, 17 October 1911. Also, G. Krumeich, 'La puissance militaire française vue de l'Allemagne autour de 1900', in P. Milza and R. Poidevin (eds), *La Puissance française à la belle époque* (Brussels, 1992), pp. 199–210; G. Krumeich, 'Le déclin de la France dans la pensée politique et militaire allemande avant la première guerre mondiale', in J.-C. Allain (ed.), *La Moyenne puissance au XXe siècle* (Paris, 1988), p. 105; and M. Hewitson, 'Images of the Enemy: German Depictions of the French Military, 1890–1914', *War in History*, 11 (2004).

34. Conservative newspapers rejecting arguments about French superiority included the *Deutsche Tageszeitung*, 26 March, 4, 11 and 12 September 1913, 2 and 6 February 1914; *Tag*, 29 March, 4 September and 5 December 1913, 5 July 1914; *Deutsche Zeitung*, 26 March 1913 and, to an extent, *Norddeutsche Allgemeine Zeitung*, 7 March 1913.

35. Schiemann in the *Neue preussische Zeitung*, June 1905, cited in Carroll, *Germany and the Great Powers*, p. 529.

36. *Post*, 13 July 1905, and *Kölnische Volkszeitung*, 16 June 1905, cited in Carroll, *Germany and the Great Powers*, pp. 529, 533.

37. Wolff in the *Berliner Tageblatt*, 24 June 1905, cited in Carroll, *Germany and the Great Powers*, p. 530.

38. *Rheinisch-Westfälische Zeitung*, cited in Carroll, *Germany and the Great Powers*, p. 530.

39. Hasse to the annual congress of the Pan-German League, 15 June 1905, in Carroll, *Germany and the Great Powers*, p. 530; *Historisch-politische Blätter*, July 1905, cited in Carroll, *Germany and the Great Powers*, p. 524.

40. *Rheinisch-Westfälische Zeitung*, March 1905, cited in Carroll, *Germany and the Great Powers*, p. 514.

41. *Neue Preussische Zeitung*, 4 July 1905.

42. *Alldeutsche Blätter*, 17 June 1905, cited in Carroll, *Germany and the Great Powers*, p. 525.

43. Delbrück in the *Preussische Jahrbücher*, 18 September 1906, cited in Carroll, *Germany and the Great Powers*, p. 555.

44. *Rheinisch-Westfälische Zeitung*, 2 July 1911, cited in Carroll, *Germany and the Great Powers*, p. 657.

45. *Alldeutsch Blätter*, 8 July 1911, cited in Carroll, *Germany and the Great Powers*, p. 657.

46. *Neue Preussische Zeitung*, cited in *Vorwärts*, 14 July 1911, in Carroll, *Germany and the Great Powers*, p. 657.

47. *Berliner Neueste Nachrichten*, 7 August 1911; *Deutsche Zeitung*, cited in *Post*, 7 August 1911, in Carroll, *Germany and the Great Powers*, p. 677.

48. *Deutsche Tageszeitung*, 30 July 1911, cited in Carroll, *Germany and the Great Powers*, p. 669.

49. See, for example the National Liberal *Börsen-Courier*, cited in the *Rheinisch-Westfälische Zeitung*, 27 July 1911, in Carroll, *Germany and the Great Powers*. Also, *Tag*, 25 July 1911, *Zukunft*, 29 July 1911, *Reichsbote*, 26 July and 27 September 1911.

50. *Neue Preussische Zeitung*, 23 September 1911.

51. *Hallesche Zeitung*, 21 September 1911.

52. *Konservative Korrespondenz*, cited in the *Rheinisch-Westfälische Zeitung*, 8 July 1911, in Carroll, *Germany and the Great Powers*, p. 657.

53. *Berliner Neueste Nachrichten*, 8 November 1911, cited in Carroll, *Germany and the Great Powers*, p. 692.

54. Ibid.

55. Heydebrand, cited in Carroll, *Germany and the Great Powers*, p. 694.

56. *Berliner Tageblatt*, 9 November 1911, cited in Carroll, *Germany and the Great Powers*, p. 694.

57. For such responses amongst liberals and Catholics, see *Berliner Tageblatt*, 26 July 1911; *Germania*, 26 July, 20 August, 8 and 16 December 1911; *National-Zeitung*, 23 August 1911, cited in Carroll, *Germany and the Great Powers*, pp. 669, 686. On the right, the reaction against Britain was much more pronounced: *Tag*, 3 October 1911; *Neue Preussische Zeitung*, 5 and 11 July, 6 and 12 September, 12 October 1911; *Hamburger Nachrichten*, 6 July 1911; *Deutsche Tageszeitung*, 11, 26 and 28 July and 3 November 1911; *Leipziger Neueste Nachrichten*, 25 July 1911; *Berliner Lokal-Anzeiger*, 26 July 1911; *Staatsbürger Zeitung*, 26 October 1911.

58. Wolff in *Berliner Tageblatt*, 3 November 1911.

59. For more on this, see Hewitson, 'Images of the Enemy'.

60. *Frankfurter Zeitung*, 4 July 1911; *Vossische Zeitung*, 10 July 1911, cited in Carroll, *Germany and the Great Powers*, pp. 658-9.

61. *Germania*, 4 July 1911, in Carroll, *Germany and the Great Powers*, p. 658.

62. *Kölnische Zeitung*, 4 July 1911.

63. *Frankfurter Zeitung*, 3 July 1911; *Vossische Zeitung*, 4 July 1911; *Freisinnige Zeitung*, 4 July 1911; *Berliner Tageblatt*, 25 July 1911; and Matthias Erzberger in *Tag*, 28 July 1911.

64. *Grenzboten*, 6 September 1911, cited in Carroll, *Germany and the Great Powers*, p. 685.

65. *Deutsche Tageszeitung*, 1 November 1911, cited in Carroll, *Germany and the Great Powers*, p. 691.

66. *Kölnische Volkszeitung*, 6 November 1911, cited in Carroll, *Germany and the Great Powers*, p. 691.

67. Goschen, 26 August 1911, cited in Carroll, *Germany and the Great Powers*, p. 683.

68. L. Kopelew, 'Am Vorabend des grossen Krieges', in M. Keller (ed.), *Russen und Russland aus deutscher Sicht*, vol. 4 (Munich, 2000), pp. 11-110, on the continuing significance of opposition to Russian 'barbarity'.

The Politics of War

69. Cited in T.R.E. Paddock, 'Deutsche Historiker als Politiker', in Keller (ed.), *Russen und Russland aus deutscher Sicht*, vol. 4 , p. 316.

70. Ibid., pp. 308-18.

71. Ibid., pp. 323, 325. Also, Bernhardi, *Deutschland und der nächste Krieg*, pp. 97-8.

72. Meinecke, cited in Paddock, 'Deutsche Historiker als Politiker', p. 307.

73. Bülow, cited in I. Geiss, *German Foreign Policy, 1871-1914* (London, 1976), p. 116.

74. *Münchener Neueste Nachrichten*, 3 June 1908, cited in Carroll, *Germany and the Great Powers*, p. 578.

75. *Vossische Zeitung*, 9 November 1907, cited in Carroll, *Germany and the Great Powers*, p. 565.

76. *Berliner Tageblatt*, 16 February 1909, cited in Carroll, *Germany and the Great Powers*, p. 625.

77. *Hamburger Nachrichten*, 24 February 1909, *Deutsche Zeitung*, 10 March 1909, *Leipziger Neueste Nachrichten*, 19 March 1909, *Alldeutsche Blätter*, 12 March 1909, and the *Rheinisch-Westfälische Zeitung*, 4 March 1909.

78. *Tägliche Rundschau*, 12 March 1909, *Deutsche Tageszeitung*, 21 March 1909, *Berliner Neueste Nachrichten*, 4 March 1909, *Kölnische Volkszeitung*, 21 March 1909, cited in Carroll, *Germany and the Great Powers*, pp. 625-6.

79. Reventlow, *Gegenwart*, 29 May 1909, cited in Carroll, *Germany and the Great Powers*, p. 628.

80. *Frankfurter Zeitung*, 29 March 1909, cited in Carroll, *Germany and the Great Powers*, p. 628.

81. *Münchener Neueste Nachrichten*, January 1912, cited in Carroll, *Germany and the Great Powers*, p. 703.

82. *Post*, 28 January 1912, cited in Carroll, *Germany and the Great Powers*, p. 710.

83. *Berliner Neueste Nachrichten*, 3 October 1912, cited in Carroll, *Germany and the Great Powers*, p. 718.

84. 16 October 1912, cited in Carroll, *Germany and the Great Powers*, p. 718.

85. *Deutsche Tageszeitung*, 3 October 1912, cited in Carroll, *Germany and the Great Powers*, p. 718.

86. *Hamburger Nachrichten*, October 1912, *Rheinisch-Westfälische Zeitung*, 3 October 1912, cited in Carroll, *Germany and the Great Powers*.

87. *Leipziger Neueste Nachrichten*, August 1913, cited in Carroll, *Germany and the Great Powers*, p. 739.

88. *Berliner Tageblatt*, 3 December 1912, cited in Carroll, *Germany and the Great Powers*, p. 727.

89. *Freisinnige Zeitung*, 13 October 1912.

90. *Frankfurter Zeitung*, 11 November 1912, *Vossische Zeitung*, 20 November 1912, *Vorwärts*, 7 and 9 November 1912, *Sozialdemokratische*

Monatshefte, 14 November 1912, in Carroll, *Germany and the Great Powers*, p. 723. The quotation came from the last mentioned publication.

91. *Grenzboten*, 23 October 1912, cited in Carroll, *Germany and the Great Powers*, p. 719.

92. R. Ropponen, *Die russische Gefahr*, pp. 82–126, 164–79.

93. *Alldeutsche Blätter*, 7 January 1906, cited ibid., p. 84.

94. Ropponen, *Die russische Gefahr*, p. 156.

95. Ibid., pp. 164–74.

96. *Germania*, 23 January 1913, cited ibid., p. 107.

97. *Zukunft*, 10 April 1909, vol. 67, cited in Ropponen, *Die russische Gefahr*, p. 92.

98. Förster, *Der doppelte Militarismus*, pp. 280–7.

99. *Berliner Tageblatt*, 3 April 1913, cited in Ropponen, *Die russische Gefahr*, p. 112.

100. On the far right: August Keim in *Tag*, 22 December 1912, 17 January 1913 and 17 June 1914, Lieutenant-General Schmitt in *Tag*, 4 February 1914, *Dresdner Nachrichten*, 23 February 1913, *Tägliche Rundschau*, 16 May 1914, *Berliner Neueste Nachrichten*, 3 May 1914. From the centre and left, *Kölnische Zeitung*, 21 February and 10 April 1913, *Vossische Zeitung*, 19 and 26 February, 2 and 15 June 1913, 15 June and 14 July 1914, *Berliner Tageblatt*, 5 and 7 March and 26 June 1913, 15 July 1914, *Frankfurter Zeitung*, 18 February and 22 May 1913, 13 March 1914, *Freisinnige Zeitung*, 12 May 1914, *Vorwärts*, 21 June 1913. On the right, but downplaying the French threat: *Deutsche Tageszeitung*, 26 March, 4, 11 and 12 September 1913 and 2 and 6 February 1914, *Tag*, 29 March, 4 September and 5 December 1913, 5 July 1914, *Deutsche Zeitung*, 23 May 1913, *Staatsbürger Zeitung*, 4 June 1914, *Berliner Lokal Anzeiger*, 8 June 1914, *Bayerische Landeszeitung*, 9 June 1914.

101. Förster, *Der doppelte Militarismus*, p. 279.

102. During the Agadir crisis, for instance, see *Tag*, 25 July 1911; *Zukunft*, 29 July 1911; *Reichsbote*, 26 July and 27 September 1911; *Germania*, 20 October 1911; *Deutsche Zeitung*, 26 October 1911; *Neue Preussische Zeitung*, 26 October 1911.

103. *Berliner Tageblatt*, 3 July 1911. *Frankfurter Zeitung*, 7 July 1911.

104. *Vossische Zeitung*, 20 July 1911.

105. *Kölnische Volkszeitung*, 9 and 13 September 1911; *Kölnische Zeitung*, 20 October 1911; *Leipziger Volkszeitung*, 28 August 1911 on the *Neue Preussische Zeitung*.

5

Militarism and Representations of Conflict

Many of the academic debates about militarism in Wilhelmine Germany seem to challenge the idea that popular and party opposition to certain types of war had increased during the decade or so before 1914. Thus, Volker Berghahn, a follower of Fritz Fischer, argued in the early 1980s – in accordance with an influential dual definition of the term – that the German military occupied an unusually powerful position in the state and that large sections of the Wilhelmine public had been inculcated with military values or, at least, were unwilling to oppose militarist policies.[1] More recently, historians such as Stig Förster and Thomas Rohrkrämer, continuing a tradition of revisionist analyses of extra-parliamentary leagues and the 'reshaped right', have added further evidence to Berghahn's case, placing greater emphasis on independent manifestations of popular militarism, which threatened at particular junctures to overcome the more conservative militarism of the state.[2] In the last few years, this 'double militarism' described by Förster has been endorsed by Hans-Ulrich Wehler, who has contended that 'social militarism' gradually eclipsed its 'old Prussian forerunner' as 'military habits in the German *Kaiserreich* forced their way ever deeper into daily life'.[3] In the context of the armaments race before 1914, which supposedly – in the view of Stevenson and Herrmann, for instance – gave the public the impression that Germany was losing out in an armed struggle for existence, popular militarism seemed to have come to rest on what Mommsen has termed 'the topos of inevitable war'.[4] Such beliefs, however, although they undoubtedly existed, were often contradicted and sometimes nullified by other predispositions, such as a fear of war or dislike of the army as an unconstitutional 'state within a state'. This chapter proposes that the existence of a 'popular', 'social' or 'folklore' militarism which crossed political, class and confessional boundaries neither ruled out opposition to

85

certain kinds of war nor drove a hesitant Reich government to risk conflict.

It is true, of course, that the army was widely acknowledged to be a fundamental pillar of the German Empire, not least because it seemed, together with the supposedly masterful diplomacy of Bismarck, to have brought about unification in 1871 through a series of *Einigungskriege*, or unificatory wars. As Frank Becker's study of public and private memories of the wars demonstrates, the army was believed within middle-class circles to have brought the nation-state into being. This was what Heinrich von Treitschke, whose state-supporting, Prussian-led history of Germany had become a dominant narrative by the Wilhelmine era, meant when he proclaimed in 1874, at the time of the debate about a new Army Law, that the military had created the state and was 'the strongest bond of national unity'.[5] The majority of his 'Borussian' and, later, neo-Rankean successors reiterated such views, producing laudatory accounts of both Wilhelm I as a warrior-king and of military commanders and war ministers such as Yorck von Wartenburg, Boyen, Scharnhorst, Roon and Moltke the Elder.[6] Treitschke's case was also corroborated by the principal political and literary representatives of the *Bildungsbürgertum*, and by soldiers themselves, whose 'recollections' continued to be published and widely read throughout the pre-war period. The argument of these testimonies was not only that the 'people and army of a nation' had 'never stood so internally united as today in Germany', as the liberal politicians Ludwig Bamberger and Eduard Lasker had claimed at the time, but also that the events leading to unification had been the corollary of the superior organization, ethos and leadership of the Prussian-German army.[7] Accordingly, celebrated writers such as Gustav Freytag and Friedrich Gerstäcker agreed with Treitschke that many 'institutions of our army, which were always offensive to the liberal bourgeoisie [*Bürgertum*], today receive their justification'.[8] A poorly trained militia, or *Volksarmee*, declared the author of *Die Ahnen*, was 'not much more useful nor much more dangerous to a disciplined army' on the Prussian and German model than 'a herd of buffaloes on the prairie'.[9] Earlier criticisms of the military had become 'peripheral', wrote Gerstäcker, compared with the courage and self-sacrifice of the officer corps:

> In any event, the officers, too, have shown themselves so brave and heroic, even in the battles to date, that they are not only able to demand the respect of the soldiers by law. The Prussian guards lieutenant with kid gloves and

a monocle in his right eye was earlier a standing comic image of arrogance and affectation; yet whoever has seen these guards lieutenants – how they stormed with such courage, and always ahead of their men, into enemy fire, so that the King himself declared that he must take measures against it or he would have no more officers – cannot deny them respect and admiration, and the small peripheral things become insignificant.[10]

As Becker proves convincingly, such sentiments met with the approval of most – predominantly educated and middle-class – soldier-diarists, even those who, like one volunteer from the Bavarian Pfalz, had been 'more of an enemy than a friend of military life', but who, by 1891, had become an admirer of the 'order, tranquillity [and] strictest precision' of the military 'machine', coming as a result of the wars of unification to 'trust in German militarism'.[11]

This trust did not derive simply from the adoption and imitation of military or aristocratic values and behaviour. Rather, it was related to the idea of a 'nation in arms' (*Volk in Waffen*), which dated back to the era of the French Revolution, but which had only gained more or less general acceptance in Germany in 1870–1. Although they could be interpreted in different ways, appeals to a *Volk in Waffen*, which proliferated after unification and the Franco-German war, invariably implied a blurring of the boundary between civilian and military spheres, with the successful establishment of liberal and middle-class histories and paintings of nineteenth-century armies and conflicts, and with the development of a genuinely popular 'folklore militarism', in the phrase of Jakob Vogel.[12] Such bourgeois or popular militarism, as Freytag pointed out in the 1870s, entailed significant compromises on all sides, including that of the 'Junker from the Mark [Brandenburg]', who had previously hated the black–red–gold flag and 'the entire German swindle'.[13] Increasingly, in preponderantly middle-class public narratives, military leaders were depicted as technical experts in 'civilian' and 'civilized' settings, and military victories were attributed to the superior education of German conscripts, who had formed a true nation in arms, in contrast to the corrupt and demoralized standing army of Napoleon III. Correspondingly, the works of Realist and Historical School painters such as Adolf von Menzel and Anton von Werner, which were amongst the most popular paintings of the Wilhelmine period, renounced the traditions of youthful heroism and the battle scene in favour of those of a mature civil society, as in the case of Menzel's *Abreise König Wilhelms für die Armee* (1871), which shows the monarch in a simple coach behind a typical Sunday crowd, or in Werner's *Graf Moltke in seinem Arbeitszimmer in Versailles* (1872), which portrays the Chief of the General Staff as a 'professor in uniform', surrounded by dispatches and telegraphs in his civilian-style study.[14] Similar types of imagery were so pervasive that Wilhelm II himself began to refer, even amongst officers, to 'our nation in arms'. Certainly, monarchist and nationalist commentators such as the historian and journalist Dietrich Schäfer, writing in 1912, had no doubt at all that the army's legitimacy and success had come to rest on popular, patriotic foundations:

> One will search history in vain for a German expression of force which was so much the common good of the entire nation and exclusively *its* achievement as was the war of 1870/71 . . . Up to the last man, one felt the historical necessity of coming to a reckoning with France and of impressing on this power once and for all that it could no longer count on German disunity. Finally there came together in one river what for so long had used up its strength in countless streams: weapon-ready courage of battle and national sentiment, raised on such rich, such diverse treasures of German culture.[15]

The fact that middle-class patriots and veterans, according to Freytag, did not see the necessity, as 'the soldier returned to his civilian occupation', of avoiding political opposition or voting for radical measures meant that left liberals, Catholics and socialists were also able to adapt, with varying degrees of discomfort, to the military traditions of the new German Empire. This adaptation was probably easiest for progressives such as Hermann Baumgarten and Theodor Mommsen, who saw the Franco-German conflict as an act of civil defence akin to that of the Greeks at Marathon or of George Washington in the American war of independence, from which 'not soldiers, but civilians come home to us', as one writer put it.[16] The 'German' idea of conscripting the whole population, however incomplete in practice, served to foster a sense of national belonging and responsibility. 'What do the mass of farmers and workers care, if France and Germany have these or those relations with each other?' Baumgarten had asked in 1870: 'But when they have their own in the army and everything for them hangs on the progress of the war, then they raise their thoughts to the sphere of great, national interests, on which they now feel their whole being for the first time dependent.'[17] Mommsen, in a speech of 1875 which was republished in a collection of 1905, went even further, arguing that the existence of a 'nation in arms' would make wars, 'although in our state order formally permissible, in fact impossible', because of the risks to which elites as well as the masses were exposed in such conflicts.[18] The support of the SPD for a *levée en masse* and, by the 1890s, for a Swiss-type militia was partly based on this belief that conscript armies would be more accountable, and partly on a long-standing admiration of civil defence and violent revolutionary elan.[19] 'We are the most convinced defenders of the introduction of universal military service', declared August Bebel, the leader of the party, in 1904. '[We] regard it as a duty of honour of every man who can bear arms that he has to do so from a given age onwards.'[20] More prag-matically, the SPD's leadership was also aware that a significant number of workers could be found attending army manoeuvres and 'Kaiser parades'.[21] As a consequence of such considerations, as well as out of fear of *lèse majesté* proceedings against explicit critics of the army, Bebel and others were anxious to point out their support for national defence, which they argued could be achieved more successfully by a fully motivated militia than the existing arrangement of a standing officer corps and incomplete conscription. 'What we are struggling against is not the fatherland in itself . . . but the *conditions* which are present in this fatherland in the interest of the ruling classes', pleaded the SPD leader in 1907.[22] After a longer period of opposition to the army, which was caused not only by the *Kultur-kampf* in the 1870s but also by the legacy of the 'civil war' between predominantly Catholic and Protestant German states during the 1860s, the Centre Party, too, had by the 1890s accepted the need for military defence of a German nation-state and support for the German army.[23]

Despite challenges to such support for the military after the turn of the century, which seemed to have come to a head with the army's abuses of its power in Alsace-Lorraine during the Zabern incident of 1913, many politicians and much of the public continued to admire the army and navy. The strength of this feeling could be observed in the public rituals and monuments of the late Bismarckian and Wilhelmine eras. These events and sites, although constantly evolving and occasionally contested, played an important role in cementing the putative relationship between unification, the Ger-man people, the military, and national defence.[24] The theme was present in many of the local obelisks, statues and plaques, which had been constructed in memory of the Franco-German war, and in many of the great national monuments, which were erected after 1871, including those of the Niederwald (1877–83), Kyffhäuser mountain (1890–6), Porta Westfalica (1892), Deutsches Eck (1894–7), and the Nationaldenkmal and Walhalla in Berlin (1890–7, 1896–1901). The statue of Hermann in the Teutoburg forest (completed in 1875), with his massive limbs and sword pointing into the distance in an act of powerful defiance of the Romans, and the Völkerschlachtdenkmal (1913), whose commemoration of the wars of liberation against France centred on a crypt of gargantuan warriors and groups of figures representing 'German virtues' of 'bravery, self-sacrifice, faith and fertility', were typical representations of the new German nation in arms, created against the wishes of surrounding enemies and united in its will to defend itself in future.[25]

Popular festivals and parades, which often drew large crowds of tens of thousands of people, imparted a similar message of voluntary, national self-defence. Some, such as the yearly Kaiser parades or the celebration of the centenary of Wilhelm I's birthday in 1897, were organized by the state as 'specifically military' spectacles, in the words of the royal Master of Ceremonies, in keeping with 'the nature, the actual origin of the new emperorship (*Kaisertum*)'.[26] Others, such as Sedan Day and the centenary celebrations of the battle of Leipzig in 1913, were mounted largely by associations and paid for by private donations. Yet they, too, put the military at the centre of the ritual, tying it even more pronouncedly to the history of the German nation. The inauguration of the Völkerschlachtdenkmal on the centenary of the battle of Leipzig in 1913 – the largest mass gathering in German history, with more than 275,000 gymnasts and many more spectators – was a case in point, designed to honour, according to the leader of the Deutscher Patriotenbund which funded and coordinated it, 'the sacrifices of goods and life for the freedom of the fatherland . . . because here our heroic fathers shattered the oppressing shackles of the occupier, here they won back such long-awaited freedom in the hard fight of body and soul, in order once more to become a nation of brothers'.[27] Wilhelm II, who resented the fact that an emphasis on the 'wars of independence' and 1813 implied a movement away from 'official', imperial and monarchical celebrations, refrained from giving a speech and bestowed the lowest possible honours on the organizers of the event. He was obliged, however, to take part in this and other similar occasions throughout Germany, such was their popularity.[28] Militarism and nationalism had, indeed, become 'social' in Wehler's sense. Thus, whilst Sedan Day, under the stewardship of the veterans associations, became more explicitly anti-socialist and was criticized vehemently by the SPD as a result, other military celebrations, including Kaiser parades, were widely accepted, to the point where Karl Liebknecht – the party's main critic of the army – lamented the 'drenching of our entire public and private national life (*Volksleben*) with a militarist spirit', characterized by 'colourful uniforms, shiny buttons and helmets, flags, parade drills, cavalry attacks and all the other bits and pieces'.[29] From the pomp and pageantry of army parades to the technological and industrial prowess of ship launches and naval regattas, most of the Wilhelmine public remained fascinated by, and supportive of, its military.[30]

Such broad support had two principal sets of consequences. First, the military – particularly the army – was able to play a central role in German society. This role owed less to the army's constitutional position under the formal jurisdiction of the Kaiser (*Kommandogewalt*) – since the Reichstag did discuss military affairs and officers did refrain from interfering in 'politics' – than to the military's prestige and popularity amongst most sections of the population.[31] Consequently, although they were often criticized by socialists and sometimes by left liberals for maltreatment of soldiers and sailors or exceeding their powers, the German army and navy were spared the type of fundamental anti-militarist attack on their institutions and practices experienced by their counterparts in France, as Moltke the Younger was well aware.[32] German officers were therefore less inclined to question or alter the value system of a separate military caste: as Erich Ludendorff recalled, 'We younger officers in general cared little about politics.' Rather, they continued to believe that the military served as a 'school of the nation', turning subjects from different backgrounds into loyal, obedient and effective soldiers and sailors.[33] One officer, writing in the main army journal in 1906, spelled out how comprehensive and inescapable such training could be:

> We indicate what Germany's Kaiser, Prussia's kings, what our fathers, our regiment have achieved in times of war and peace; we speak of the solemn oath of the soldier and of the flag, the sacred object of the unit; we emphasise the necessity of unconditional subordination to the will of one's superior, of iron-like discipline; we mention – and call it by its real name – attempts at insurrection, which we characterise as mistaken theories whose goals are unsustainable and therefore unattainable, and are opposed to our duties and goals.[34]

The effects of such military service were considerable, if difficult to gauge. They were reinforced in the Wilhelmine period by military-style discipline in schools, which to the playwright Gerhard Hauptmann was 'just like the instruction hour in the military'; by the development of youth organizations under the umbrella of the Jungdeutschland-Bund, which had 750,000 members by 1914 and received official state backing in 1911; and by the dense network of veterans associations, which counted almost 3 million members and had become increasingly politically active during the 1890s.[35] The historian Otto Hintze taunted the SPD that 'even Social Democracy, which is fundamentally against everything to do with militarism, . . . not only owes its discipline to it, but also has unconsciously incorporated in its vision of the future a strong element of that coercion of the individual by society which stems from the Prussian military state'.[36] He went on: 'Militarism still today permeates our state body and our national life (*Volksleben*) generally, and in many ways sets the tone.'[37] It is probable that such respect for and obedience to military norms worked against insubordination and desertion, once war was declared. To what extent they helped to cause the outbreak of war remains unclear, especially since many similar forms of deference and discipline – notwithstanding the German army's predilection for drill – existed, as Markus Ingenlath has pointed out, in other states as well.[38]

Second, the linkage in many Wilhelmine onlookers' minds between the military and the establishment of a German nation-state helped to ensure that war, on the whole, was still perceived to be a heroic affair. Thus, the majority of adolescents' novels examined by Marieluise Christadler and most of the 'war scare' literature analysed by I.F. Clarke perpetuated the supposedly glorious history of 'German' wars, from Arminius's defence of Germania against the Romans, via the wars of Barbarossa and the German knights, and of Friedrich the Great, to the wars of 'independence' and of 'unification' in the nineteenth century.[39] The principal German textbook, describing the Franco-German war of 1870–1, gave a good idea of how myths of historical conflicts were tied to each other and to the putative history of a German nation:

A storm of enthusiasm went through the German land. Once again, the classrooms and the professorial chairs emptied, ploughshares and shops were abandoned, and from the grand country houses and tiny cottages everyone rushed to the colours to serve in the same army and fight for the same goal. In every square and street one heard the clatter of arms and the sounds of war, and in quiet chambers clasped hands were raised in prayer. The people and the army congregated in the houses of God for a universal day of prayer to implore the help of the Almighty; with faith in God and their hearts steeled for battle, the warriors flocked around their banners. The fiery iron horses drew thousands westwards; and from the cars there echoed 'Lieb Vaterland, magst ruhig sein, fest steht und treu die Wacht am Rhein'. At every station the soldiers were met with loud cheers; men and women surged forward to offer them refreshments. In a fortnight nearly half a million soldiers stood ready to meet the enemy, while just as many waited in reserve.[40]

The passage hints at many of the attributes of heroism in Wilhelmine war literature and monuments. Like the novels of Felix Dahn, a volunteer in 1870 and best-selling author of *Der Kampf um Rom* (1876) and other popular works, the extract hints – 'once again', 'warriors', 'banners', 'Die Wacht am Rhein' – at a series of wars in the ancient, medieval and modern past, conflating them as if they constituted one great struggle, as in historical works for youths such as *Mit Kreuz und Schwert* and *Arminius, Germaniens Befreier*.[41] What was more, these wars were national, drawing strength from enthusiasm throughout 'the German land' and uniting different generations (students and professors) and occupations (farmers and shopkeepers) from town and country alike in the defence of their 'dear fatherland' (*Lieb Vaterland*). This sense of national unity had been cemented by soldiers' recollections of 1870–1, which talked of a war involving 'all Germany's tribes (*Volksstämme*)', where all 'stood shoulder to shoulder, the son of the wage labourer and of the nobleman', as if it were 'sweet and honourable to die for the fatherland'.[42] Monuments to the dead of the Franco-German war, with inscriptions referring to 'heroic sons' or simply 'heroes' of a 'glorious war' or a 'struggle for the fatherland' in the name of 'unity and greatness' and 'Germany's prestige and honour', also alluded, like the passage, to the support of God in such a 'holy struggle', for national wars were both sacred and mystical.[43] It was for this reason that the Völkerschlachtdenkmal was constructed to resemble a Germanic pyramid, replete with a Gothic-decorated Roman vault and Egyptian-scale statues in the form of medieval knights.[44] All such elements were typical of the purported pathos of war for the majority of artists and authors and, perhaps, readers and spectators. Consequently, the style and mood of the textbook passage are epic and optimistic ('loud cheers', 'refreshments'), in spite of the incursion of modern technology, with trains romanticized as 'fiery iron horses', and the mobilization of massive armies pointing to the power and imminent victory of German troops, not to their mass slaughter.

'War scare' literature, although on the surface stressing the dangers of conflict, usually served to promote belligerence and, as a result of increased vigilance, to maintain the possibility of military victory. Thus, army officers and militarist publicists like Colmar von der Goltz, whose *Das Volk in Waffen* (1883) went through many editions before 1914, and Friedrich von Bernhardi, the author of *Deutschland und der nächste Krieg* (1912), repeatedly urged that 'we must work incessantly' towards 'a final struggle for the existence and greatness of Germany' so that 'loyalty towards the emperor, passionate love for the fatherland, determination not to shrink from hard trials, self-denial and cheerful sacrifice may wax ever stronger in our hearts and in those of our children'.[45] Only in such a way, went on von der Goltz, 'will the German army, which must be and shall ever remain the German nation in arms, enter upon the coming conflict with full assurance of ultimate victory'.[46] By 1912, Bernhardi was more aware of the potential destructiveness of modern warfare, but his aim remained the same: to prevent the warlike qualities of the German population from disappearing and to maintain its 'proud consciousness of strength, of regained national unity, and of increased political power', from which it had benefited since the 'age-long dream' of unification.[47] Despite signs to the contrary, Bernhardi continued to believe, like the retired Chief of the General Staff Alfred von Schlieffen and most other generals, that wars could be relatively short, decisive and morally justifiable, not least because military leaders, aware of their new power, would act responsibly.[48]

Most civilian authors of 'war scare' literature, which began to appear from the late 1890s onwards, agreed with their military counterparts. Their works were either intended to shock readers into making greater preparations for war, as in the case of Gustav Erdmann's naval propaganda *Wehrlos zur See* (1900), or they envisaged a German victory, as in Karl Bleibtreu's *Die 'Offensiv-Invasion' gegen England* (1907) or Adolf Sommerfeld's *Frankreichs Ende im Jahr 19??* (1912). Numerous less well known or anonymous authors described similar outcomes, marvelling at new inventions like aeroplanes and dreadnoughts, rather than anticipating the mass killing and industrialization of warfare, which technological advances, full conscription and the arms race facilitated. Technology and armament appeared to allow more room for adventure, for example in adolescent literature about the colonies (*Jungdeutschland-in-Afrika, Peter Moors Fahrt nach Südwest*) and the navy (*Auf blauem Wasser, Willi der Schiffsjunge*). Alternatively, they were treated anachronistically, as if modern weapons were still forged by blacksmiths (*Der Gott der Eisen wachsen liess, Der Waffenschmied*) or as if they would have little impact on a war of swords, banners and cavalry charges (*Deutschland in Waffen, Unter flatternden Fahnen, Unter Fahnen und Standarten, Die drei Kürassiere*).[49] As a result, war was to be awaited eagerly, in the words of one writer for the mass-circulation, middle-class magazine *Die Gartenlaube* in 1913, as 'the happy, great hour of struggle', since it was 'more beautiful, more magnificent to live forever on the plaque of heroes in the church than to die a hollow death without a name in bed'.[50] Few things, implied one of the most famous war authors, August Niemann, in the preface to his book *Der Weltkrieg* (1904), could be more glorious than fighting for the expected victory – and post-war utopia – of the German nation-state:

> Almost all wars have, for centuries past, been waged in the interests of England, and almost all have been incited by England. Only when Bismarck's genius presided over Germany did German Michel become conscious of his own strength and wage his own wars. Are things come to this pass that Germany is to crave of England's bounty – her air and light, and her very daily bread? . . . My dreams, the dreams of a German, show me the war that is to be, and the victory of the three great allied nations – Germany, France and Russia – and a new division of the possessions of the earth as the final aim and object of this gigantic universal war.[51]

Victory, or the possibility of eventual triumph, remained an essential ingredient of most war literature. When William Le Queux's *Invasion of 1910* (1906) was translated into German, as *Der Einfall der Deutschen in England*, the editor left out the last two hundred pages, which described how the British counter-attacked against the invading Germans and massacred them in the streets of London.[52]

The existence of such sanguine views of military conflict helped to prevent the formation of a strong anti-war movement and to thwart resistance to the outbreak of war in July and early August 1914. It did not mean, however, that war had come to seem 'inevitable', nor that the German government was pushed by a militarist public into risking war, as Mommsen claims. Critically, although the peace movement was marginal and heroic depictions of war were preponderant, there were well-known warnings of a coming apocalypse, which appear to have given rise to private anxieties amongst a significant number of Wilhelmine commentators and readers. Thus, even a warmonger such as Bernhardi admitted that war could occasion great misery.[53] Famously, from a similar quarter, Moltke the Elder had warned the public in 1890 of the horrors of 'a people's war (*Volks-krieg*)': 'it may be a war of seven years' or of thirty years' duration – and woe to him who sets Europe alight, who first puts the fuse to the powder keg!'[54] Members of the German Peace Association such as Bertha von Suttner and Alfred Fried published much fuller and even bleaker prophecies, reaching a broad public despite their organization's small membership, which was a mere 7,000 in 1907.[55] Suttner's *Die Waffen nieder!* (1889), for example, was one of the main war novels of the Wilhelmine era, going through several editions and being translated into twelve languages before 1914. In it, she described the blood and dirt, disease and death, loss and mourning surrounding characters involved in the Franco-Austrian conflict of 1859 and the 'wars of unification' in the 1860s. The Polish banker Ivan Bloch, whose six-volume work *Der Krieg* (1899) attracted much attention in Germany's press, and the novelist Wilhelm Lamszus, whose *Menschenschlachthaus* was published in 1912, pointed respectively to the terrible possibility of a war of attrition, with trenches, artillery and commercial collapse, and to the actuality of industrial killing, with '240 bullets or more per minute' and 'our millions of corpses shovelled into the earth with burying machines', as if 'death . . . had now become a machine operator'.[56] The socialist journal *Neue Zeit* acclaimed Lamszus's work as 'one hundred and eleven pages of "poetry" of mechanical mass murder', arguing that 'when modern Great Powers clash with one another with their war machines, then it looks like this or even madder'.[57] Looking back to Friedrich Engels's prediction in 1887 of 'famine, epidemics, general barbarization of armies and the masses, . . . utter chaos in our trade, industry, and commerce . . . [and] the collapse of the old states', SPD leaders such as Bebel reinforced the case and gave it still greater publicity, foreseeing 'a terror without end'. 'Then comes the catastrophe', declared Bebel to the Reichstag in 1911. 'Then general mobilisation in Europe is ordered, on which 16 to 18 million men, the male stock of the various nations, armed with the best tools of murder, go into the field against each other as enemies . . . The end of the bourgeois world is nigh.'[58] Not many non-socialist deputies or newspaper readers agreed with the SPD leader's peroration, but most had already heard accounts of the potential destructiveness of a European or world war. The majority of them appear to have discounted such an eventuality 'rationally'. From their reactions in July 1914, however, few seem to have been able to banish such thoughts entirely.

Even on the right, the idea that the scale of destruction caused by a European war would be unprecedented was widely accepted. Indeed, many nationalist and Conservative commentators saw such destruction – or, at least, the risk of destruction – as a necessary component of international relations. Social Darwinism was frequently perceived to give added weight to this argument. Thus, Bernhardi believed war to be 'a biological necessity of the first importance' because it tested the mettle of states, favouring the strong and destroying the weak.[59] In nature and in the life of states, 'the struggle for existence' was 'the basis of all healthy development'.[60] Conflicts, he held, could be successful, as in the cases of the Great Elector, Friedrich II and Bismarck; they could avert threatening systems of alliances or ruin an increasingly powerful neighbouring state; or they could strengthen a nation's hand, even in defeat, as in the case of the Boers, who had been granted self-government after 1902.[61] More importantly, war was essential in order to uphold the state's duty to protect its own subjects against the often immoral tenets of international law, to oppose materialism and reinvigorate a sense of national idealism, to counter the tendency of modern 'social' states to protect the weakest members of society, and to promote the strongest nations and their 'national missions' for the 'health' of humanity as a whole. Since the world had already been divided up amongst the major powers, states now had a 'duty of self-assertion', wrote Bernhardi, to accommodate the need for demographic, economic and territorial growth.[62] In the years after 1871, Germans had allegedly been deflected from their original warlike purpose by an extended period of peace, which had led to increased materialism, political horse-trading, diminishing patriotism and foreign-policy failures.[63] If this trend were to continue, Bernhardi implied, the Germans would suffer the type of racial and moral degeneration which had led to the eclipse of the Dutch.[64] Wars ensured that the strongest states and the best ideals survived and prospered. Bernhardi, like many right-wing nationalists, saw this struggle for states' survival as an unchanging 'law of development'.[65]

Not all right-wing commentators were as convinced as Bernhardi of the biological benefits of war, but most saw conflict as an inevitable and natural component of interstate relations. Historically, as Treitschke pointed out, states seemed to have emerged primarily to defend families, tribes and peoples against external threats.[66] 'Power is the principle of the state', he continued, and 'if the state neglects its power in favour of the ideal endeavours of humanity, then it denies its essence and goes under', as the Athenians had been defeated by the Spartans, the Greeks by the Romans, and Florence by Venice.[67] In recent times, it was evident to the Berlin historian, 'all the states known to us came about through wars', including Germany, in which the small states had been won over to the leadership of Prussia only in the 1860s.[68] Because of its geographical position, Treitschke agreed with colleagues like Hintze, the *Kaiserreich* had continued, to a large degree, to be a military state, ready to defend itself against attack, but also prepared to countenance an offensive war to 'defend' its interests.[69] International law should not rule out such conflicts, since wars were the means by which cultured states had triumphed and had come to dominate the world.[70] Cultures, morality and law could only develop within well-ordered states, which went on to establish voluntary international treaties and legal codes. Consequently, contended Treitschke, to try to enforce the precepts of international law against the freedom of states to compete and come into conflict with each other was contradictory, mistaking cause and effect. War had created states and, via the state, culture. Accordingly, reason was exhibited most commonly in armed conflicts, he proposed: when cultured states went to war, they rarely contravened the tenets of internationally agreed codes of conduct.[71]

Sharing similar premises to those of Treitschke or Bernhardi, many right-wing politicians, journalists, readers and voters made regular and uninhibited references to war. 'It is no different in the life of states than in the life of individual people', observed the Conservative deputy Elard von Oldenburg-Januschau: 'Even the most peace-loving person will in the end be threatened by a ruffian. Then he must fight for his life.'[72] The feeling that war was unavoidable found regular expression in a broad right-wing public, encompassing much of the commercial, educated and professional middle classes, as well as landowners, farmers and some farm labourers, artisans and shop-keepers. There is disagreement amongst historians about the size of this public, with estimates ranging from the 3 million or so involved in the veterans' associations to the several hundred thousand active members of 'national associations' such as the Navy and Army Leagues, yet there is little doubt that it was vocal, influential and increasingly radical. Thomas Rohrkrämer has shown how such radicalization occurred within the Deutscher Kriegerbund, with the gradual exclusion of socialists and a growing willingness to contemplate war by the turn of the century, after a generation of resistance on the part of veterans of the 'wars of unification'.[73] Thus, by the 1900s, allusions to the 'suicide' of killing 'the bellicose spirit of the nation (*Volk*)' and to war as a 'test' of 'strength, unity and greatness of will' were commonplace in the association's mouthpiece *Die Parole*.[74] Similar references punctuated the speeches of right-wing politicians. For Conservatives, as Oldenburg-Januschau intimated, war was a familiar and cherished subject. Accordingly, when Bülow asked him what the public was saying about Morocco during the crisis of 1905, he replied: 'if you want to make war, then you have much nicer ground'.[75] His own preference was 'to take Morocco from the French after a successful war with France'.[76] From the perceived failure of the German delegation at the Algeciras conference onwards, Conservatives became more and more shrill in their calls for brinkmanship and the use of arms, although they did not, as has been seen, support war indiscriminately. By the second Moroccan crisis of 1911, the Conservative Party leader, Ernst von Heydebrand und der Lasa, had attacked government foreign policy for the first time, implicitly admonishing Bethmann Hollweg for not threatening the use of 'our good German sword'. He hoped 'to see a government which is determined not to let this sword rust at the given moment', he went on.[77] Whatever the precise balance of their motives, Conservative politicians like Heydebrand, Kunow von Westarp and Hans von Kanitz-Podangen persisted in calling for war until 1914, sometimes in opposition to the *Reichsleitung* and sometimes in spite of their dislike of the taxation policy underpinning arms increases.

In this respect, Conservatives followed the lead of the National Liberals, who had broken in 1905 with the 'state-supporting' parties' tradition of almost automatic consent in the realm of foreign policy. Subsequently, Ernst Bassermann – a 'civilian Moltke', in Matthias Erzberger's jibe – and other right-wing liberals had criticized official timidity during pre-war diplomatic crises, backed arms increases and consolidated their links with nationalist leagues such as the Alldeutscher Verband and the Deutscher Wehrverein.[78] The point of these stances was explicitly bellicose, as the leader of the Badenese National Liberals made plain during Reichstag debates about the Army Law in 1913. Assurances of peace-loving intentions, he claimed, had called forth the impression of extraordinary weakness (quite right!), had called forth the impression that we do not want to use our weapons any more at all – an impression that stands in full contradiction to the fact that the German nation has always passed army and navy increases straightaway. We continue to arm and say: we want to have more soldiers, we want to have more ships, but believe us – we will not use them. So, good riddance to these assurances of peace (quite right!). Let us say to the nation once again: we have our weapons, and we want to use them, and the devil knows what will happen if we don't again get what we got in 1870 (applause)![79]

The right-wing press, conservative Catholics and Protestant pastors all spoke in favour of war, albeit often in a less aggressive tone, in the decade before 1914.[80]

Increasing belligerence has also been seen by historians like Förster as a feature of Centre Party and, even, left-liberal foreign-policy platforms. However, most in the centre and on the left – comprising two-thirds or more of the electorate – were concerned about the human and material costs of conflict, opposing all but an unambiguously defined defensive war. 'Much is now said [in the 'nationalist' press] of the possibility of war, but the great majority has no intention of fighting except in self-defence', recorded the Catholic journal *Historisch-Politische Blätter* at the height of militarist agitation in August 1913. 'Of those who are the most bellicose, more than three-quarters would draw back at the prospect of immediate hostilities.'[81] Although there was considerable discussion of power politics, imperialism, armament and the possibility of conflict by politicians such as the liberal Friedrich Naumann and the Catholic Georg von Hertling, most of their policies were designed to avoid or avert war. The 'democratic' Centre Party leader, Erzberger, despite helping to overcome his party's traditional scepticism about armament, nevertheless went on believing that war was avoidable:

A weak Germany was always the greatest danger of war for the whole of Europe and the bloody battlefield of the European masses. A strong German Reich has become, by contrast, a bulwark of world peace, bought at the cost of its growing defence forces and capability, and its army. Bought at the cost of expensive sacrifices – certainly, but not too expensive, as proved by the growth of our national income and wealth. Forty years of high military burdens are cheaper than half a year of victorious war, not to mention the sacrifices of a defeated campaign, for this sacrifice would be the continuation of the unified Reich.[82]

Erzberger prided himself on his realism, criticizing the premises of disarmament and understanding German unification in terms of power politics, but he also deplored the rise of militarism on the right and remained optimistic about the possibility of increasingly democratic and wealthy – albeit armed – states reconciling their differences.[83] Likewise, left liberals consistently repudiated the case for war and abhorred, in the words of their spokesman in 1911, 'chauvinist agitation'.[84] During Reichstag debates about the 1913 Army Bill, which they eventually came to support, left-liberal speakers agreed with Erzberger that, at such a tense juncture in foreign relations, armament served as a deterrent against war, given its terrible and unpredictable consequences. This support for arms increases was strictly conditional and was intended to rule out international attempts to achieve disarmament.[85]

The SPD was quick to criticize the liberal and Centre parties for supporting arms increases, which in turn helped to reinforce its own reputation as an unpatriotic and even treasonous group of revolutionaries.[86] In fact, beyond the tumult of domestic politics, socialist leaders like Bebel were anxious to prove their military credentials, partly – as has been seen – because they believed that international tension required a more effective, less ceremonial militia-type army, and partly because they feared prosecution or proscription for attacks on the armed forces. Famously, the SPD opposed the idea of a general strike and direct action as a means of opposing war at the main meetings of the Second International, culminating in a blocking motion during the six-day headline debate about militarism at the Stuttgart congress of 1907.[87] The German Social Democratic Party also, of course, voted for war credits on 4 August 1914. These actions, however, did not betray a latent militarism, nor did they indicate that the party was resigned to the ineluctability of war, notwithstanding Bebel's occasional predictions of a European conflagration.[88] Instead, the SPD's leadership put forward compelling arguments why direct action and disarmament were counterproductive in the changed circumstances of the early twentieth century: both would favour 'barbaric' powers, since a state such as tsarist Russia would be less willing to comply with restrictions on armament and conscription and it would, as Georgi'i Plekhanov had told the Second International, not be vulnerable to the effects of a general strike, unlike advanced capitalist economies such as Germany, France and Britain.[89] Resistance to war in a modern military state like Germany, in which 2 million Social Democrats would immediately be enlisted, would be impossible, as had already been the case in 1870.[90] 'Who believes, then, that at a moment when a violent agitation, a fever shakes the masses to the deepest depths, when the danger of an enormous war . . . stands before our eyes, who believes that it is possible at such a moment to stage a mass strike?' demanded Bebel in 1906.[91] Faced with the destructive power of modern warfare, utopianism – whether pacifist or revolutionary – seemed out of place to pragmatic SPD leaders such as Philipp Scheidemann, Hugo Haase, Georg von Vollmar and Ignaz Auer, and to revisionists such as Eduard Bernstein, Joseph Bloch, Karl Leuthner and Max Schippel. Most were convinced that the party should work through the Reichstag and the press for the democratization of the army and that it should act – by persuasion and demonstration, not strikes and sabotage – to prevent the outbreak of a European or world war.

In general, German socialists had distanced themselves from war as the horrific consequences of modern weaponry and mass armies began to be heeded in left-wing circles from the late 1880s onwards. In such conditions, even Engels, who had earlier – with Marx – been a supporter of war as a means of accelerating the outbreak of revolution, now warned of a conflict's humanitarian and strategic disadvantages, leading to

> a severe and general suppression of our movement, a strengthening of chauvinism in all countries and finally a weakening, a period of reaction ten times worse than after 1815, as a consequence of the exhaustion of the people bled white [by the war] – and all this against the slender chance that a revolution comes out of this awful war – this horrifies me. Especially because of our movement in Germany, which would be repressed, smashed and forcibly annihilated, whereas peace brings us virtually certain victory.[92]

Unsurprisingly, revisionists like Bernstein concurred with Engels that parliamentary opposition to the arms race, militarism and war-mongering constituted the most effective way of countering the deleterious effects of nationalism and the states system.[93]

For his part, Karl Kautsky, the foremost Marxist in the SPD, saw military matters through the prism of economic theory, as did radicals like Rosa Luxemburg. Unlike Luxemburg, however, he came to understand militarism as an adjunct of capitalism rather than as an integral part of it, altering his position in the late 1900s, as a result of the findings of Austro-Marxists such as Rudolf Hilferding, from a belief that army expenditure and colonies absorbed surplus production to the idea that extra products could be reinvested and, consequently, were not primarily responsible for economic crises. Military spending therefore was no longer seen as a temporarily ameliorative mechanism in capitalist crises of over-production, but as a political choice of the ruling classes – to create a praetorian guard – which made crises worse by preventing reinvestment. Kautsky's revised theory appeared, in other words, to leave open the possibility of challenging and curtailing militarism – and the risk of war which it entailed – before the end of capitalism.[94]

The radical socialist Karl Liebknecht explored this possibility in his pamphlet on *Militarismus und Antimilitarismus*, which was published in 1907 and led to an eighteen-month period of imprisonment for its author. His main purpose was to show that militarism could be understood as a form of mass psychosis, separable from – though not unrelated to – the workings of capitalism. According to Liebknecht, whose treatise was disowned by the SPD, workers were virtually hypnotized *en masse* – in schools, churches and the army itself – into accepting the irrational and evil forces inherent in the military spirit: 'It stands before the proletariat as a robber armed to the teeth, and its ultimatum is not "la bourse ou la vie" (your money or your life), but "la bourse et la vie" (your money and your life) – which goes further than the morality of robbers.'[95] Such militarism, together with the menace of war, was 'a great danger for the future', of which socialists were acutely aware.[96]

SPD opposition to war reached its height on 28 and 29 July 1914, when more than 750,000 people across Germany joined anti-war demonstrations, far exceeding the numbers involved in simultaneous nationalist gatherings. Historians such as Wolfgang Kruse and Jeffrey Verhey have recently re-examined both sets of demonstrations, as well as other reactions to the July crisis, questioning received wisdom about popular, cross-party 'war enthusiasm'.[97] Although they recognize the depth of support for war in large sections of Germany's *Bürgertum*, especially amongst middle-class youth and intellectuals, both point out that active backing of anti-war rallies was numerically greater, corresponding to working-class criticism of warmongers and sabre-rattling before 1914.[98] 'We're warned not to demonstrate', complained one Hamburg worker, comparing his own fate with that of 'hurrah-patriots', 'and they can do what they want, just because they're for the war and sing the "Watch on the Rhine".'[99] Even amongst those who accepted the call to arms, there was often little more than resignation: 'It's all the same to me whether I die at work or for the fatherland,' confided another worker to his drinking partner, overheard by police spies, 'and you're going as well as me.'[100] There is similar evidence, furnished by priests and other observers, from rural localities.[101] The majority of those in the big-city crowds, it appears from a reading of eye-witness accounts and press reports collected in regional case studies, came to the main squares and thoroughfares in a desperate attempt to find out whether war would be declared or not, precisely because they had been caught unawares by the possibility of armed conflict and persisted in viewing it as avoidable.[102] 'Our people had heavy hearts; the possibility of war was a frightening giant nightmare which caused us many sleepless nights', wrote Theodor Wolff, the editor of the left-liberal *Berliner Tageblatt* in 1916:

> The determination with which we went to war sprang not from joy, but from duty. Only a few talked of a 'fresh, wonderful war.' Only a very few, too, in comparison to the great masses, found flags immediately after the Austrian ultimatum and marched in front of the allied embassies, including the Italian, and in front of the Chancellor's office, screaming themselves hoarse.[103]

Eugen Schiffer, a previously bellicose National Liberal, made similar jottings in his diary as the events in Berlin unfolded, noting 'the deadening seriousness which has settled down upon the people' as mobilization was ordered.[104] On 1 August, the SPD mouthpiece, *Vorwärts*, reported that

> the hurrah atmosphere has gone and a leaden presentiment of an approaching and nameless calamity weighs upon the great multitude of those who wait for the latest news. The sixteen year olds have completely disappeared, and the streets are dominated by adults. A massive river of people populates the Linden and the area around the palace; however, the basic mood is serious and depressed. A few young people attempt to rouse an ovation, but it peters out sadly. Before the extras appear, a man who was standing on a street corner read aloud the Kaiser's speech from a stenogram. Two timid bravos were heard and then the crowd dispersed. Spirits were depressed by ton weights. And we are only at the start of events.[105]

Newspapers with other party leanings also noted the 'seriousness of the hour', with tears and forebodings, as well as more occasional flowers and music, which had characterized the departure of troops in 1870.[106]

Neither the militarist sentiments of the masses nor the warmongering of a majority of political parties, then, had pushed the government and the army to war in 1914. In spite of the unsettling effects of the arms race, most Wilhelmine onlookers still seemed to believe that a conflict was unlikely to occur and, if it did, that Germany would be the victor. War was not seen by the majority of commentators to be inevitable. Instead, in contradistinction to those on the increasingly extreme and belligerent right, most in the centre and on the left of the political spectrum remained sceptical of calls for war. They were certainly not pacifist, often supporting armaments programmes and resenting threats to Germany's position in an era of international tension, but they usually acted in the expectation of avoiding conflict, even if this required arms increases in order to reinforce a policy of deterrence.[107] At most, many liberals, Catholics and Social Democrats were only willing to fight a 'defensive' war against a threatening enemy, remaining wary of other types of military entanglement in Europe, partly out of a half-suppressed fear of their terrible human cost. Such caution amongst significant sections of the electorate placed constraints on the strategies and policies of the military and the civilian government.

Notes

1. V.R. Berghahn, *Militarism: The History of an International Debate, 1861–1979* (Leamington Spa, 1981).
2. S. Förster, *Der doppelte Militarismus: Die deutsche Heerestüstungspolitik zwischen Status-quo-Sicherung und Aggression*, 1890–1913 (Stuttgart, 1985), and T. Rohrkrämer, *Der Militarismus der 'kleinen Leute'. Die Kriegervereine im Deutschen kaiserreich, 1871–1914* (Munich, 1990)
3. H.-U. Wehler, *Deutsche Gesellschaftsgeschichte, 1849–1914* (Munich, 1995), p. 881.
4. See Introduction, and D. Stevenson, *Armaments and the Coming of War: Europe, 1904–1914* (Oxford, 1996), and D.G. Herrmann, *The Arming of Europe and the Making of the First World War* (Princeton, 1996). W.J. Mommsen, 'Der Topos vom unvermeidlichen krieg', in J. Dülffer and K. Holl (eds), *Bereit zum Krieg: Kriegsmentalität im wilhelminischen Deutschland, 1890–1914* (Göttingen, 1986), pp. 194–224.

5. Cited in F. Becker, *Bilder von Krieg und Nation: Die Einigungskriege in der bürgerlichen Öffentlichkeit Deutschlands, 1864–1913* (Munich, 2001), p. 322.

6. On the former, see H. v. Sybel, *Die Begründung des Deutschen Reiches durch Wilhelm I.*, 7 vols, 4th edn (Munich, 1892–5), E. Brandenburg, *Die Reichsgründung*, 2 vols (Leipzig, 1914), and E. Marcks, *Kaiser Wilhelm I.* (Leipzig, 1897); on the latter, see J.G. Droysen, *Das Leben des Feldmarschalls Yorck von Wartenburg*, 2 vols, 11th edn (Leipzig, 1913), F. Meinecke, *Das Leben des Generalfeldmarshalls Hermann von Boyen* (Stuttgart, 1895–9), F. Meinecke, 'Boyen und Roon, zwei preussische Kriegsminister', *Historische Zeitschrift* 77 (1896), M. Lehmann, *Scharnhorst*, 2 vols (Leipzig, 1886–7), H. Delbrück, 'Moltke', in *Erinnerungen, Aufsätze und Reden* (Berlin, 1902), pp. 546–75.

7. Lasker citing Bamberger in Becker, *Bilder von Krieg und Nation*, p. 324.

8. Ibid., p. 288.

9. Freytag's account of the war was published as a book in 1914. Cited ibid., p. 229.

10. His recollections of the war were published in Leipzig in 1908. Ibid., pp. 285–6.

11. Published in 1891, cited ibid., p. 271.

12. J. Vogel, *Nationen im Gleichschritt: Der Kult der 'Nation in Waffen' in Deutschland und Frankreich, 1871–1914* (Göttingen, 1997); J. Vogel, 'Der "Folklorenmilitarismus" und seine zeitgenössische Kritik: Deutschland und Frankreich, 1871–1914', in W. Wette (ed.), *Militarismus in Deutschland 1871 bis 1945. Zeitgenössische Analysen und Kritik* (Münster, 1999), pp. 277–92.

13. Cited in Becker, *Bilder von Krieg und Nation*, p. 286.

14. Ibid., pp. 455–6, 460–1. Also, P. Paret, *German Encounters with Modernism, 1840–1945* (Cambridge, 2001), pp. 7–45, and R. Lenman, *Artists and Society in Germany, 1850–1914* (Manchester, 1997).

15. Becker, *Bilder von Krieg und Nation*, p. 322.

16. Karl Frenzel's memoirs of 1873, cited ibid., p. 352.

17. H. Baumgarten, *Wie wir wieder ein Volk geworden sind* (Leipzig, 1870), cited in Becker, *Bilder von Krieg und Nation*, p. 336.

18. Becker, *Bilder von Krieg und Nation*, p. 217.

19. See N. Stargardt, *The German Idea of Militarism: Radical and Socialist Critics, 1866–1914* (Cambridge, 1994), pp. 50–4; and J. Rojahn, 'Arbeiterbewegung und Kriegsbegeisterung: Die deutsche Sozialdemokratie, 1870–1914', in M. van der Linden and G. Mergner (eds), *Kriegsbegeisterung und mentale Kriegsvorbereitung: Interdisziplinäre Studien* (Berlin, 1991), pp. 57–71.

20. Cited in Vogel, *Nationen im Gleichschritt*, p. 223.

21. Ibid., pp. 221–7.

22. Cited in Rojahn, 'Arbeiterbewegung und Kriegsbegeisterung', p. 58.

23. A.-H. Leugers, 'Einstellungen zu Krieg und Frieden im deutschen Katholizismus vor 1914', in Dülffer and Holl, *Bereit zum Krieg*, pp. 56–7.

24. For the ways in which Sedan Day was contested at different points, for example, see U. Schneider, 'Einheit oder Einigkeit: Der Sedantag im Kaiserreich', in S. Behrenbeck and A. Nützenadel (eds), *Inszenierungen des Nationalstaats. Politische Feiern in Italien und Deutschland seit 1860/71* (Cologne, 2000), pp. 27–44.

25. T. Nipperdey, 'Nationalidee und Nationaldenkmal in Deutschland im 19. Jahrhundert', in *Gesellschaft, Kultur, Theorie* (Göttingen, 1976), pp. 133–73.

26. Cited in Vogel, *Nationen im Gleichschritt*, p. 144.

27. Clemens Thieme, cited in S.-L. Hoffmann, 'Sakraler Monumentalismus um 1900: Das Leipziger Völkerschlachtdenkmal', in R. Koselleck and M. Jeismann (eds), *Der politische Totenkult. Kriegerdenkmäler in der Moderne* (Munich, 1994), p. 277.

28. See, for example, T. von Elsner, *Kaisertage. Die Hamburger und das Wilhelminische Deutschland im Spiegel öffentlicher Festkultur* (Frankfurt a. M., 1991).

29. Vogel, 'Der "Folklorenmilitarismus" und seine zeitgenössische Kritik', p. 277. On SPD criticism of Sedan Day, see H. Müller, 'Die deutsche Arbeiterklasse und die Sedanfeiern', *Zeitschrift für Geschichtswissenschaft*, 17 (1969), pp. 1554–64.

30. J. Rueger, '"Naval Spectacle": The Celebration of the Navy in Germany and Britain, 1897–1914' (unpublished paper). This covers some aspects of Jan Rueger's Cambridge dissertation on the same subject.

31. For more on the army's constitutional position and the powers of the Reichstag in this area, see H.W. Koch, *A Constitutional History of Germany in the Nineteenth and Twentieth Centuries* (London, 1984), pp. 164–8.

32. Moltke, 29 January 1913, A A R6755, A2556; Mutius, 16 January 1906, A A R6601, A1307.

33. H. Ostertag, *Bildung, Ausbildung and Erziehung des Offizierkorps im deutschen Kaiserreich, 1871 his 1918. Eliteideal, Anspruch und Wirklichkeit* (Frankfurt a. M., 1990), on the caste-like nature of the officer corps. Also, M. Kitchen, *The German Officer Corps, 1890–1914* (Oxford, 1968) and H.H. Herwig, *The German Naval Officer Corps: A Social and Political History, 1890–1918* (Oxford, 1973).

34. *Militärisches Wochenblatt*, vol. 91 (1906), cited in Ostertag, *Bildung, Ausbildung und Erziehung*, p. 233.

35. Hauptmann cited in A. Kelly, 'The Franco-German War and Unification in German Schoolbooks', in W. Pape (ed.), *1870/71–1989/90: German Unifications and the Change of Literary Discourse* (Berlin, 1993), p. 39; C. Berg (ed.), *Handbuch der deutschen Bildungsgeschichte. Von der Reichsgründung bis zum Ende des Ersten Weltkriegs* (Munich, 1991), vol.

4, pp. 70-3, 136-7, 501-24; Rohrkrämer, *Der Militarismus der 'kleinen Leute'*, pp. 27-54, 229-35.

36. Hintze in 1906, cited in Berg, *Handbuch der deutschen Bildungsgeschichte*, p. 72.

37. Ibid., p. 70.

38. M. Ingenlath, *Mentale Aufrüstung. Militarisierungstendenzen in Frankreich und Deutschland vor dem Ersten Weltkrieg* (Frankfurt a. M., 1998).

39. M. Christadler, *Kriegserziehung im Jugendbuch. Literarische Mobilmachung in Deutschland und Frankreich vor 1914* (Frankfurt a. M., 1979); I.F. Clarke, *Voices Prophesying War, 1763-1984* (Oxford, 1966).

40. Textbook by Weigand and Tecklenburg, cited in Kelly, 'The Franco-German War and Unification in German History Schoolbooks', p. 49.

41. Other similar works include *Germanische Urkraft und Tatenlust, Germaniens Heldenschicksal, In Kampf um die Heimat, Kampf und Sieg vor 100 Jahren*, and *Der deutsch-französische Krieg*. R. Kripper, 'Formen literarischer Erinnerung an den Deutsch-Französischen Krieg von 1870/71', in H. Berding, K. Heller and W. Speitkamp (eds), *Krieg und Erinnerung. Fallstudien zum 19. und 20. Jahrhundert* (Göttingen, 2000), pp. 28-33. Christadler, *Kriegserziehung im Jugendbuch*, pp. 106-22.

42. Various war memoirs, cited in Becker, *Bilder von Krieg und Nation*, pp. 213, 326, 329-30.

43. On monument inscriptions, see K. Latzel, *Vom Sterben im Krieg. Wandlungen in der Einstellung zum Soldatentod vom Siebenjährigen Krieg bis zum Zweiten. Weltkrieg* (Warendorf, 1988), p. 53.

44. Hoffmann, 'Sakraler Monumentalismus um 1900', pp. 265-75.

45. Von der Goltz, *Das Volk in Waffen*, cited in Clarke, *Voices Prophesying War*, p. 139.

46. Ibid.

47. F. von Bernhardi, *Germany and the Next War* (London, 1913), pp. 9-14.

48. For more on the discrepancy between generals' awareness of the implications of new technology and their unwillingness to alter their overall view of war, see G. Krumeich, 'Vorstellungen vom Krieg vor 1914', in S. Neitzel (ed.), *1900: Zukunftsvisionen der Grossmächte* (Paderborn, 2002), pp. 173-86.

49. All titles examined by Christadler, *Kriegserziehung im Jugendbuch*, pp. 65-199.

50. Ibid., p. 72.

51. Cited in Clarke, *Voices Prophesying War*, p. 143.

52. Ibid., p. 148.

53. Bernhardi, *Germany and the Next War*, pp. 39-53.

54. Cited in S. Förster, 'Dreams and Nightmares: German Military Leadership and the Images of Future Warfare, 1871-1914', in M.F. Boemeke, R.

Chickering and S. Förster (eds), *Anticipating Total War: The German and American Experiences, 1871–1914*, p. 347.

55. D. Riesenberger, *Geschichte der Friedensbewegung in Deutschland. Von den Anfängen bis 1933* (Göttingen, 1985), p. 67.

56. Lamszus cited in Krumeich, 'Vorstellungen vom Krieg vor 1914', p. 184.

57. Ibid., p. 185.

58. Engels cited in Förster, 'Dreams and Nightmares', p. 347; Bebel in Mommsen, 'Der Topos vom unvermeidlichen Krieg', p. 205.

59. Bernhardi, *Germany and the Next War*, p. 18.

60. Ibid.

61. Ibid., pp. 39–53.

62. Ibid., p. 21.

63. Ibid., especially pp. 241–59.

64. Ibid., pp. 246–47.

65. Ibid., p. 50.

66. H. von Treitschke, *Politik*, 2nd revised edn (Leipzig, 1899), vol. 1, p. 32.

67. Ibid., pp. 33–4.

68. Ibid., p. 72.

69. bid., pp. 86–7. O. Hintze, 'Das monarchische Prinzip und die konstitutionelle Verfassung' (1911), in G. Oestreich (ed.), *Otto Hintze. Staat und Verfassung*, 2nd revised edn (Göttingen, 1962), p. 377.

70. Treitschke, *Politik*, vol. 1, pp. 13–137.

71. Ibid., vol. 2, pp. 518–50.

72. E. von Oldenburg-Januschau, *Erinnerungen* (Leipzig, 1936), p.125.

73. Rohrkrämer, *Der Militarismus der 'kleinen Leute'*, pp. 229–62.

74. Ibid., pp. 256, 258.

75. Ibid., p. 123.

76. Ibid.

77. K.von Westarp, *Konservative Politik im letzten Jahrzehnt des Kaiserreiches* (Berlin, 1935), vol. 1, p. 155.

78. Erzberger cited in Förster, *Der doppelte Militarismus*, p. 204.

79. Edmund Rebmann, cited ibid., p. 279. See Förster for further details on conservative and National Liberal positions. For an analysis of the Pan-German platform, see R. Chickering, 'Die Alldeutschen erwarten den Krieg', in Dülffer and Holl, *Bereit zum Krieg*, pp. 20–32.

80. See the press reaction to the Agadir crisis, for example: *Tag*, 25 July 1911; *Zukunft*, 29 July 1911; *Reichsbote*, 26 July, 27 September 1911; *Germania*, 13 October 1911; *Deutsche Zeitung*, 26 October 1911. For Protestant and Catholic reactions, see M. Greschat, 'Krieg und Kriegsbereitschaft im deutschen Protestantismus' and A.-H. Leugers, 'Einstellungen zu Krieg und Frieden im deutschen Katholizismus vor 1914', in Dülffer and Holl, *Bereit zum Krieg*, pp. 33–73.

81. Cited in E.M. Carroll, *Germany and the Great Powers, 1860-1914: A Study in Public Opinion and Foreign Policy* (New York, 1938), p. 758.

82. K. Epstein, *Matthias Erzberger und das Dilemma der deutschen Demokratie* (Frankfurt a. M., 1976), pp. 97-8.

83. Ibid., pp. 91-102.

84. Otto Wiemer cited in Förster, *Der doppelte Militarismus*, p. 215.

85. Ibid., pp. 243-5. J. Dülffer, *Im Zeichen der Gewalt. Frieden und Krieg im 19. und 20. Jahrhundert* (Cologne, 2003), pp. 66-78.

86. See, for example, Erzberger, cited in Epstein, *Matthias Erzberger*, p. 114.

87. J. Braunthal, *History of the International* (London, 1967).

88. See Mommsen, 'Der Topos vom unvermeidlichen Krieg', pp. 203-4, for a counter-argument.

89. Stargardt, *The German Idea of Militarism*, pp. 49-71.

90. Rojahn, 'Arbeiterbewegung und Kriegsbegeisterung', pp. 62-3.

91. Ibid., p. 62.

92. Engels in 1889 cited in Stargardt, *The German Idea of Militarism*, p. 67.

93. W. Wette, *Kriegstheorien deutscher Sozialisten: Marx, Engels, Lassalle, Bernstein, Kautsky, Luxemburg* (Stuttgart, 1971), pp. 125-44.

94. Ibid., pp. 145-90, on Kautsky and Luxemburg. Also, Stargardt, *The German Idea of Militarism*, pp. 72-90.

95. K. Liebknecht, *Militarism and Antimilitarism with Special Regard to the Young Socialist Movement* (Cambridge, 1973), p. 127. See also Stargardt, *The German Idea of Militarism*, pp. 91-107.

96. Liebknecht, *Militarism and Antimilitarism*, p. 127.

97. J. Verhey, *The Spirit of 1914: Militarism, Myth and Mobilisation in Germany* (Cambridge, 2000); W. Kruse, *Krieg und nationale Ingegration. Eine Neuinterpretation des sozialdemokratischen Burgfriedenschlusses 1914/1915* (Essen, 1993); W. Kruse, 'Die Kriegsbegeisterung im Deutschen Reich zu Beginn des Ersten Weltkrieges: Entstehungszusammenhänge, Grenzen und ideologische Strukturen', in Linden and Mergner, *Kriegsbegeisterung und mentale Kriegsvorbereitung*, pp. 73-87; W. Kruse (ed.), *Eine Welt von Feinden. Der Grosse Krieg, 1914-1918* (Frankfurt a. M., 1997), pp. 159-66, 196-204.

98. R.J. Evans, *Proletarians and Politics: Socialism, Protest and Working Class in Germany before the First World War* (London, 1990), p. 178. On youthful and intellectual support for war, see E.J. Leed, *No Man's Land: Combat and Identity in the First World War* (Cambridge, 1979); R.N. Stromberg, *Redemption by War: The Intellectuals and 1914* (Lawrence, 1982).

99. Evans, *Proletarians and Politics*, p. 183.

100. Ibid., pp. 182-83.

101. B. Ziemann, *Front und Heimat. Ländliche Kriegserfahrungen im südlichen Bayern 1914-1923* (Essen, 1997), pp. 39-54.

102. On the avoidability of war, reversing Mommsen's claim, see C. Geinitz, *Kriegsfurcht und Kampfbereitschaft. Das Augusterlebnis in Freiburg* (Essen, 1998), pp. 93–9. For other regional studies, see M. Stöcker, *Augusterlebnis 1914' in Darmstadt. Legende und Wirklichkeit* (Darmstadt, 1994); K.-D. Schwarz, *Weltkrieg und Revolution in Nürnberg* (Stuttgart, 1971); V. Ullrich, *Die Hamburger Arbeiterbewegung vom Vorabend des Ersten Weltkrieges bis zur Revolution 1918/19* 2 vols. (Hamburg, 1976); J. Reulecke, 'Der Erste Weltkrieg und die Arbeiterschaft im rheinisch-westfälischen Industriegebiet', in *Arbeiterbewegung an Rhein und Ruhr* (Wuppertal, 1974), pp. 205–40.

103. Cited in Verhey, *The Spirit of 1914*, p. 7.

104. Cited ibid., p. 69.

105. Cited ibid., pp. 62–3.

106. See, for example, the *Karlsruher Zeitung*, 8 August 1914, cited ibid., p. 79.

107. J. Dülffer, *Im Zeichen der Gewalt*, pp. 66–78, 107–23.

6

Strategies of War: The Army
and the Navy

The German military argued most consistently for war. In particular, officers in the Great General Staff, it is held, were most bellicose, since they realized that Germany's land forces, on which the Reich's national security depended, were being progressively and irreversibly outnumbered by those of the Entente powers. The arms race on the eve of the First World War, which the German Empire was allegedly losing, was both an effect and a proof of this military disequilibrium in the European states system. Consequently, Germany's military spending and strategy, which had shifted from the army, the focus in the Bismarckian and Caprivi eras, to the navy during a period of *Weltpolitik* from 1897 onwards, now purportedly reverted to the army after 1911.[1] Volker Berghahn has made this case most forcefully, extending his early studies of the Tirpitz plan to an analysis of Anglo-German naval antagonism and a subsequent 'retreat to the European continent' as the principal features of the 'approach of war in 1914'.[2] Not only followers of Fischer like Paul Kennedy, but also more recent critics such as Rolf Hobson have accepted the main elements of such a narrative.[3] Their assumptions are shared by historians of the armaments race such as Stevenson and Herrmann, and by historians of the army such as Förster and Mombauer. All emphasize that the General Staff and the War Ministry were gradually convinced of the necessity of war during the course of the 1900s for 'defensive' reasons – or, at least, they believed that their existing desire for an armed conflict had been reinforced – because the Reich's power base on the Continent had come to be threatened by the expanding armies of the Entente.[4] Desperate to wage war whilst Germany was still strong enough to stand a chance of winning, the generals supposedly colluded with Bethmann Hollweg to restore the continental basis of foreign policy and to push the Reich into a European conflagration.

The boasts and recriminations of navy and army officers at the time seem to support Berghahn's case about the shifting military premises of policy-making. Tirpitz, for instance, writing in 1895, shortly before becoming State Secretary of the Navy Office, was certain that the Reich had to redirect the focus of its external policy away from continental Europe and its standing armies, and towards Africa, Asia, the Americas and the navy. 'In my view', he wrote, 'Germany will, in the coming century, rapidly drop from her position as a Great Power unless we begin to develop our maritime interests energetically, systematically and without delay.'[5] He continued four years later: 'In view of the changes in the balance of power in Asia and America, the navy will, in the coming century, become increasingly important for our defence policy, indeed for our entire foreign policy.'[6] By the turn of the century, it seemed that Britain had become the principal object of that policy, as Germany began to concentrate – according to Tirpitz's marginal notes on secret documents – all its 'efforts on the creation of a battle-fleet against England which alone will give us a maritime influence vis-à-vis England'.[7] In his memoirs, Bülow reiterated the same points, recalling that 'the task set for me when I was recalled from Rome to Berlin [in 1897] was to make possible the strengthening of the fleet, which had become a question of our existence, without, however, allowing its construction to lead to a war with England'.[8] The construction of a powerful navy, he recorded in *Deutsche Politik*, which was written in 1913, had been 'the next great task of post-Bismarckian policy'.[9] Against such an apparent change of course, as the Navy Bills of 1898 and 1900 allocated 228 million marks per annum – or about one-fifth of the military budget – for the construction of three large ships per year, the War Minister, Heinrich von Gossler, was forced to accept that 'a considerable increase for the army was for the time being out of the question'.[10] 'In view of the great financial requirements of the navy,' he continued in the Prussian State Ministry of January 1900, 'the army administration would have to be as frugal as possible.'[11] After 1911, when extra expenditure was channelled towards the army again, particularly with the unprecedented growth of military spending in 1913 from 1,781 million marks to 2,406 million marks, admirals likewise lamented that, 'under the pressure of the Army Bill and the financial situation, we had to limit ourselves to the utmost'.[12] From a reading of such accounts, it could seem that the navy and the army were rivals, competing for the same resources and favouring different foreign policies.

Competition between the army and navy had the potential to affect the formulation and conduct of foreign policy, since the Navy Office and Admiralty Staff were less bellicose than the War Ministry and General Staff. At critical junctures after the turn of the century, Tirpitz argued against war. 'The building of the fleet needed peace to succeed', he wrote in his memoirs.[13] From a position of weakness in 1898, when the Reich had only nine large naval vessels compared with Britain's seventy-four and France's fifty-two ships of 6,000 tons or more, Germany had to construct a strong fleet without giving opponents an opportunity of destroying it with impunity, as was alleged to have happened in the much-cited legend of 'Copenhagen', which recalled the Royal Navy's surprise attack on the Danish fleet a century earlier.[14] In other words, Tirpitz warned, German statesmen should avoid risking war until the *Reichsmarine* had emerged from a 'danger zone', during which time the British navy could 'annihilate' it at will:

> The circumstances of my area of responsibility allow me to criticise any world-political stand in double measure. On the other hand, I saw with trepidation how little, in general, one was aware of the political, strategic and economic whole, its enormous prospects and particular pitfalls. The danger of a blockade for example, of any kind of war with England, which could have cut away our entire standing in the world and our future as if with a knife, was not acknowledged, as I was often forced to observe, with appropriate gravity. In the face of English attempts to bind us through a coalition, it was a question of keeping our nerve, to arm ourselves liberally, to avoid provocation and to wait without apprehension until the advancing consolidation of our sea power caused the English peacefully to give us enough air to breathe.[15]

The problem for those who wanted war was that Tirpitz's notion of a 'danger zone' and the avoidance of 'provocation' was elastic, stretching into the more and more distant future as Britain began to expand its own fleet at a similar rate. By 1909, he estimated that 'the danger zone in our relationship with England' would not be overcome until 1915.[16] Thus, during crises in 1908, 1911 and July 1914, the Secretary of State at the Navy Office counselled peace on the grounds that the *Reichsmarine* was not strong enough to defend itself against a British attack.[17] Such caution led Moltke to complain – at the so-called 'War Council' of 8 December 1912, which Wilhelm II had called after British support for France in any future continental war had been revealed – that the navy would never be ready and that war should not be postponed for this reason.[18]

It can be contended that war had never been postponed because of Tirpitz's reluctance, however. The fleet was built in Germany, as in other continental states such as Russia, to supplement a powerful army, not to compete with it. This, at least, was the intention of Bülow and the Kaiser, who encouraged Tirpitz to go ahead with the project, and of political parties, who sanctioned the naval budget. Throughout the period, cuts in spending on one part of the military in order to fund another were carefully avoided. Rather, as the military budget increased – from 841 million marks in 1896–1900 to 1,163 million in 1901, and from 1,781 million in 1912 to 2,406 million in 1913 – the navy and the army respectively benefited from the new funds. In the late 1890s and early 1900s, when extra expenditure was devoted to the *Reichsmarine*, the War Ministry had already decided that 'the German army has in its war formation now gained an extent which has exceeded its limits', as Heinrich von Gossler put it in 1899.[19] His successor Karl von Einem was likewise confident in 1904 that 'the development of the army in the direction of the establishment of new formations and the setting up of new troop units can for the time being be regarded as essentially completed'.[20] Although Tirpitz and other naval officers were less satisfied with the existing rate of warship production, as the army began to demand more funding from 1911 onwards, they were nevertheless aware that Bethmann and Wilhelm II continued to recognize the need for a powerful fleet. 'We must now certainly *always* have to count on both, even in an attack against us!' declared the Kaiser in 1911. 'This requires an entirely unusual increase of the *army* and navy in the form of a defence bill.'[21] It was obvious to the Bavarian military attaché that such a pause in naval increases would be short-lived. It 'seemed to be better tactics to concentrate at first on the improve-ment of the shortcomings and gaps of the army, while temporarily reducing the naval requests', he recorded in 1912. 'Through the German army increase the desire of the French to take the English chestnuts out of the fire would perhaps disappear altogether. Then it would be time to speed up the completion of the navy to one's heart's content without any danger of war.'[22] From the late 1890s onwards, the principle of navy and army expansion had been accepted by Germany's ruling elites. The fact that the former gained the greater part of budget increases in the 1900s, and the latter in the early 1910s, should not obscure the significance of – and continuity of funding to – both parts of the military throughout the entire period.

The army, however, remained the dominant partner, in part because the *Reichsmarine* was not designed to defeat the Royal Navy as much as to threaten it with the possibility of losses so great that it would hesitate to open hostilities, for fear of laying itself open to subsequent attack by a third party. Tirpitz explained this 'risk theory' to Wilhelm II in September 1899, pointing out that when the Reich's construction programme was completed it would have forty-five ships of the line, second only to Britain. Consequently, he went on, 'England will have lost [any] political or economic . . . inclination to attack us.'[23] The Secretary of State's aim, as he had already revealed to the Prussian Minister of Finance, was to make the German fleet 'a true power factor among the world powers' by 1905 and not, 'in the eyes of expert Englishmen, . . . a mere plucking object'.[24] Although at Tirpitz's desired ratio of 2:3 the German navy would have had a chance of defeating its British counterpart, it was admitted that such a chance was small. The army, therefore, continued to constitute German diplomats' principal instrument of coercion, even in a war against Britain, as Schlieffen spelled out in 1897:

> England's might rests in her fleet. To defeat it or to seize it must be the task of every power that fights with the island state.
>
> Germany in a war against England unfortunately has no fleet which is strong enough to carry out the battle of destruction against the hostile fleet. Her ships, ready earlier, better prepared for battle, and commanded more skilfully, can only hope to defeat one part of the overwhelmingly superior might of the enemy and drive it back. The sea cannot be held against the later emerging mass of English naval power by the small number of German ships. After the extensive losses which even the victor will have suffered in the initial stage of war, he must flee to a protecting harbour.
>
> The rest of the task of the war will fall to the German army. It is to use the hoped-for partial victory of the navy for landing on the hostile coast. However great the victories it might win over the hostile army, it cannot do anything to the English fleet, the real enemy . . . As long as the English fleet exists and the island state rules the surrounding seas, the victorious German army is the prisoner of the conquered state . . . It will gradually be starved, not through it being cut off from its food supplies . . . but through the cutting off of any replacement of personnel and *matériel*, but particularly munitions.[25]

The Chief of the General Staff saw no reason up until his retirement in 1906 to revise his view that Germany could not defeat Britain on its own soil because of British naval supremacy.

The upshot of such a conclusion was the prominence and popularity in diplomatic and military circles of the so-called 'hostage theory'. Devised for the first time in the Admiralty Staff in 1897, the theory was based on an admission of military inferiority vis-à-vis the Royal Navy: in order to exert diplomatic leverage and military power, even against the United Kingdom, the Reich would be forced to attack France, damaging British interests on the European mainland, altering the continental balance of power and drawing London into a continental war. Since the 'English' army was much too small to 'undertake to come to Germany' and 'the German [army] will not be able to reach its opponent on the other side of the Channel', noted Schlieffen in 1904, 'France will surely be an ally of England' and, 'were England to declare war on Germany, France would shortly follow the given example'.[26] Bülow outlined the advantages of such a strategy for the Reich in December of the same year:

> In case of an English attack on us is France also to be drawn into the war? The argument against this is that the General Staff thinks France is a very serious adversary, more so than in 1870, that a move against France could bring in Russia against us unless we had previously come to some sort of agreement with her; that perhaps even Italy might side with England and France. The argument in favour is that if the war remained confined to ourselves and England we are practically powerless against England. By capturing our colonies and shipping, destroying our navy and trade, and paralyzing our industry, England could in a foreseeable time force us to a disadvantageous peace. But if France is involved, and particularly if we also bring in Belgium and Holland, we increase our risk, but we would at least have a chance of achieving military successes, obtaining guarantees, and exercising pressure.[27]

To the Chancellor and other diplomats, the possibility of military success and the consequent exercising of pressure were essential components of foreign policy, which only the army could underwrite. 'In the light of this situation it appears that in a future war, whether it be between Germany and Britain or between Germany and France, the decision will fall on land and must be brought about by the army', wrote Moltke in a memorandum of 1911. 'It is on the strength of its army that Germany's power continues to rest.'[28] This principle remained in place until 1914. Thus, during the second Moroccan crisis, naval officers reported without further comment that 'Kiderlen said that if the situation became more acute we should declare war on England on the assumption that France would then declare war on us.'[29] Like their counterparts in the Foreign Office, War Ministry and General Staff, many at the Admiralty Staff and Navy Office seem to have accepted the predominance of the army as a consequence of the 'hostage theory'. Certainly, as Ivo Nikolai Lambi has shown, the objections to the risk of war which were raised by Tirpitz and other admirals in 1905, 1908, 1911 and July 1914 were overruled by the joint efforts of diplomats and generals.[30]

As the ultimate resort of German diplomacy, the army could look back on a long tradition of bellicosity. During most major crises between 1871 and 1914, German generals advocated a pre-emptive strike against the Reich's enemies. Usually, they justified such calls by referring to a growing future menace to national security, which might, at a later date, be difficult, if not impossible, to overcome. This was Moltke the Elder's argument for attacking France during the 1875 War-in-Sight crisis and, together with his successor' Alfred von Waldersee, for launching a war against Russia in 1887.[31] Likewise, during the first Moroccan crisis in 1905, 'it was completely natural and understandable even to any layman that the Chief of the General Staff wanted to see the reckoning with France, which was equally unavoidable, before England had openly crossed over to Germany's enemies, especially at a point in time at which France's ally [Russia] was herself embroiled in a war in the Far East and France thus stood isolated', in the words of Schlieffen's son-in-law. 'Count Schlieffen alerted Prince Bülow to this militarily favourable situation at the right time in a matter-of-fact and sober manner.'[32] Schlieffen's successor, Moltke the Younger, very much regretted, after the peaceful resolution of the Bosnian crisis in 1908–9 'that an opportunity has passed unused that might not present itself again under such favourable conditions in the near future';[33] and, after contending that the time was right for a 'reckoning with England' during the second Moroccan crisis in 1911, he warned his wife that, 'if we once again emerge from this affair with our tail between our legs, if we cannot bring ourselves to make energetic demands which we would be ready to force through with the sword', then 'I will leave', making 'a request to get rid of the army and to have us placed under a Japanese protectorate'.[34] Finally, during the Balkan wars, at the 'War Council' convened by Wilhelm II on 8 December 1912, the Chief of the General Staff pushed for war 'the sooner the better'.[35] He was supported, as his predecessors had been, by high-ranking officers throughout the military establishment.[36]

Such calls for war, which were made at times of strategic defens-iveness under Moltke the Elder and in a period of acknowledged German ascendancy after the turn of the century, do not in them-selves prove that the Reich's military leadership was motivated primarily by fear of a future defeat. There were, of course, well-known expressions of anxiety and pessimism. The majority of those cited in the literature, however, are either appendices to arguments for a pre-emptive strike, instrumental exaggerations to gain support for increases in conscription and armament, or retrospective justifica-tions of pre-war bellicosity. Thus, Jagow's recollection of a conversa-tion with Moltke in May 1914, in which the latter argued that Russia would have completed her armament in two to three years and that 'the military superiority of our enemies would then be so great that he did not know how we would overcome them', belonged to the immediate post-war era of blame and exculpation.[37] Similarly, the recently returned files of the Reichsarchiv, including General Wil-helm von Dommes's supposed certainty in July 1914 'about the difficulties that the war would entail for us considering the numerical superiority of our enemies', were part of an attempt by the army to clear its name during the Weimar period.[38] Such 'certainty', it is true, can also be found in the records of the pre-war years, but it was almost always linked directly to a demand for war in the midst of an international crisis – a practice which went back to the years of Moltke the Elder and beyond – or it was connected, more or less transparently, to campaigns for army increases, which gathered momentum from 1911 onwards. The memorandum of the Director of the General War Department of the Prussian War Ministry, Franz von Wandel, on 29 November 1911, which evoked the threat of an attack in the West by France, Britain, Belgium and the Netherlands; Moltke and Ludendorff's 'Great Memorandum' of 21 December 1912, which asserted that the Reich's position was weaker than that of its enemies because of the defensive nature of the Triple Alliance, the entanglement of Austria–Hungary in the Balkans, and the German army's numerical inferiority when compared to France or to Russia; and War Minister Josias von Heeringen's speech to the Reichstag committee on the Army Bill on 24 April 1913, in which he pointed to improvements in Russian and French mobilization, conscription and armament, all arose from the need to convince sceptics that German army increases were required.[39] The Chief of General Staff's prediction in the 'War Council' of 1912 'that the army would be getting into an increasingly disadvantageous position, because our enemies are increasing their armies more than us, since we are financially very restricted', was both a demand that the German army be expanded and a call for war.[40] Such statements should, as a consequence, be treated with caution.

Few historians would now disagree that the relative military power of the *Kaiserreich* and its allies diminished on the eve of the First World War. Scholars such as Förster, Mombauer, Herrmann, Stevenson and Ferguson, however, postulate that this relative decline constituted – and was perceived to constitute – a genuine threat to the Reich's future security. The gravamen of their case rests on the gloomy forebodings of military leaders during pre-war crises and debates about universal conscription, including newly exhumed memorandums such as that produced by Quartermaster General Georg von Waldersee in May 1914, which declared that it would 'soon no longer be the case' that Germany could come out of 'a great European war quickly and victoriously'.[41] Similar views – many only recorded during or after the war – were expressed by Schlieffen, especially during the early 1890s and 1910s, Moltke the Younger, Ludendorff and Groener.[42] Yet there was very little talk, even in private, of the possibility of a German defeat. Rather, most asserted, like Waldersee, that 'the prospects . . . are *today* still very favourable for Germany and also for the Triple Alliance'.[43] Such words were redolent of Moltke's assurance to the 'War Council' in 1912 that 'there had not been a more favourable opportunity' for an immediate attack 'since the formation of the Triple Alliance' in 1882.[44] This absence of defeatism derived, above all, from what the Belgian ambassador, in 1913, termed the generals' belief in 'Germany's hegemony', and from their expectation of an absolute – or, at least, decisive – victory in Schlieffen's and Moltke's strategies for a war of annihilation.[45] Thus, Ludendorff's aim in pushing for general conscription in 1912 was not to stave off the prospect of defeat, but to retain the means, with or without allies, to force the complete surrender of the Reich's enemies:

> We must adopt measures that will keep the country free from attacks in breach of international law and that will make us independent of the measures adopted by our opponents. We must go further than this and give our entire army the strength that alone can guarantee ultimate success in the next war, a war that we will have to wage with [our] allies, but on the whole with our own strength for [the purposes of] Germany's grandeur. We must make the decision to use our human resources (*Menschenbestand*). We must again become the people in arms that great men made of us in the great days of the past.[46]

Germany, Ludendorff implied, had the resources to 'guarantee ultimate success in the next war', above and beyond the ability to defend itself – or to remain 'independent' of its opponents' actions. In other words, the Reich would be able to prosecute a rapid, offensive war of annihilation. This is also what Waldersee meant when he referred to Germany emerging from a European conflict 'quickly and victoriously'. Russian armament and a shifting balance of power in the Balkans might – by 1917, if Moltke were to be believed – threaten the Reich's 'hegemonic' position and its ability to achieve a complete victory in accordance with Schlieffen's shifting strategies, unless German conscription and armaments were increased. Such warnings did not signify that Germany might, in the foreseeable future, be defeated, as recent historiography has suggested.

Three sets of circumstances militated against pessimism and despair amongst the Reich's military leaders: belief in an offensive strategy and a short campaign in the West; trust in Germany's military resources and domestic morale; and improving military assessments of the *Kaiserreich*'s position vis-à-vis its enemies between the late 1890s and the early 1910s. The first set, concerning a so-called 'ideology of the offensive' and a blind adherence to a tradition – created during the 1860s – of short wars, has been re-examined by Förster, who has argued that the notion of *Blitzkrieg* – already abandoned by Moltke the Elder after his experiences of a Franco-German *Volkskrieg* in 1871 – had been privately discarded by German military leaders in the years before the First World War, and that trust in the viability of an offensive war was temporary, since it would be challenged by the completion of Russian armament and railway-building in 1916–17. Given that an offensive strategy was allegedly the only way to overcome the Reich's numerical inferiority and that a modern economy like that of Germany was supposedly ill-suited to sustain a long war, such doubts amongst the military leadership are held to have created a sense of despair.[47]

It is true that Schlieffen, the main architect of Germany's pre-war strategy, was conscious of the greater number of soldiers in the French and Russian armies, as he began to devise various plans, which involved first annihilating French forces in the West, before attacking and defeating Russian forces in the East. 'We have two opponents against us, whose forces are only tied up by our allies to a very small degree', wrote the Chief of General Staff to his sister Luise in November 1892. 'What is counted on our bill alone constitutes almost double what we possess.'[48] He was not sure, as he had conceded to his other sister, Marie, two days earlier, that the German army 'is so much better' than those of its enemies – 'something like Europeans against Indians and negroes' – that it would be able to overcome such a numerical imbalance.[49] Schlieffen also admitted that a small but effective army was favoured by many contemporaries and that the imbalance was 'in general completely unknown' to virtually all except those in the General Staff.[50] Nevertheless, notwithstanding Terence Zuber's persuasive arguments about the absence of a single 'Schlieffen plan', which could have guaranteed Germany's success in a future war, there is little evidence that the Chief of the General Staff's offensive strategies were conceived as a desperate measure to stave off an envisaged defeat.[51] Rather, they sought to restore the possibility of a decisive victory. 'Necessity forces us to think of ways to win with inferior numbers', he told his fellow-officers after an exercise in 1901. The work of Arden Bucholz and Jehuda Wallach, in particular, has shown the lengths to which the Chief of the General Staff went in order to assure the predominance of this 'principle of annihilation, which distinguished all the battles of Friedrich the Great, which prevailed in all the operations of Napoleon and on whose basis Field Marshal Moltke achieved his exemplary successes'. His emphasis was on a great tradition of heroic and politically critical victories:

> All great commanders have done essentially the same thing. When Friedrich the Great on a foggy December morning marched around the flank of the Austrians, when Napoleon in October 1806 moved down the Saale, and when Field Marshal Moltke in the August days of 1870 went over the Mosel, their actions appeared very different but fundamentally all . . . were based on a single idea: the enemy shall be attacked on one flank and defeated.[52]

The enemies of the Reich were convinced that the German officer corps had inherited the legacy of the 'great man of Sedan' and were to be found in safe possession of the secret of victory, declared Schlieffen on his retirement. 'There is great honour in this, but also a great duty: the duty to make this secret one's own.'[53] Such mystical ideas of military glory constituted the cornerstone of military planning between 1891 and 1914. Wilhelm Groener, who became head of the Railway Department of the General Staff in 1912, evinced how certainty of victory had become closely interwoven with the historical reputation of Schlieffen by the eve of the First World War:

'none of us feared war, but contemplated it, holding it to be inevitable, calmly; not with the certainty which, being armed, boasts loudly, but with the calm of a good conscience and trust in our own strength. To me, too, our victory was a certainty, as long as we stuck to the teachings of Schlieffen.'[54] Despite changing the details of his predecessor's planned campaign against France, Moltke adhered to its core of flanking movements, annihilation and complete victory, such as had been achieved by Hannibal over the superior forces of Rome. Thus, the Chief of the General Staff's gift to his son Adam on entering the War Academy was a copy of Schlieffen's seminal work, *Cannae*.[55]

There was, of course, a well-established alternative within the German army to Schlieffen's aim of rapid wars of annihilation and the complete surrender of opponents. For most of the 1870s and 1880s, Moltke the Elder, confronted by improved fortifications, armament, railways and conscription, had contended that 'the tactical defensive had gained a great advantage over the tactical offensive'.[56] By the 1890s, chided Schlieffen in his summation of tactical–strategic exercises in 1893, 'the defensive idea occupies much more space in men's hearts than seems desirable'. Even with superior numbers in a favourable strategic position, many generals preferred not to act. 'This is surprising; for only 22 years have passed since the time when the notion of the offensive resonated in all, from the first to the last', he concluded.[57] Such defensive preferences and habits did not simply disappear during Schlieffen's period of office. The memorandum in 1895 of Major General Friedrich Köpke, Quartermaster of the General Staff, was typical of many, resigned to the fact that 'only a sum of partial and small successes' was possible: 'We cannot expect rapid and decisive victories.'[58] The Boer and Russo-Japanese wars, which showed the difficulties of attacking against heavy infantry fire and carrying out flanking manoeuvres against extended fronts, gave further credibility to Köpke's line of argument, with articles in military publications such as the *Militärzeitung* openly reassessing the viability of an offensive strategy.[59] 'In recent staff exercises', the Chief of the General Staff warned his fellow-officers in 1905, 'I have only twice seen the goal expressed: I will destroy the enemy.'[60] Thus, although Schlieffen was successful in creating a cult of the offensive during the late 1890s and early 1900s, which was then maintained by Moltke until the outbreak of the First World War, there was always a legitimate alternative tradition of tactical defence, often in combination with subsequent limited offensives, to which the Chiefs of the General Staff could have reverted.

In war games, Schlieffen appears, at times, to have attempted to fix the forces and tactics of France and Germany in order to rule out a defensive strategy. Even then, as General Hermann von Kuhl reported in 1905, French attacks frequently failed.[61] This was in keeping with Clausewitz's famous dictum, explicitly acknowledged by Schlieffen, 'that an offensive war demands and uses very many forces, [and] that these diminish just as steadily as those of the defender increase'.[62] Schlieffen and Moltke the Younger applied such a doctrine to a French defensive, but refused to consider a German defensive in the same light. Arguably, the main reason, hinted at by Kuhl, was that both men believed that a war of annihilation and an absolute victory were still possible: 'the defensive is merely frontal resistance and cannot annihilate the adversary. Annihilation can only be achieved by movement, not immobility.'[63] Neither Schlieffen nor Moltke wanted to admit the feasibility of a defensive – or limited – campaign, not least to stifle challenges to their offensive plans. Yet there were times – for example, as Moltke pushed for army increases from a reluctant War Ministry in 1913 – when they did betray the possibility of defence: 'Since the War Ministry's intended Army Bill falls considerably short of my demands, the completion of our national security (*Landesbefestigung*) is pushed sharply into the foreground, so that Germany as a result can at least successfully carry out a war of defence.'[64] Needless to say, the Chief of the General Staff had no intention of waging such a war, but merely raised its spectre in order to retain the means to launch an offensive.

Schlieffen's offensive design was predicated on a series of short campaigns. The fact that Moltke the Younger realized, like his uncle, that any future European war would be 'a people's war that cannot be won in one decisive battle but will turn into a long and tedious struggle' was not necessarily, as Förster implies, a cause of despair.[65] He had come to such a realization, after all, before he had accepted the post of Chief of the General Staff in 1906. Moreover, by upholding the basic principles of his predecessor's strategy, he effectively repudiated Schlieffen's argument that long wars 'are impossible at a time when the existence of a nation is founded on the uninterrupted progress of commerce and industry'.[66] Schlieffen himself had first articulated this claim in 1901, years after he had decided on an offensive strategy.[67] Instead, Moltke and Ludendorff pressed the War Ministry to stockpile ammunition and encouraged the Secretary of

State for the Interior to make economic preparations for an imminent conflict. 'A perhaps lengthy war on two fronts can only be sustained by an economically strong people', recorded the former in May 1914.[68] Like Schlieffen, whose famous 'plan' of 1905 – entitled 'War against France' – dealt solely with the campaign against the Reich's western neighbour, Moltke concentrated on a quick defeat – or near-defeat – of France, leaving the precise course of the second stage of the war – against Russia – much more open-ended. 'Once France is defeated in the first big battles, then this country, which does not have great reserves of people (*Menschenmaterial*), will hardly be able to continue a long war, while Russia can divert the war after a lost battle towards the interior of her vast terrain and can drag it out for an unforeseeable length of time', reported the Chief of the General Staff in a memorandum of December 1911. 'However, Germany's entire ambition must be to end the war on at least one side with a few big strokes as soon as possible.'[69] The tone of this and other memorandums suggests that Moltke looked on a longer conflict, especially in the East, with a degree of equanimity – certainly not in a panic, which might have been provoked if he had suddenly and belatedly become aware that a long war was possible.

According to Förster and Ferguson, one of the main reasons why Moltke supposedly clung to the idea of a short war, leading him to call for war sooner rather than later, was his conviction that the German army was constrained financially and politically. Both postulate that the Reich's military leaders – in particular, those in the Great General Staff – were driven to despair by the inability of the chaotic and interest-based political system to keep pace with France and Russia in the arms race, and to make adequate provision for war.[70] At the outbreak of the First World War, the German army lacked between 20 and 50 per cent of necessary reserves of ammunition.[71] However, there are a significant number of indications – the second set of circumstances militating against pessimism – that German generals continued to believe in the efficacy of reform and in the country's resources. Thus, Moltke and Schlieffen repeatedly drew attention to the fact that Germany possessed a larger population than France and a more powerful and modern economy than Russia, which, they implied, ought to be more fully utilized than in the past. What was more, they appeared to believe that the army – and military increases – could count on public support. Accordingly, Moltke was confident in 1912 that the Army Bill would be 'seemingly straightforwardly passed': 'The people has a more healthy sensitivity to our international position (*Weltlage*) than its appointed leaders.'[72] Financial constraints had surfaced only during the latter part of Bülow's period of office and they became a potential obstacle to a reform of conscription, military organization and armament only from 1912 onwards, as the War Ministry began to pass on the General Staff's demands to the government and Reichstag. As a consequence, military leaders had had little time to become thoroughly disenchanted with the Reich's fiscal regime, notwithstanding their long-standing scepticism of parties and politics. In addition, they had witnessed the successful passage through the Reichstag of the largest military increases in modern German history in 1913, which, even if falling considerably short of full conscription, offered the prospect of further reform in the future. In a letter to the Chancellor on 18 July 1914, in which he pointed to the numerical superiority of Russia and France, the Chief of the General Staff made it clear that 'what is possible in Russia and France will not be difficult for us': 'the necessary financial means . . . are – as far as I am informed – available in abundance in the country'. 'In any case', he continued, showing a traditional military disregard of politics and economics, 'the question of money must in my opinion not hinder us from executing immediately a measure that is considered essential for the security of the Reich.'[73] Just a fortnight before Germany went to war, Moltke still seemed confident that the *Kaiserreich* had the domestic resources to keep up with France and Russia.

The main opposition to Moltke, argues Förster, was the Prussian War Ministry rather than the Reichstag or the electorate. Conservative militarists in the army itself, he contends, consistently refused to increase the number of conscripts, since they would be obliged to draft larger numbers of 'socialist' workers. Similarly, they refrained from extending the officer corps, because they were fearful of destroying its aristocratic code of honour and duty. There is ample evidence to suggest that conservative-minded generals, particularly those in the War Ministry and Military Cabinet, were reluctant, on social grounds, to expand the army, but there is little proof that domestic considerations overrode the imperatives of foreign policy and military strategy, as Förster implies. Rather, such generals were certain that the Reich would be victorious in a future conflict, as the War Minister Karl von Einem made plain in 1903: 'Our present army organization is so secure that all eventualities can be looked upon calmly.'[74] Consequently, War Ministers were often the most bellicose members of the military establishment, from Einem himself, who told the Bavarian representative in Berlin in 1906 that 'war will and must come' – when 'we are militarily fully ready' – in twelve or eighteen months, to Erich von Falkenhayn, who complained throughout the latter part of the July crisis that Moltke was too ambivalent about war.[75]

On becoming Chief of the General Staff in 1906, Moltke had, for the first six years, toed the War Ministry's line on army increases, joining forces with Bethmann and Josias von Heeringen in 1910, for instance, to dissuade Wilhelm II from pursuing his goal of large-scale military expansion. In 1912, after the War Ministry had scaled down the proposals of the General Staff, Moltke was persuaded, without obvious signs of coercion, that the military situation was reassuring and that the increases of that year had been adequate.[76] It was only by mid-October 1912, after the head of the mobilization section, Ludendorff, had revealed important deficits, that the Chief of the General Staff distanced himself from the War Minister and began to call for full conscription.[77] The Ministry's initial response was disbelief, accusing the General Staff, with some justification, of exaggerating the gravity of Germany's external military position in order to force through conscription during a period of international crisis.[78] When Moltke reported to Bethmann that Heeringen's resistance to increases brought national security into question, the representative of the army section of the War Ministry wrote the sarcastic rejoinder 'sad view!' in the margin.[79] In the same tone, the War Minister rejected the General Staff's request that three new army corps be formed in 1913, arguing that no one would believe that they were necessary, and understandably, 'for it is in fact false': 'No earthly mortal can know what the future will bring.'[80]

Nevertheless, in the years between the Agadir crisis and the outbreak of the First World War, there are numerous signs, not least their acceptance of three unprecedented Army Bills in succession, that officers in the War Ministry had begun to recognize that the Reich's position had worsened. As early as November 1911, therefore, the Director of the General War Department at the Ministry had reported that 'we are surrounded by enemies, that a conflict with them will be difficult to avoid and that this will involve Germany's position in the world (*Weltstellung*)'.[81] By 1913, the same department was examining in a balanced way the feasibility of three more army corps. Even Heeringen, who opposed the formation of extra corps, was willing to describe to a Reichstag committee how the French and Russian armies had become stronger and more mobile, necessitating a further expansion of the army in 1913. That he did not go as far as Moltke in demanding full conscription – 300,000 men rather than the 117,000 granted – was partly a result of competing domestic and foreign priorities, echoed in regular assertions that the 'limits of trainability (*Ausbildungsmöglichkeit*)' had been exceeded, but also partly the corollary of a belief, as he told the committee, that the German army could still regain its 'quantitative advantage'.[82] War Ministers had, at the very least, shifted their position considerably within a short period of time. Although they remained sceptical of General Staff 'exaggerations', it is unlikely that their scepticism led Moltke to despair of keeping up with France and Russia in the pre-war arms race.

Reports from abroad furnished a further – and third – set of reasons for qualified optimism. Arguably, for the first time since the early 1870s, the Reich's military leadership had good grounds to believe by the 1900s that Germany's borders were secure. As was to be expected, the two principal continental enemies of the Reich, France and Russia, were the main focus of the German army's attention. Britain was usually discounted as a land force, despite being viewed as a malevolent instigator of conflict and a likely combatant in a future European war from 1905 onwards.[83] Schlieffen ignored 'England' almost entirely in his military calculations, mentioning it in a continental context for the first time in December 1905, a few days before he retired. Moltke considered the intervention of the British army on the European mainland at greater length, but continued to assure the Foreign Office, according to Jagow's recollection in 1920, that Britain was a *quantité négligeable*: 'Well, I think if need be we would be able to deal with those 150,000 Englishmen, too.'[84] In the West and South, the neutral power Belgium and the ally Italy were likewise treated as marginal factors in a continental war.[85] In the East, the rise of Serbia, the decline of Austria–Hungary and the defeat of Turkey were taken more seriously, but they were nearly always subordinated to assessments of the only threatening power in the region, Russia. Thus, in a memorandum to the Chancellor at the time of a meeting with Wilhelm II in May 1914, in which he again sought to press the case for full conscription, Moltke disclosed that Germany's ally Romania would probably join enemy forces in a future war. The significance of such betrayal was that Austrian troops would be prevented from attacking Russia, allowing 'the offensive of almost the entire Russian army . . . against our forces which remain in the East'.[86] Similarly, in Moltke and Ludendorff's 'Great Memorandum' of

December 1912, the anticipated victory of Serbia and the other Balkan states in their war against Turkey would, it was claimed, tie down most of the Austro-Hungarian army. This was important, above all, because it coincided with Russian rearmament, the memorandum implied.[87] As the second Balkan war broke out in the summer of 1913, Moltke's priority was to find out 'how far this war would affect the conduct of the Great Powers'.[88] 'One would do best to surround the entire Balkans with a fence and not to open it again before all had killed each other', he wrote in July of the same year. 'As long as Austria and Russia do not get involved in the confusion, I see no danger of a European conflict.'[89] In themselves, the Balkan states were regarded as an irritant rather than as a menace. The General Staff's calculation of forces in the East depended on an assessment of Russian strength. Re-alignment within the Balkans – with Moltke prophesying further internecine conflicts between Germany and Austria's current enemies there – only became critical when Russia was perceived to be powerful on its own account.[90]

For most of the 1900s and early 1910s, France was seen by the military to be the Reich's principal opponent, not Russia. During the first Moroccan crisis in 1905, Schlieffen reportedly described in private how 'we are surrounded by a huge coalition; we are in the same position as Friedrich the Great before the Seven Years War'. Yet, he also went on: 'Russia will not be capable of action for years; we could now call to account our most bitter and dangerous opponent France and we would be completely justified in doing so.' France, he went on, contradicting his earlier statement about the Seven Years War, would not hesitate for a moment if it had a chance of success.[91] His views had not changed by 1912, in his final memorandum to the General Staff: 'The *whole* of Germany must throw itself on *one* enemy – the strongest, most powerful, most dangerous enemy: and that can only be the Anglo-French!'[92] Looking back on international crises during the previous decade, he remained convinced that 'The power and prestige of the German army proved their worth in 1905 and 1909. Neither France nor Russia was willing to take up arms once Germany left no doubt about her determination to fight back.'[93] In a similar way, Moltke believed that France would have attacked in 1905, but that it had been too weak, even with the support of Russia; in 1909, he was said by the Chief of the Military Cabinet not to 'fear the French and the Russians', believing that the French army was 'capable' but inferior and that its Russian counterpart 'had still not overcome the repercussions of the years of war and revolution'; and in 1911, he declared that 'on the fight against France depends the outcome of the war'. [94] 'The Republic is our most dangerous opponent,' he went on, 'but we can hope to achieve a decision here quickly.'[95] To military leaders, France remained the main enemy of the *Kaiserreich* until 1913. Accordingly, the Austrian Foreign Minister, Leopold von Berchtold, returning from his first state visit to Berlin in May 1912, was certain 'that all the calculations of German policy were directed from beginning to end towards the eventuality of a clash with France', just as the Belgian delegation, including King Albert, reported the Chief of the General Staff saying in November 1913 that 'the war with France is inevitable', since the neighbouring state was 'obstructing and provoking us'.[96] His comment at that date that 'we will win' and that 'we are certain of victory' adumbrated his judgment on 29 July 1914 that the situation was 'unusually favourable' and that Germany should 'bring about a war'. France, he concluded, 'is at the moment in military difficulties' and 'Russia does not feel militarily secure at all.'[97] Viewed in this light, the German army's response to the events of the July crisis was the culmination of a decade of military assessments of France and of the perceived military superiority of the *Kaiserreich*.

During the period between the Dreyfus Affair in the late 1890s and the outbreak of the First World War, France was viewed by German generals and attachés, more and more pronouncedly, to be a state in military decline. Such assessments, although drawing on long-standing stereotypes of French decadence, seem to have been cautious in their judgements of France's army until a surprisingly late date.[98] The official verdict of German military superiority, which had been implicit since the Dreyfus Affair, had become unambiguous by the mid-1900s, after a succession of mutinies appeared to have given substance to warnings against 'politicization' during the 'affaire des fiches'. Even in 1904, the Reich's attaché admitted that he had 'often' drawn attention to 'the split within the French officer corps, in which there is no comradeship as we know it'.[99] Yet he also repeatedly added the caveat that 'we have no right . . . to infer the inferiority of the [French] army'.[100] Initially, his successor in 1906 adopted a similar line of argument, despite coming to France with a 'superficially' critical view of the French army, akin to that – or so he claimed – of most of his contemporaries. 'The radical regime and its War Ministers', he recorded, 'work in ignorance of the true needs of the army', wasting time playing games and training soldiers for civilian occupations, which was, 'from a military standpoint, extremely

questionable'.[101] He concluded, however, that, 'for the moment, these
tendencies only touch the surface; they are more or less sizeable
obstacles, which are not able to prevent all the serious military circles
working assiduously'.[102] Although 'doubts were justified about
whether radical-democratic propaganda had not also disturbingly
loosened discipline in the army', the attaché knew of no case of
disobedience, even during 'the delicate tasks' of policing worker
uprisings or religious demonstrations.[103] When such disobedience did
occur, during mutinies in the south of France in 1907, the balance
of military reports, which had long been ambivalent, altered definitively, confirming 'earlier impressions' that 'the obedience of the
French soldier is no longer fully unconditional'.[104] 'The soporific
democratic system', he continued, 'has caused officers, at first in the
daily round, to try to win them [soldiers] over by means of leniency;
then, in the moment of danger, they have no longer been able to call
upon stronger force.'[105] The last days had shown, the attaché concluded, 'that the present national army [*Volksheer*] is a mirror image
of the people itself and that it is impossible, in spite of the honest
efforts of the officer corps, to maintain the level of an army when
the moral resources of the people itself are not fostered'.[106] By 1910,
after other mutinies, the next attaché needed no convincing that the
'interference of politicians in military affairs' constituted 'a real
cancer for the French army', irresistibly undermining discipline.[107]

The shift in military evaluations of France can be witnessed in
the principal reports filed during the two Moroccan crises. The first,
which was written in August 1905, warned against an uncritical
acceptance of the view that the French army was 'demoralised' and
'morally degenerate', which had become a slogan of the French press
and which had been 'carried abroad, where it was unfortunately all
too often welcomed, without closer verification.'[108] In fact, the
attaché went on, 'I have become convinced that the French officer
takes his duties very seriously', and 'the French officer corps would
stand united to a man on the battlefield, without political division'.[109]
All the same, he conceded that the *état-major* was, indeed, divided
politically and its authority had been undermined by egalitarianism
and anti-militarism within civil society and the political establishment
of the Third Republic.[110] By August 1911, when the attaché's successor sent in his main dispatch about the second Moroccan crisis,
such 'political influences of all kinds', which had been introduced
into military ranks and which had 'lamed the running of the service
and spoiled the officer's satisfaction in his vocation', were now

uppermost.[111] Ambition and obsequiousness vis-à-vis political power-brokers, he went on, led 'to unjust acts of favouritism and provoke bad blood and profound discouragement in the circle of those who have character and take their service and the army seriously'.[112] This was partly the consequence of the fact that 'the prestige of the army had been systematically lowered in comparison to that of the civil power'.[113] The attaché's summing-up resembled most other diplomatic and military reports which were filed in the years before 1914:

> The French army is by no means poor, but ours is considerably better and for these reasons: because it is more thoroughly and more carefully trained, has firm discipline and possesses an officer corps which, in terms of thrust, professionalism and patriotism, does not, at the very least, stand behind its French counterpart and which is morally superior in its loyalty to its Commander-in-Chief and in its internal coherence.[114]

On the basis of this and other military intelligence, Moltke had good grounds to be confident about the outcome of any future war against France. The so-called 'réveil national' from 1912 onwards and the passing of the Three Year Law in 1913, which extended the length of military service in France by a year, made little difference to the Chief of the General Staff's appraisal. In his annual report, submitted in January 1913, the military attaché had played down the risk of French chauvinism leading to conflict, arguing that most of the populace shied away from war, fearing defeat.[115] Likewise, throughout the debate about extending the length of conscription in France, the attaché left no doubt in his readers' minds that the measure was at once defensive and inferior to the German Army Bill of the same year:

> Germany . . . has . . . no cause to believe the French military law more threatening than it actually is. Given my existing Parisian experience, I believe . . . that the practical results of the last German military bills will be considerably more real, after they have been successfully carried out, than any benefit that the French will ever derive from their three-year period of conscription, which has been bought with such disproportionately great sacrifices.[116]

After doubting for a long time that the French government would manage to pass the Three Year Law at all, he remained certain that the country, given its demographic deficit and political weaknesses, was 'overstretched' and in search of 'peace and quiet'. The legislation bore the hallmark of 'the tortured, the cobbled-together, the "expédi-ent"', since 'France has not been in a position for a considerable time, as is well-known, to draw on plentiful resources in its military competition with Germany.'[117] These reports were backed up by the General Staff's own reading of French military journals. Thus, in 1913, Moltke knew that France was able to mobilize 939,000 troops immediately, whereas Germany could call up more than 1.5 million men without delay, even though both countries had similar peace-time forces, because of the Reich's superior system for mobilizing and exploiting trained reservists.[118] Given such a numerical imbalance in the critical early period of any campaign, together with the supposed long-term structural weaknesses of the French army, Moltke had many reasons to believe that the Reich could achieve decisive victories in the West, before transferring troops to the East.

France's weakness was not balanced by Russia's strength. Military reports between 1905 and 1913 showed the shortcomings of the Russian army, after it had been defeated by Japan and undermined by revolution. One of the main memorandums was composed by Schlieffen in June 1905, following a request from Bülow. Outwardly, expounded the Chief of the General Staff, Russia's 'old army' could be reconstituted in a relatively short period but, 'internally, consider-able differences have been introduced'.[119] It had been known for a long time, he continued, that the Russian army lacked leadership, 'that the majority of officers were of little worth and that the training of the troops could only be seen as inadequate'.[120] Obedience was conditional and resignedly fatalistic, threatening to degenerate into uncontrollable brutality. Uneducated and poorly trained soldiers could not use advanced weapons, making them ill-suited to modern warfare. To the offensive, in particular, 'they are not at all suited'.[121] The Russo-Japanese war, Schlieffen concluded, had not only proved that the Russian army was even worse than had been generally accepted, it had also further weakened the army, as trust and obedience had been destroyed. Since Russian officers did not look to reform the organization of the military, blaming defeat on numeri-cal inferiority rather than internal flaws, it would be 'in the natural course of things, if the Russian army in future, too, does not become better, but worse'.[122] Subsequent reports by military attachés during the late 1900s made similar points, alluding to the 'completely outdated' condition of Russian artillery, the 'grave lack of young officers', a complete dearth of 'usable NCOs', and the necessity of leaving 'strong forces to guard against an internal revolution'.[123] Other dispatches passed on, in apparent agreement, Russian estimates that it would take fifteen or twenty-five years, or more, to recover.[124] The notion of 'military impotence' was commonly linked during these years to the peaceable intentions of Russia's officer corps and government.[125] It remained, perhaps, the principal reason why the German military, despite misgivings about popular pan-Slavism, was confident during the Bosnian crisis in 1908-9 and the Balkan wars in 1912-13 that Russia would not go to war.[126]

Moltke, in particular, eventually came to revise his assessment of the Russian military. At times, of course, he exaggerated his anxiety about the economic and demographic growth of a state whose 'internal conditions and naval powerlessness' had so concerned him, in 1905, that he did not want to sign a treaty with it.[127] As had occurred in German assessments of France in 1911-13, the General Staff seem deliberately to have exaggerated the Russian menace in 1913-14 in order to achieve unprecedented military increases. Holger Herwig has shown how unrealistic predictions about Russia's ability to bring eleven army corps into the field against Germany's meagre twelve divisions by the eighth day of mobilization were handed on to the War Ministry for use in the Reichstag and were published in the *Vierteljahreshefte für Truppenführung und Heereskunde* in order to convince doubters within the army itself.[128] In the event, the Niemen and Narev armies took, respectively, seventeen and twenty-one days to mobilize. Moltke's memorandum of May 1914, in which he talked forebodingly of the extension and expansion of Russian conscription, was – in a similar way – probably an overstatement of the balance of forces, designed to convince Wilhelm II of the necessity of full conscription: 'the entire Russian army will be directed against our forces which remain in the East – to be precise, a Russian army which will, from about 1917 onwards, probably already be fully fitted out and equipped in everything in a modern way, and which will be able to cross the border in the shortest time'.[129] Nevertheless, from a reading of more sober assessments, such as that which he drafted for Jagow in February 1914, it seems likely that Moltke was genuinely concerned about the strengthening of the Russian army as a result of the 'Great Programme'. It had taken until 1912, he wrote, for the neighbouring state to make good the losses suffered against Japan in 1904-5. Since then, there had been 'a whole series of decisive measures', including better training for augmented reserves and the improvement of mobilization, which meant that 'Russia's war-readiness had made massive advances since the Russo-Japanese war and had today reached a level never known before'.[130]

The question, however, was whether such an increase in Russia's military strength was seen to entail the possibility of a future defeat for Germany, as Förster, Mombauer, Stevenson and Herrmann imply.[131] This seems unlikely, given that the Reich's military leaders had begun to take note of the neighbouring state's 'recovery' as late as 1912 or 1913, if at all. On perhaps the sole occasion that Moltke mentioned the possibility of a 'lost war', as he tried to convince the Chancellor to accede to full conscription, Falkenhayn taunted him that 'such a small increase (of our peace-time strength by 30–40,000 men) will not deter our opponents from striking in the spring of 1916 if, as Your Excellency's hints suggest, they are determined to do so'.[132] Clearly, the War Minister, who arguably still saw Britain as more of a threat than Russia, did not believe that the latter would attack, since it had little chance of success. Between the lines of the campaign for more conscripts, the Chief of the General Staff's own evaluation of Russia seemed to coincide with that of Falkenhayn. Even in the 'Great Memorandum' of December 1912, he asserted merely that 'an offensive war into Russia would have no foreseeable end', not that the neighbouring state would be victorious.[133] Other officers understood Moltke's strategy in the same terms. 'The Russians would probably indeed have retreated into the centre of their country in case of a German offensive', recalled one major of the year or so before the First World War. 'Thus the possibility of a decisive success was lacking.' For this reason, he went on, the General Staff had, in 1914, finally abandoned Plan II, which foresaw an offensive in the East, and an initial defensive campaign in the West.

As Adolf Gasser has argued, it is possible that the jettisoning of the eastern deployment plan, which had long been overlooked in favour of an offensive in the West, might have been intended to preclude reconsideration of a more defensive, eastward-looking strategy, at precisely the moment when Russian armaments, conscription and railway-building looked destined, by 1916–17, to bring Plan I – or Moltke's adaptation of Schlieffen's western strategy – into question, if further German military increases were not forthcoming.[134] In other words, the General Staff wanted to retain the chance of complete victory after a war of annihilation, to which it had become accustomed during the decade before 1914, when a supposedly declining French state had been the main enemy of the *Kaiserreich*. Russia's 'Great Programme' of military reform imperilled the planned rapid defeat of France by obliging German planners to leave more troops in the East in order to counter the less cumbersome mobilization of the Russian army. Consequently, Moltke's famous admission to Jagow in May 1914 that 'Russia will have completed her armaments in two or three years' and that 'there was no alternative to waging a preventive war in order to defeat the enemy as long as we could still more or less pass the test' was, if the recollection was accurate at all, an expression of 'anxiety' about the viability of Plan I and the possibility of absolute – or decisive – victory.[135] It is highly improbable that it was a premonition of defeat. German war planners had not yet had time to despair of passing further army increases and they had not yet seen the necessity of considering in detail military strategies which fell short of a war of 'annihilation'.

Unlike Tirpitz, who advised against war 'sooner rather than later', the leading officers of the German army continued to believe that they would be victorious in a future conflict. It was this belief, rather than anxiety about the Reich's declining military position, which motivated their calls to arms before 1914. There is little indication that such officers had given serious consideration to the finitude of Germany's financial and demographic resources or to its worsening international position. As a consequence, it is unlikely that they would have been able to answer the indignant question of the Reich's ambassador in London about how anyone could know what would happen by 1916.[136] At most, they were conscious of conservative and nationalist analyses of foreign affairs. Yet even these 'political' accounts, which officers commonly professed to despise, were not universally pessimistic, as will be shown in the next chapter. 'Military' affairs remained uppermost for the Great General Staff and the War Ministry, and it was because of military assessments and traditional military aggressiveness that they called for war.

Notes

1. For example, M.S. Seligmann and R.R. McLean, *Germany from Reich to Republic, 1871–1918* (London, 2000), pp. 138, 141.

2. F. Fischer, *War of Illusions* (London, 1975), studies 'German Policies from 1911 to 1914'; V.R. Berghahn, *Der Tirpitz-Plan. Genesis und Verfall*

einer innenpolitischen krisenstrategie under Wilhelm II (Düsseldorf, 1971), and V.R. Berghahn, *Germany and the Approach of War in 1914* (London, 1973), especially pp. 125–44 on the 'Retreat to the European Continent'.

3. P.M. Kennedy, *The Rise of the Anglo-German Antagonism 1860–1914* (London, 1980); R. Hobson, *Imperialism at Sea: Naval Strategic Thought, the Ideology of Sea Power and the Tirpitz Plan, 1875–1914* (Boston, 2002).

4. See the Introduction for more details of D. Stevenson, *Armaments and the Coming of War: Europe, 1904–1914*; D.G. Herrmann, *The Arming of Europe and the Making of the First World War* (Princeton, 1996); S. Förster, 'Dreams and Nightmares: German Military Leadership and the Images of Future Warfare, 1871–1914', in M.F. Boemeke, R. Chickering and S. Förster (eds), *Anticipating Total War: The German and American Experiences*; S. Förster, 'Der deutsche Generalstab und die Illusion des kurzen Krieges, 1871–1914', *Militärgeschichtliche Mitteilungen*, 54 (1995), pp. 61–95; A. Mombauer, *Helmuth von Moltke and the Origins of the First World War* (Cambridge, 2001). It is important to remember that Stig Förster and Annika Mombauer do not argue that this was the sole reason for the sabre-rattling of the generals, but rather they maintain that such predictions of a future threat to the Reich increased the urgency and resolve with which they acted.

5. Tirpitz, cited in Berghahn, *Germany and the Approach of War in 1914*, p. 29.

6. Ibid., p. 36.

7. Ibid., p. 38.

8. Bülow, cited in I.N. Lambi, *The Navy and German Power Politics, 1862–1914* (London, 1984), p. 157.

9. Ibid.

10. Gossler, from the protocol of the Prussian State Ministry, 20 January 1900, cited ibid., p. 163. The figures are from N. Ferguson, *The Pity of War* (London, 1998), p. 129, and V.R. Berghahn, *Modern Germany: Society, Economy and Politics in the Twentieth Century*, 2nd edn (Cambridge, 1987), p. 296.

11. Lambi, *The Navy and German Power Politics*, p. 163.

12. Eduard von Capelle, head of the *Etatabteilung* of the Reich Navy Office, May 1912, cited in Berghahn, *Germany and the Approach of War in 1914*, p. 127.

13. A. v. Tirpitz, *Erinnerungen* (Leipzig, 1919), p. 163.

14. The estimates of French and British strength come from the Reich Navy Office; and those of German strength from *Brassey's Naval Annual*. See Lambi, *The Navy and German Power Politics*, p. 142.

15. Lambi, *The Navy and German Power Politics*, p. 165.

16. Tirpitz to a meeting convened by Bülow, 3 June 1909, cited ibid., p. 301.

17. Ibid., pp. 296, 363, 426–7; Kennedy, *The Rise of the Anglo-German Antagonism*, p. 457. Such accounts convincingly revise the account given by Tirpitz himself in his memoirs, in which he claims that Germany had emerged from the 'danger zone' by 1912: Tirpitz, *Erinnerungen*, p. 170.

18. Lambi, *The Navy and German Power Politics*, pp. 382–3.

19. Gossler, 8 June 1899, cited ibid., p. 160.

20. Einem, 19 April 1904, cited ibid., p. 161.

21. Wilhelm II, November 1911, ibid., p. 368.

22. K. Wenninger to Bavarian War Minister, 24 February 1912, ibid., pp. 372–3.

23. Tirpitz to Wilhelm II, 28 September 1899, ibid., p. 146.

24. Tirpitz to J. v. Miquel, n.d., ibid., p. 142.

25. Schlieffen to E. v. Knorr, 14 December 1897, ibid., p. 127.

26. Schlieffen to War Ministry, 7 October 1904, ibid., pp. 243–4.

27. Bülow to F. v. Holstein, 15 December 1904, cited ibid., p. 240.

28. Moltke, 2 December 1911, cited in Fischer, *War of Illusions*, p. 119.

29. H. v. Seebohm to Tirpitz, 10 August 1911, cited in Lambi, *The Navy and German Power Politics*, p. 319.

30. Ibid., pp. 241–68, 287–331, 361–89, 416–29.

31. Förster, 'Dreams and Nightmares', p. 351; G.E. Rothenberg, 'Moltke, Schlieffen and the Doctrine of Strategic Envelopment', in P. Paret (ed.), *Makers of Modern Strategy from Machiavelli to the Nuclear Age* (Oxford, 1986), p. 309.

32. Mombauer, *Helmuth von Moltke*, p. 44.

33. Ibid., p. 112.

34. Ibid., pp. 123–4; T. Meyer (ed.), *Helmuth von Moltke, 1848–1916: Dokumente zu sienem Leben und Wirken*, vol. 1 (Basel, 1993), p. 283.

35. J.C.G. Röhl, 'An der Schwelle zum Weltkrieg: Eine Dokumentation über den "Kriegsrat" vom 8. Dezember 1912', *Militärgeschichtliche Mitteilungen*, 21 (1977), p. 100.

36. Mombauer, *Helmuth von Moltke*, pp. 42–181.

37. Cited in J.C.G. Röhl (ed.), *From Bismarck to Hitler: The Problem of Continuity in German History* (London, 1970), p. 70. For the extent of distortion in this period, see G. v. Jagow, *Ursachen und Ausbruch des Weltkrieges* (Berlin, 1919).

38. Dommes, recollections from 1919, cited in Mombauer, *Helmuth von Moltke*, p. 209. Mombauer's excellent biography draws extensively on the *Reichsarchiv* files.

39. J.R. Dukes, 'Militarism and Arms Policy Revisited: The Origins of the German Army Law of 1913', in J.R. Dukes and J.J. Remak (eds), *Another Germany: A Reconsideration of the Imperial Era* (Boulder, 1988), pp. 19–39; S. Förster, *Der doppelte Militarismus: Die deutsche Heeresrüstungspolitik zwischen Status-quo-Sicherung und Aggression*, 1890–1913 (Stuttgart, 1985), pp. 266–7, 286.

40. Röhl, 'An der Schwelle zum Weltkrieg', p. 100.

41. Mombauer, *Helmuth von Moltke*, p. 178.

42. On Schlieffen, F. v. Boetticher, *Schlieffen* (Göttingen, 1973), pp. 52–5; E. Kessel (ed.), *Generalfeldmarschall Graf Alfred von Schlieffen: Briefe* (Göttingen, 1958), pp. 298, 316–17; on Moltke, Mombauer, *Helmuth von*

Moltke, pp. 172, 175-6, M. Kitchen, *The German Officer Corps, 1890-1914* (Oxford, 1968), p. 146, N. Ferguson, *The Pity of War*, pp. 97-101; for Ludendorff's views, E. Ludendorff, *Kriegführung und Politik* (Berlin, 1922), pp. 52-6; for Groener, W. Groener, *Lebenserinnerungen*, in F. Hiller von Gaertringen (ed.), *Deutsche Geschichtsquellen des 19. und 20. Jahrhunderts*, vol. 41 (Osnabrück, 1972), pp. 85, 135-6.

43. Mombauer, *Helmuth von Moltke*, p. 178.

44. Bavarian military attaché, cited in Fischer, *War of Illusions*, p. 163.

45. Cited ibid., p. 228.

46. Cited in Mombauer, *Helmuth von Moltke*, p. 148.

47. Förster, 'Dreams and Nightmares', pp. 343-76; S. Förster, 'Facing "People's War": Moltke the Elder and Germany's Military Options after 1871', *Journal of Strategic Studies*, 10 (1987), pp. 209-30; Förster, 'Der deutsche Generalstab und die Illusion des Kurzen Krieges, pp. 61-98.

48. Kessel (ed.), *Generalfeldmarschall Graf Alfred Schlieffen*, p. 298.

49. Boetticher, *Schlieffen*, p. 54.

50. Ibid. Kessel, *Generalfeldmarschall Graf Alfred Schlieffen*, p. 298.

51. T. Zuber, *Inventing the Schlieffen Plan: German War Planning, 1871-1914* (Oxford, 2002); T. Zuber, 'The Schlieffen Plan Reconsidered', *War in History*, 6 (1999), pp. 262-305, and T. Zuber, 'Terence Holmes Reinvents the Schlieffen Plan', *War in History*, 8 (2001), pp. 268-76; for the case against Zuber, see T.M. Holmes, 'The Reluctant March on Paris: A Reply to Terence Zuber's "The Schlieffen Plan Reconsidered"', *War in History*, 8 (2001), pp. 208-32.

52. A. Bucholz, *Hans Delbrück and the German Military Establishment: War Images in Conflict* (Iowa City, 1985), p. 67. Also, A. Bucholz, *Moltke, Schlieffen and Prussian War Planning* (Oxford, 1991), pp. 109-213; J.L. Wallach, *Das Dogma der Vernichtungsschlacht: Die Lehre von Clausewitz und Schlieffen und ihre Wirkungen in zwei Weltkriegen* (Frankfurt a. M., 1967), pp. 52-122; J.L. Wallach, 'Feldmarschall von Schlieffens Interpretation der Kriegslehre Moltkes d. Ä', in R.G. Foerster (ed.), *Generalfeldmarschall von Moltke. Bedeutung und Wirkung* (Munich, 1991), pp. 54-66.

53. M. Salewski, 'Moltke, Schlieffen und die Eisenbahn', in Foerster, *Generalfeldmarschall von Moltke*, p. 96.

54. Groener, *Lebenserinnerungen*, pp. 136-7.

55. Wallach, *Das Dogma der Vernichtungsschlacht*, p. 145.

56. Moltke the Elder in 1874, cited in Wallach, 'Feldmarschall von Schlieffens Interpretation der Kriegslehre Moltkes d. Ä', p. 55.

57. Ibid., p. 56.

58. Cited in Förster, 'Dreams and Nightmares', p. 355.

59. B.-F. Schulte, *Die deutsche Armee: 1900-1914. Zwischen Beharren und Verändun* (Düsseldorf, 1977), pp. 184-5, 202-3. See also M. Howard, 'Men against Fire: Expectations of War in 1914', in Miller et al. (eds), *Military Strategy and the Origins of the First World War* (Princeton, 1991), pp. 3-19, and A.J. Echevarria II, 'A Crisis in Warfighting: German Tactical Discussions

in the late Nineteenth Century', *Militärgeschichtliche Mitteilungen*, 55 (1996), pp. 51-68, on the nature of the problem posed by the Boer and Russo-Japanese conflicts.

60. Cited in Bucholz, *Hans Delbrück and the German Military Establishment*, p. 67.

61. Cited in J. Snyder, *The Ideology of the Offensive: Military Decision-Making and the Disasters of 1914* (Ithaca, 1984), pp. 143-4.

62. Schlieffen in 1905, cited in Wallach, *Das Dogma der Vernichtungsschlacht*, p. 116.

63. Cited in Snyder, *The Ideology of the Offensive*, p. 144.

64. Moltke, 30 January 1913, cited in Förster, *Der doppelte Militarismus*, p. 272.

65. Moltke to his wife, 29 January 1905, reporting a conversation with Wilhelm II, cited in Förster, 'Dreams and Nightmares', p. 363. According to Groener, Schlieffen himself had not insisted on a short war, but 'as short a war as possible', cited in Mombauer, *Helmuth von Moltke*, p. 95.

66. Förster, 'Dreams and Nightmares', p. 359.

67. Snyder, *The Ideology of the Offensive*, p. 139.

68. Förster, 'Dreams and Nightmares', p. 370.

69. Cited in Mombauer, *Helmuth von Moltke*, p. 91.

70. See L. Burchardt, *Friedenswirtschaft und Kriegsvorsorge: Deutschlands wirtschaftliche Rüstungsbestrebungen vor 1914* (Boppard, 1968).

71. Förster, 'Dreams and Nightmares', p. 371.

72. Moltke, 24 April 1912, cited in Meyer, *Helmuth von Moltke*, p. 284.

73. Cited in Mombauer, *Helmuth von Moltke*, p. 179. For similar views from Ludendorff, see Förster, *Der doppelte Militarismus*, p. 267.

74. Einem to Bülow, 3 June 1903, cited in V.R. Berghahn and W. Deist (eds), *Rüstung im Zeichen der wilhelminischen Weltpolitik* (Düsseldorf, 1988), p. 68.

75. Gebsattel, 30 March 1906, cited ibid., p. 148; H. Afflerbach, *Falkenhayn: Politisches Denken und Handeln im Kaiserreich* 2nd edn (Munich, 1994), pp. 147-71.

76. Förster, *Der doppelte Militarismus*, p. 251.

77. Dukes, 'Militarism and Arms Policy Revisited', p. 29.

78. Moltke made this point himself in 1913: see Förster, *Der doppelte Militarismus*, p. 270.

79. Ibid., p. 272.

80. Ibid., p. 269.

81. F. v. Wandel, 29 November 1911, cited in Berghahn and Deist, *Rüstung*, p. 379.

82. Förster, *Der doppelte Militarismus*, pp. 270, 286.

83. Meyer, *Helmuth von Moltke*, pp. 247, 259-61; Afflerbach, *Falkenhayn*, pp. 78-9; F. Uhle-Wettler, *Erich Ludendorff in seiner Zeit. Soldat, Stratege, Revolutionär* (Berg, 1995), p. 86; Mombauer, *Helmuth von Moltke*, pp. 77-9, 116-17, 132, 159-60.

84. Mombauer, *Helmuth von Moltke*, p. 160. On Schlieffen, ibid., pp. 78.
85. Ibid., pp. 153–70.
86. Cited ibid., p. 176.
87. Förster, *Der doppelte Militarismus*, p. 267.
88. Moltke, 16 May 1913, cited in Meyer, *Helmuth von Moltke*, p. 290.
89. Ibid., p. 292.
90. Mombauer, *Helmuth von Moltke*, p. 152.
91. Obergeneralarzt z. D. Hugo Rochs, cited in Groener, *Lebenserinnerungen*, pp. 85–6.
92. Cited in G. Ritter, *The Schlieffen Plan: Critique of a Myth* (London, 1958), p. 172.
93. Ibid., p. 171.
94. Moltke, 31 March 1905, cited in Meyer, *Helmuth von Moltke*, p. 253; M. v. Lyncker and Moltke respectively, in 1909, cited in Mombauer, *Helmuth von Moltke*, p. 112; Moltke in 1911, cited ibid., p. 91.
95. Moltke, 1911, cited in Mombauer, *Helmuth von Moltke*, p. 91.
96. Berchtold, cited in Fischer, *Germany's Aims in the First World War* (London, 1967), p. 30; the Belgian military attaché, cited in J. Stengers, 'Guillaume II et le Roi Albert à Potsdam en novembre 1913', *Bulletin de la classe des lettres et des sciences morales et politiques*, 7–12 (1993), p. 246.
97. The Bavarian Military Plenipotentiary in Berlin to the Bavarian War Ministry, 29 July 1914, cited in Kitchen, *The German Officer Corps*, p. 111.
98. G. Krumeich, 'Le déclin de la France dans la pensée politique et militaire allemande avant la premiere guerre mondiale', in J.-C. Allain (ed.), *La Moyenne puissance au XXe siecle* (Paris, 1988)', p. 112, on the resonance of the idea of French decadence; G. Krumeich, 'La puissance militaire française vue de l'Allemagne autour de 1900', in P. Milza and R. Poidevin (eds) *La puissance française á la belle époque* (Brussels, 1992), pp. 199–209, on German caution.
99. Hugo, 24 January 1905, AA R6746, A1446.
100. Ibid. Also, 12 August 1905, AA R6747, A14624.
101. Mutius, 29 April 1906, AA R6748, A7988.
102. Ibid. Also, 22 March 1907, AA R6749, A4862.
103. Mutius, 29 April 1906, AA R6748, A7988.
104. Mutius, 29 June 1907, AA R6749, A10256.
105. Ibid.
106. Ibid.
107. Winterfeld, 27 May 1910, AA R6751, A9196.
108. Hugo, 12 August 1905, AA R6747, A14624.
109. Ibid.
110. Ibid.
111. Winterfeld, 30 August 1911, AA R6753, A13921.
112. Ibid.
113. Ibid.
114. Ibid.

115. Winterfeld, 13 January 1913, AA R6754, A1268.

116. Winterfeld, 20 August 1913, AA R6756, A17204.

117. Ibid. Also, 14 February 1913, AA R6755, A3519, 5 March 1913, AA R6755, A4773, 1 March 1913, AA R6755, A4503, 12 March 1913, AA R6755, A5341.

118. H.H. Herwig, 'Imperial Germany', in E.R. May (ed.), *Knowing One's Enemies: Intelligence Assessment before the Two World Wars* (Princeton, 1984), pp. 67–8. The extent to which Schlieffen relied on reservists is shown by Zuber, *Inventing the Schlieffen Plan*, pp. 135–219.

119. Schlieffen to Bülow, 10 June 1905, in J. Lepsius et al. (eds), *Grosse Politik der Europäischen Kabinette* (Berlin, 1922–7), vol. 19, no. 6195, p. 423.

120. Ibid.

121. Ibid., 424.

122. Ibid.

123. Posadowsky-Wehner to Wilhelm II, 10 December 1908, GP, vol. 26, no. 9149, pp. 325–6. See also Jacobi to Wilehlm II, 4 July 1908, vol. 25, no. 8826, p. 488.

124. Hintze to Wilhelm II, 29 May 1909, GP, vol. 26, no. 9545, p. 806; also, 24 March 1910, GP, vol. 27, p. 521.

125. Ibid.

126. For the latter crisis, see Moltke, 6 February 1913, GP, vol. 34, no. 12480, p. 319, and the dispatches cited above for the former.

127. Bülow to the Foreign Office, 9 August 1905, GP, vol. 19, no. 6235, p. 488.

128. Herwig, 'Imperial Germany', p. 69.

129. Cited in Mombauer, *Helmuth von Moltke*, p. 176.

130. Moltke to Jagow, 24 February 1914, GP, vol. 39, no. 15839, pp. 533–4.

131. All of these authors maintain that most generals thought that the Reich would be victorious in and before 1914, but that they feared defeat in the future. The argument put forward in this chapter is that such generals did not seriously consider the possibility of defeat, but were anxious about giving up the chance of an absolute or decisive victory intrinsic to a war of annihilation. The possible future renunciation of such a decisive victory was not the same thing as accepting defeat.

132. Cited in Mombauer, *Helmuth von Moltke*, p. 180. See also, Afflerbach, *Falkenhayn*, pp. 134–5.

133. Mombauer, *Helmuth von Moltke*, p. 158.

134. A. Gasser, *Preussischer Militärgeist und Kriegsentfesselung 1914: Drei Studien zum Ausbruch des Weltkrieges* (Basel, 1985).

135. Ferguson, *The Pity of War*, p. 100.

136. Prince K. M. Lichnowsky, cited in J. C. G. Röhl (ed.), *1914: Delusion or Design?* (London, 1973), p. 104.

7

Imperialism and Conceptions of Diplomatic Relations

Both Fischer and his opponents have contended that the achievement of world power became the decisive question for the leaders – and, indeed, public – of the German Reich in the two decades before the First World War. New conceptions of diplomatic relations based on the idea of 'world empires' supposedly upset the nineteenth-century notion of a balance of power within the concert of Europe or pentarchy. Germany, as F.H. Hinsley wrote shortly after the publication of *Griff nach der Weltmacht*, 'at last approached a degree of material primacy in Europe which no power had possessed since 1815 – and did so at a time when her power beyond Europe was negligible and when the prospects of enlarging it there were rapidly diminishing'.[1] Fischer, who had made the putative choice between world power or decline the title of a book (*Weltmacht oder Niedergang?*) in 1965, argued that Germany already occupied a hegemonic position in Europe and implied that German leaders' aspirations for the status of a world empire were the consequence of a catastrophic act of self-delusion and domestic manipulation, as the Reich government sought to deflect attention from political deadlock and social stasis at home.

Schöllgen and other critics of the Hamburg school have countered that the predicament faced by Bülow and Bethmann was real, not imaginary: Wilhelmine statesmen had good grounds for believing that the Reich needed to become a world power in order to guarantee access to raw materials and markets during a period when Germany was increasingly reliant on exports, yet any attempt to gain power on the world stage, either in Europe or beyond it, met the resistance of the traditional Great Powers, whose leaders feared that the European balance of power would be overturned.[2] Sönke Neitzel, in particular, has sought to show that the notion of world empires had been widely accepted by the turn of the century, not just in Germany, but in Britain, the United States and elsewhere.[3] Despite much miscalculation and exaggeration, it appeared necessary at the time – to 'the mass of middle-class and conservative forces' – to ensure that 'the German Reich join the exclusive club of world empires'.[4] 'It was not a question of simply reiterating a slogan', proposes Neitzel. 'Rather, the idea of so-called world empires (*Weltreichslehre*) stood behind it, a theory according to which, not the military disputes of nation-states, but the economic conflicts of vast, powerful empires and trading blocs would determine the twentieth century.'[5] The perceived need to acquire the status of a world power, it is held, pushed both government and public towards colonialism overseas, which led to the country's diplomatic isolation by 1911, and towards an increasing concentration on *Mitteleuropa* and the Near East, which purportedly came to constitute the Reich's last chance of becoming a world empire. As a consequence, challenges to German or Austrian interests on the Balkan 'land bridge' to the Near East allegedly proved more and more difficult to accept.

Few, if any, historians deny that there was a turn towards *Weltpolitik* around the turn of the century, which appealed to a broad cross-section of political parties. The roots of this world policy were disparate, entangled and well established, with the quest for colonies or the dream of creating a Central European trading bloc against Britain and the United States, for instance, going back to the 1830s and 40s. Yet, as Konrad Canis points out, a series of events converged in the late 1890s which helped to create a shift in policy: most notably, the expansion of the US economy and the passage of the protectionist McKinley and Dingley tariffs in 1890 and 1897; Russian industrialization under Sergei Witte; the rise of Japan as a significant power and the related fear in Germany of a 'yellow peril'; and British aggression in the Transvaal, as well as discussion in London of protective tariffs and of 'Greater Britain'.[6] The Reich government, the navy and the Kaiser, which together did most to bring about the shift in policy, were certainly aware that such events had begun to alter Germany's international position. In his first speech to the Reichstag on 6 December 1897, as he justified the seizure of Kiaochow as a naval base and entry-point into China, in his new role as Secretary of State at the Foreign Office, Bülow signalled the change:

> We must demand that the German missionary and the German entre-
> preneur, German goods, the German flag and German ships in China are
> just as respected as those of other powers. We are finally very willing to

give recognition to the interests of other Great Powers in East Asia, in the certain prospect that our own interests will likewise find the credit that they are due. In a word: we don't want to put anyone in the shadow, but we too demand our place in the sun. In East Asia as in the West Indies, we will endeavour, true to the traditions of German policy, without unnecessary sharpness, but also without weakness, to defend our rights and interests.[7]

This moment was seen at the time – and subsequently – to mark a break in the conduct of German foreign policy. 'Some fortunate phrases in his short, succinct speech – like, for example, "we don't want to put anyone in the shadow but we too demand our place in the sun" and "the times when the German left the earth to one of his neighbours, the sea to the other, and reserved for himself the heavens where pure doctrine reigns – these times are over" – have already become almost proverbial and are on everyone's lips', noted Württemberg's Minister to Berlin later that month.[8] Looking back in 1909, Bülow claimed that the task put before him in 1897 was 'the development of our commerce, transition to *Weltpolitik* and, especially, the creation of a German fleet without a collision with England'.[9] 'We can do nothing other than pursue *Weltpolitik*', he wrote in 1900, echoing Wilhelm II's boast that Germany 'had great tasks to accomplish outside the narrow boundaries of old Europe', with its future lying 'less in Europe than the entire world'.[10] Although avowedly more cautious, urging that 'we must drive forward quietly and patiently', Bethmann, too, aimed 'to be able to realise greater aims in colonies and world trade', adding the hope that he would not, by such means, have 'to risk our existence'.[11] Indeed, David Kaiser has argued that the last peacetime Chancellor, who came from the domestic civil service rather than the diplomatic corps, was more detached from the traditional – and implicitly 'European' – tenets of German foreign policy than any of his predecessors.[12]

There is abundant evidence, as Kaiser rightly assumes, that middle and lower-middle-class public opinion enthusiastically endorsed the government's transition to *Weltpolitik*. Its support for the new policy could be divined from the extensive coverage given in the mass press to colonial affairs, wars and exploration, and from the strength of nationalist leagues such as the Flottenverein, whose doggerel pro claimed that 'for German strength and German tongue/There must be room still on this earth'.[13] Germany's most famous explorer and imperial publicist, Carl Peters, helped to set the tone of such reportage and articulated some of its assumptions. Britain and the United States – the 'Anglo-Saxons' – constituted Germany's principal model and menace:

> The advantage of entering upon the coming centuries as a giant national empire is obvious. It must result in the monopolisation, by the Anglo-Saxons collectively, of two-sevenths, and by the English themselves of two-eighths of the surface of the earth, for their own species. Another result will be that within measurable time the Anglo-Saxon race will form a political community of greater extent than any possible combination of foreign nations; nay, that perhaps the mere existence of foreign nations will solely depend on England's discretion; or that ultimately this planet will be inhabited exclusively by the English and their slaves . . . It is, therefore, generally accepted that the union of the British Empire will confer great material advantages upon every single British subject wherever he may have been born.[14]

If Peters's predictions were to be believed, Joseph Chamberlain's plans for an imperial tariff would be realized, the United States would 'monopolise' South America, possibly joining Great Britain in 'a great federal state' of 'the Anglo-Saxon world'.[15] Meanwhile, the German Empire, unless it acted to avert such a state of affairs, would be 'wedged in, as it is, between France and Russia, and by nature a continental power disinclined to take the offensive'.[16] Peters's message to his public was that German leaders had to act decisively and immediately if the Reich were to retain its freedom in a world divided between imperialist powers.

The opinion-makers and political leaders of the Wilhelmine public were equally receptive to, if often more circumspect about, the necessity of the Reich becoming a world power. As was to be expected, this was true of right-wing liberals such as Ernst Hasse, the first head of the Pan-German League, and of Ernst Bassermann, the pre-war leader of the National Liberal Party and a vociferous critic of the 'timidity' of German foreign policy under Bülow and Bethmann. 'The twentieth century is dominated by the imperialist idea', wrote Bassermann at the end of 1912. 'The nations are carried away by the aim of world power and power at sea. The concept of international brotherhood and the idea of disarmament are increasingly forced into the background by harsh reality.'[17] The necessity of imperialism was also accepted by historians and publicists like Hans Delbrück, the editor of the prestigious, moderate right-wing journal the *Preussische Jahrbücher*, who warned, in 1897, that 'huge land masses in all parts of the world are going to be divided up. The nationality which comes away empty-handed will, in the succeeding generation, be excluded from the ranks of the great nations which determine the spirit of humanity (*Menschengeist*).'[18] Throughout all of Delbrück's weekly columns, which were amongst the most influential – if not most widely read – foreign-policy commentaries of the pre-war period, ran a common thread: the Reich had to challenge British domination overseas and compete for world power. 'What the world strives for is not a reversal and the destruction of the great position which the English have won for themselves on the globe, but only the wish to compete equally in the division of the countries and territories which can still be gained by the cultured world (*Kulturwelt*)', he explained in 1902.[19] In the decade of diplomatic incidents involving Britain and Germany which followed, Delbrück's sense that 'England or perhaps England and the United States together would make the entire extra-European world English' became a matter of conviction.[20] In December 1913, in a notorious attack on the 'hypernationalist' Pan-Germans, whom he perceived to be more of a danger to the Reich's interests than the socialists, he nevertheless remained convinced that 'the political task of Germany can be no other than striving undeterred for the goal of a great colonial empire, and not to tolerate the carrying out of further "partitions" or the putting aside of "spheres of interest" in the world, without us being involved at the same time'.[21] A policy of armament was needed in order to exert 'sufficient pressure' on the other powers to allow German participation, although war would only be a last resort, if there was no 'other way out with honour'.[22]

Conservative journalists like Theodor Schiemann, the Berlin historian who wrote the regular foreign affairs section of the *Kreuz-Zeitung*, and politicians such as Westarp and Heydebrand, although referring to it less frequently and fervidly than far-right-wing nationalists and National Liberals, generally supported the policies and adopted the phrases of *Weltpolitik* on behalf of their largely rural voters and often aristocratic readers. Terms such as 'competition of the peoples' (*Wettbewerb der Völker*) and 'partition of the world' (*Erschliessung der Welt*) could be found in Schiemann's articles and those of fellow journalists in other Conservative journals like *Grenzboten*.[23] 'What we strive for', wrote the historian-cum-columnist, 'is freedom of the seas and the partition of the world with equal rights for the strong (*Tüchtigen*).'[24] 'Our reputation abroad and our strength at home depend on German policy becoming world policy, just as

German trade has become world trade', he had already written in 1896.[25] On a party level, such support for *Weltpolitik*, though long a feature of Conservative rhetoric, became most salient during the second Moroccan crisis, as Heydebrand announced his party's first full criticism of government foreign policy in November 1911:

> The German nation now knows when it will expand in this world, when it will seek its place in the sun, which is its right and purpose – we now know, then, where that person [David Lloyd George] is who is to be asked whether he will allow it or not. (Lively applause on the right, in the centre and amongst National Liberals.) Gentlemen, we Germans are not used to having to put up with this, and the German nation will know what answer to give.[26]

In this fashion, Heydebrand and other Conservatives combined a traditional dislike of liberal, industrial 'England' with the Reich's 'right' to achieve world power. Sir Edward Grey had presumed, noted Westarp, to warn Germans against aggression, yet it was Britain which had threatened to bring to an end the German Empire's forty-year history of peace:

> the opinion that England has intended to create difficulties for our development in recent years – right up to the present – is now deeply rooted in the German people, and the belief that a powerful opponent has stood in our way, wherever we, following the inclination of our own needs, show ourselves on the world stage, must have an influence on our internal and external policy.[27]

Longstanding antipathy towards Britain had helped to convince Conservatives during the 1900s and 1910s of the rectitude of German *Weltpolitik*, bringing them closer in the realm of foreign policy to the nationalist leagues and to the National Liberal Party.

Although for the most part abandoning the anti-imperialist stance of Eugen Richter, the leader of the left liberals until his death in 1906, a new generation of progressive politicians and intellectuals such as Friedrich Naumann and Max Weber remained critical of what the former's journal, *Die Hilfe*, termed 'nationalist super-patriots and the hysteria of friends of the military' during the Agadir crisis of 1911.[28] They were also well disposed towards Britain, on the whole, as a parliamentary, liberal state, individualist and open society, and free-trade, industrial economy. However, Naumann was convinced like Weber that German unification would have been a 'youthful spree', if it were not 'the starting-point for German power politics on a global scale', in the words of the latter's celebrated inaugural lecture in Freiburg in 1895.[29] 'We Germans are the newest revolutionaries in the European family, the people who have disturbed the sleep of this region of the earth for the last time in a decisive way', recorded the editor of *Die Hilfe* in his treatise on *Demokratie und Kaisertum* (1900). 'That our nation did this was its well-earned right before God and humanity – it, too, wanted, after long centuries of misery, to have its place in the sun.'[30] Naumann rejoiced in the 'unity and power of the Reich', repudiating the view that it could have been achieved without 'troubling any waters' as 'naïve sentimentality'. Indeed, he applauded Peters's necessary brutality as late as 1907 and maintained that a war with Britain was 'certain', opening the way for German colonial acquisitions.[31] In 1911, in spite of his reservations about the destructiveness of nationalist agitation, he still objected 'that Germany had, objectively, been short-changed in the partition of Africa'.[32] Naumann, like the academics and publicists – Lujo Brentano, Max and Alfred Weber, Friedrich Meinecke, Gerhart von Schulze-Gävernitz, Ernst Jäckh and Paul Rohrbach – to whom he was close and whose articles he published, continued to believe that world-power status, a fleet and access to foreign markets were essential interests of the German Reich. None of these 'liberal imperialists', despite their disillusionment with Tirpitz and Wilhelm II, gave up their hope that Germany should become what Rohrbach – the most well-known liberal commentator on colonial affairs – called a 'world people' (*Weltvolk*):

> Today it is necessary to be clear about the fact that we must stake our claim in the politics of the world and amongst those world peoples by whom *Weltpolitik* is made, and that we must not allow ourselves to be pushed back into the number of merely European peoples, whose place in the extra-European world is prescribed by the leading world nations, and whose circle we have in fact already outgrown.[33]

Like the left liberals, the deputies of the Zentrumspartei had largely overcome their scepticism of navalism and imperialism by the early 1900s, at least in public, in order to prove their credentials as a national-minded, state-supporting party. Consequently, when the 'democratic' Catholics Matthias Erzberger and Hermann Roeren launched a campaign against corruption and inhumanity in the German colonial service in 1906, giving Bülow an additional pretext to break with the 'unpatriotic' Centre and call new elections for the following year, the majority of the party leadership moved to disown them.[34] Yet, although the Chancellor encouraged the formation of a 'national bloc' of conservatives, National Liberals and progressives in explicit opposition to the Centre Party in the so-called 'Hottentot' elections of 1907, there is little evidence that Catholic politicians were deterred from giving their broad, if sometimes not particularly heart-felt, backing to government *Weltpolitik*. Thus, Erzberger himself was a vocal advocate of Germany's national mission, which included the acquisition of colonies overseas.[35] Britain, he believed, was attempting to thwart the Reich's justified efforts to become a world power. As a result, 'there cannot, in our opinion, be an agreement with England at the price of German sea defences', on 'German-national grounds' alone: 'The renunciation of our sea defences, which are a proper part of our power position, would reduce the German nation to a vassal state of England.'[36] Conflict with Britain was not inevitable, but it should not be avoided at all costs, for example by giving way to Winston Churchill's view that the German navy was merely an expendable luxury, as Erzberger spelled out in a Reichstag speech in April 1912:

> When the sentence is uttered that our fleet in Germany is a luxury, I, too, must say a word against this. Our fleet can only be seen as a luxury by someone who takes the standpoint of the arsonist and who holds that the fire service is a luxury (laughing), not by anyone else. We shall not let ourselves be influenced by such speeches, even if they come from such influential positions in foreign countries, in recognition of the fact that the German nation, in the development which it has experienced, with all its existential needs, which it has as a great power and world nation, needs a great fleet.[37]

Some Social Democrats, despite the party's official international-ism, were ready to agree. In particular, revisionists around Joseph Bloch, editor of the *Sozialistische Monatshefte*, presented a similar case to that put forward by those on the right. Imperialism, they argued, was not economically determined – as an outgrowth of capitalism – but historically specific, deriving from the actions of individuals and non-economic circumstances, such as those imposed by geography.[38] Given its central position, Germany had a duty to unify Europe and consolidate its territory in the Near East and Africa, and at the same time to escape threats to its own existence. Imperial-ism, wrote one of the principal 'socialist imperialists' Karl Leuthner, had produced large-scale government, protectionism, nationalism and a new sense of vitality, all of which were preferable to the decadence, laissez-faire capitalism and selfish individualism of inward-looking liberal states.[39] Even more radically, Leuthner called for a wholesale redistribution of overseas colonies, implicitly after a successful continental war, and a Europe of client states dominated by a 'Greater Germany'. In the latter respect, he was adapting the ideas of Richard Calwer, who had argued from 1897 onwards that the Central European lands 'must aim to expand their own economic area through mutual trade-policy mergers, gradually dismantle the tariff walls between the united states, in order externally . . . to be able to compete with commercial–political rivals'.[40] In his injunction to acquire colonies, Leuthner was articulating ideas put forward by Gerhard Hildebrand and others:

> Even from a socialist standpoint, the acquisition of colonial domains has become a present economic necessity . . . We Germans, severely disadvantaged and repressed for decades by France and England, must, if it comes to the crunch, unanimously stand up for the long-term vital interests of our people . . . Only by means of a consolidation of Western Europe through the final resolution of its internal difficulties will it be possible to present a solid counterbalance to the Russian advance in the East and the North American advance in the West . . . The socialist labour movement must decide on its fate. If it makes the wrong decision, it condemns itself to opposition and impotence. If it does what is necessary, it can rapidly win undreamt-of success in the domestic arena as well. Here there is only an either-or.[41]

Ideologically, few leaders in the centre or on the left of the SPD agreed with the 'reactionary' conclusions drawn by 'socialist imperialists', proposing instead that imperialism was either the extension of capitalism to the whole world, which was the thesis of Rosa Luxemburg in *Sozialreform oder Revolution* (1899) and in later works, or that it was an ephemeral aberration of capitalism created by pre-industrial elites in order to defend their own social, political and economic position, as Karl Kautsky contended in the years after 1911.[42] However, SPD theoreticians had, at the very least, come to pay far greater attention to imperialism as an economic and political problem in the decade before the First World War, and the party's leaders, pushed by the unions and rank and file, arguably became less willing, though still critical of Germany's colonial administration, openly to challenge *Weltpolitik* as a set of ideas or, even, as a series of policies. Significantly, during the second Moroccan crisis in 1911, the SPD's organ, *Vorwärts*, and its leader, August Bebel, rejected Ramsay MacDonald's request for a special meeting of the Second International and defended the German government's policy of maintaining an 'open door' in Morocco.[43] Like many of his party colleagues, Bebel was anxious about the apparent movement towards world empires and protectionist trading blocs.

In addition to cross-party anxiety about the political and economic rise of British, American and Russian world empires, there were three other popular components of *Weltpolitik*. The first concerned the construction of a large navy under Tirpitz, which was founded on the Navy Laws of 1898 and 1900. The purposes of the programme are still disputed, with some evidence pointing to a deliberate manipulation of domestic public opinion, including the rallying of working-class voters to the monarchy, and some indicating self-interest or technical enthusiasm on the part of naval officers, who were able under Tirpitz to gain the ear of the Kaiser and his government.[44] 'No one amongst us', recorded Admiral Eduard von Capelle, Tirpitz's closest aide, 'knew the final aims of the fleet-building master.'[45] From the outset, however, it was obvious that the principal target of Tirpitz's navy was Britain, which he had felt obliged to hint in public was the 'actual cause' of the 1900 bill, and that one of the reasons – probably the primary one – for its construction was the desire to break free of Britain's naval 'stranglehold' in order to be able to acquire colonies in the rest of the world on equal terms.[46] Commissioning three new ships per year for the next twenty years, the German Navy Bills were designed to establish a 2:3 ratio with Britain, since it was believed that a navy which was two-thirds of the strength of its British opponent was the minimum requirement for a possible victory.

With the odds still stacked against the *Reichsmarine* defeating the Royal Navy at this ratio, however, it is likely that Tirpitz envisaged the German navy largely as a deterrent to be deployed in a policy of brinkmanship. According to such a 'risk theory', as has been seen, London would prefer to treat German claims seriously rather than take the chance of entering into a war which it could lose outright or in which a third power – for example, Russia or France – would be able to profit from Britain's momentary naval weakness, seizing colonies or naval bases overseas. When Germany had attained the 2:3 ratio and had escaped the 'danger zone', within which its navy could be destroyed pre-emptively and without military risk by Britain, it could then 'expect "fair play" from England', predicted Tirpitz in 1909.[47] At this point German leaders would be in a strong enough position to negotiate equally with their British counterparts and to safeguard the goals of *Weltpolitik*, whether partition – in the case of Portuguese and Belgian colonies – or free access to markets – in the case of the Ottoman Empire, South America, and China. 'If one disregards the military position, which is by no means hopeless', Tirpitz informed the Kaiser in 1899, alluding to the possibility of an eventual German naval victory, 'England will have lost, for general political reasons and because she will view the situation from the purely sober standpoint of a businessman, all inclination to attack us.' Rather, 'she will concede to Your Majesty such a measure of maritime influence which will make it possible for Your Majesty to conduct a great overseas policy'.[48] There is every indication after the launch of Tirpitz's propaganda campaign to 'warm up great numbers of the nation for this action', including articles by a phalanx of 'fleet professors', that the joint cause of the navy and *Weltpolitik* took on a popular momentum of its own.[49] Certainly, Rosa Luxemburg thought that the SPD made itself 'really risible in broad sections of the population' by 'thundering' against *Weltpolitik* and militarism, but not acting when conflicts did occur.[50] 'I bring this up', she continued in 1900, 'because the era of world politics is now here to stay.'[51] Although there were disagreements between ardent naval and colonial enthusiasts, navalism and imperialism were usually elided under the more general popular heading of *Weltpolitik* in contemporaries' minds.

A second component of *Weltpolitik* concerned what has since been labelled 'social Darwinism'. As Alfred Kelly has demonstrated, the use of bowdlerized Darwinian theory – or merely its catchphrases such as 'struggle for existence' and 'natural selection' – was common on both the left and right of the political spectrum and characterized different types of social explanation.[52] Woodruff Smith, amongst others, has attempted to link such explanations to particular varieties of imperialism. Thus, the well-known *Lebensraum* or 'living space' hypothesis of the Leipzig zoologist, political geographer and ethnologist Friedrich Ratzel has been associated with migratory or settlement imperialism, where the struggle for a state's existence was mainly a question of gaining territory and where colonies were to act as a repository for the surplus population of a 'race', akin to the competition of animals and plants for territory or space for the species.[53] 'The growth of political territories in Asia and America has given territory

(*Raum*) itself a degree of attention and study in our time, as never before', wrote Ratzel in his textbook on political geography in 1897. 'Great spaces are more and more becoming the current tendency of national and state development.'[54] Similarly, supposedly natural domestic economic competition, with individual capitalists and companies vying to formulate the best survival strategies, has been connected to free-trading and neo-mercantilist types of economic imperialism, with the former supported by scholars like Lujo Brentano, who urged the government to use its leverage to keep open markets and form low tariff areas, and with the latter backed by those such as Gustav Schmoller, who advised ministers to accept 'the irresistible tendency towards the creation of large markets' and to recognize that Europe had to compete with 'the great world trade empires'.[55] Finally, Darwinian struggles for world power have been equated with the traditions of *Realpolitik*, according to which Borussian and neo-Rankean historians explained the rise and fall of states and empires by referring to actual levers of power and the readiness of leaders ruthlessly to use them. Treitschke, who had done more than any other historian to lay the foundations of *Realpolitik* between the 1860s and late 1890s, showed in his lectures on politics, published in 1897, how the advent of *Weltpolitik* seemed to have made the existence of nation-states even more precarious: 'It is very easy to imagine that, one day, a country which has no colonies will not be counted amongst the European Great Powers any more, however powerful it might otherwise be.'[56] Such states, he wrote, 'will play a pitiful part at some later day'.[57]

In practice, of course, commentators and their readers rarely fell into just one of Smith's – and other historians' – categories of imperialists, and they deployed a multitude of overlapping arguments in defence of their version of the colonial project. To a large number of writers, though, Darwinism seemed to add a modern, uncontroversial and scientific verisimilitude to already existing assumptions about the territorial, economic and historical struggle of states for predominance. Unsurprisingly, among such writers were right-wing militarists such as Bernhardi, who extended his belief that 'the struggle for existence is, in the life of nature, the basis of all healthy development' to justifications of war and aggrandisement; but there were also moderate conservatives like Delbrück, who was certain that France would 'with natural necessity sink deeper and deeper in the competition of the peoples', and Rohrbach, who contended that French demographic stagnation resulted from 'an atrophy of natural-moral sensitivity'.[58] By contrast, he went on, 'our growth is an occurrence of elemental natural force', which called for a corresponding position in the world economy and sufficient land if Germany was to remain 'healthy'.[59] Even the doctrinally incorruptible *Neue Zeit*, the mouthpiece of German Marxism, could occasionally be found putting forward 'Darwinian' explanations of rising and falling empires. 'The political changes of the last years have further sharpened the unfavourable position of the Latin peoples', it commented in 1899. 'The preponderance of the Germanic . . . race is more and more apparent, whilst the hegemony of the Slav nationalities stands menacingly in the background.'[60] The idea that racial groups – however defined – were engaged in a struggle for world power was widely entrenched by the turn of the century and remained so until 1914 and beyond.

A third common component of *Weltpolitik*, related to the Darwinian struggle of races, concerned the notion of a balance of power. Germany, it was repeated throughout the press, was a 'young' power, not 'saturated', in Rohrbach's phrase, as it had been under Bismarck, but rather needing to expand in order to provide food, outlets for manufactured goods and sources of raw materials for its growing population.[61] It was for this reason, stated the liberal publicist, that 'all questions of foreign policy for Germany come under the aspect of creating and retaining markets'.[62] In contradistinction to the Reich, Britain was regularly depicted as an old, conservative power, jealously defending its empire and monopoly of the seas by upholding a European balance of power which allowed it to dominate the rest of the world. As overseas territories became more and more important for the international power and status of all states during the late nineteenth and early twentieth centuries, a continental balance seemed to the majority of journalists and academics to be redundant – little more than a façade for a British policy of divide and rule on the European mainland.[63] The historian Otto Hintze, one of the least radical academic commentators on foreign affairs, demonstrated how Wilhelmine views of foreign affairs had altered from the 1890s onwards. Looking back in 1915, he explained:

Scarcely had we won the normal nation-state-type form, which countries like France and England have had for centuries, when we saw ourselves forced by fate into a new change of form, in order to maintain ourselves as one of the leading powers, as a 'world power', in the emerging system of world states. This is the meaning of 'Weltpolitik', which characterised the era of Kaiser Wilhelm II. It is a policy which aims to claim for us the same position and status that we had achieved in the old European states system from the time of the Great Elector and Friedrich the Great in the more distant spheres of the new system of world states, too.[64]

Hintze had formulated most of this argument before the First World War. Notably, in an article on 'Imperialismus und Weltpolitik' in 1907, he described how the development of the European states system had led to Britain's 'universal dominance of the seas', as the other powers were embroiled in a series of wars on the Continent, ending in stalemate, or a balance of power, within the European pentarchy. Napoleon I had attempted to escape Britain's maritime and commercial dominance, continued Hintze, by seeking to subjugate the Continent in the early nineteenth century. Having successfully resisted French forces, Europe's monarchies spent much of the rest of the century re-establishing domestic order and coexisting peacefully within the framework of the concert of states. In recent decades, however, this equilibrium had been disturbed by the creation of nation-states in Italy and Germany, the traditional 'buffer zone' of the pentarchy; by colonization and the emergence of world powers; and by industrialization and increased commercial competition, provoking 'the jealous anxiety of England', which 'is today no longer the only great trading and sea power, as at the start of the nineteenth century', but which 'is determined to keep and safeguard an absolute superiority in areas of interest'.[65]

The imperialist movement seems to us to be the introduction to a new epoch of political balance. A new system of world states wants to take the place of the old European states system; the powers begin to group themselves on this new basis and to demarcate their spheres of interest amongst each other. What is characteristic of this process, as in the 17th and 18th centuries, lies in the dual quest for concentration and expansion, and indeed in the economic as well as in the political sphere. New powers like Japan have joined, enormous empires like America, England with its colonies and Russia encircle the core of old Europe, whose states appear to have shrunk together, as it were, in an extended political world. Which powers are able to maintain themselves as Great Powers in the future system of world states will depend on the energy of their economic and political activity. The struggle for such a Great Power position is the actual significance of the imperialist shift in the modern world. It is not a question of the world domination of a single people, as in antiquity, but a selection of nations, which will take up a leading position in the world. When we speak of world empires, we mean these Great Powers of the future. The goal of modern imperialism is not *one* world empire, but a number of world empires side by side, of equal independence and in a similar balance of power as the Great Powers in the old European states system.[66]

The assumption that *Weltpolitik* had made the old European balance of power redundant, together with the belief that the Russian, American and British empires were rising and that the other powers might fail to survive over the long-term according to Darwinian or historical 'laws', served to alter the parameters within which foreign policy was formulated, allowing policy-makers greater room for manoeuvre, but also rendering political and public reactions to policy more difficult to predict. The shift to *Weltpolitik*, however, did not 'revolutionize' Wilhelmine policy-making, nor was it sufficient in itself to push German statesmen into risking a European or world war. A number of questions remain unanswered. One is: to what extent did the adoption of a world policy entail a disavowal of the traditional precepts of European diplomacy? Historians such as Hintze doubted that the practical implications of the change were great, predicting that a balance of power would be established between the new world powers similar to that which had existed between the states of the concert of Europe. 'The quest for supremacy is not irreconcilable with this', he went on. 'It has been, as it were, the motor of political progress in the history of states up until now, yet it has not led to the dominance of a single power, but rather to increased counter-efforts which have, indeed, always reconstituted and maintained the balance-of-power system.'[67]

Delbrück and Schiemann, who – as the most prominent moderate right-wing commentators – together exercised a significant amount of influence over government foreign policy, agreed with Hintze that the old states system was in the process of being replaced by a new order of world empires, even though they disputed the fact that the balance of power would be restored. In the first major 'world crisis' involving Germany, in Morocco in 1905, the *Kreuz-Zeitung*'s commentator on foreign affairs, was already certain that 'a political balance of power has not existed for a long time'.[68] But the new order was still essentially European, as Schiemann made plain: 'We have an English superiority (*Übermacht*) on the seas, a Russian superiority in the Orient, a French–English superiority in Africa, and the superiority of Germany on the European continent, which today again claims its rights, but which was artificially held back.'[69] 'England is above all a sea power, as we are above all a land power, England an island and colonial empire, we a continental power', he concluded at the end of the crisis, 'and the geographical position of Germany, like its history, point to the fact that our centre of gravity must remain here, just as theirs must remain the seas.'[70] As a consequence, Schiemann assumed that conflict during both the first and the second Moroccan crises – although unlikely to occur on such a flimsy colonial pretext – would be European in cause and effect, involving continental armies and deriving from the relations between European states. The Reich should use its continental superiority to gain concessions overseas, but it would probably not need to go war to achieve such aims, which were, in any case, secondary to its continental interests.[71] Delbrück, for the most part, concurred. War was unlikely, he wrote, even though the European balance of power, to which he had continued to subscribe until the first Moroccan crisis, had now ceased to be relevant, except insofar as it guided the actions of the other European powers, convincing them of the need to unite against the single most powerful continental state, Germany.[72] The principal danger of war, however, was not to be found in 'individual questions' such as those of Morocco or Turkey, nor any longer in 'the thirst for revenge of the French or the desire of the Russians for Constantinople', but in 'the jealousy of England towards Germany', which in turn stemmed from British fears that the Reich's navy constituted a threat to the country's own security – 'a question of life or death' (*Lebensfrage*).[73] In other words, Delbrück explained even the Anglo-German antagonism in terms of European politics, not colonial rivalries.

Bülow, Bethmann and most German diplomats acted on similar premises. The Reich Foreign Office was, to a greater extent than its more colonial-minded foreign counterparts, founded on the primacy of European affairs. Thus, the Political Division (IA), which was comprised of the Secretary and Under-Secretaries of State, together with about thirty counsellors, assistant directors and directors, plus junior staff, constituted the fulcrum of the policy-making apparatus, specializing in Europe, providing nearly all foreign diplomats and consuls, and drawn largely from French-speaking, cosmopolitan noble or diplomatic families.[74] The other departments, including the Kolonial-Abteilung, which was established in 1890 and only became an independent Colonial Office in 1907, were housed in separate buildings from the secretaries of state, contained fewer nobles – 27 per cent in the Colonial Department between 1890 and 1914 compared to 61 per cent in Division IA between 1881 and 1914 – and were openly held to be repositories for the least talented members of the service. All the secretaries of state after the turn of the century, as well as Bülow, had passed through European embassies, which continued to be the most prestigious and the best staffed. It was not surprising, therefore, that policy-makers went on thinking primarily in terms of long-established, 'high-political' relationships between major European states.

Bülow, who boasted that 'I have written and spoken French as fluently as my mother tongue' from childhood, is the most significant representative of such a diplomatic corps, since he oversaw the shift to *Weltpolitik* after 1897.[75] In private correspondence, he made it quite clear that, although the task he was set 'was to make possible our transition to *Weltpolitik* (trade, shipping, overseas interests, the consequences of the huge development of our industry, our increasing prosperity, the increase in our population) and above all the building of the German navy', he also had to persist in 'preserving German dignity and our position on the Continent'.[76] In his public account, which came out first in an English translation early in 1914, the former Chancellor was even more emphatic:

> We did not plunge into world politics, we grew, so to speak, into our task in that sphere, and we did not exchange the old European policy of Prussia and Germany for the new world policy; our strength today is rooted, as it has been since time immemorial, in the ancient soil of Europe.
>
> 'It is the task of our generation at one and the same time to maintain our position on the Continent, which is the basis of our international position, and to foster our interests abroad as well as to pursue a prudent, sensible and wisely restricted international policy, in such a way that the safety of the German people may not be endangered, and that the future of the nation may not be imperilled.' With these words I attempted on 14 November 1906, towards the close of a detailed exposition of the international situation, to formulate the task which Germany must perform at the present time, and, as far as man can judge, will have to perform in future: an international policy based on the solid foundation of our position as one of the Great Powers of Europe.[77]

Such an international policy meant transcending the limits of Bismarckian precedents, given that German industry had since

created interests 'in all quarters of the globe', but it did not mean
abandoning continental policy altogether, because the Reich's
military power on the Continent remained - and, even after the
German navy had crossed the 'danger zone' by 1917, would remain
- the country's main source of diplomatic leverage, as Bülow was
well aware.[78] Bethmann, despite his previous lack of contact with the
Foreign Office, retained his predecessor's policy: the pursuit of a
strong world policy by staying strong on the European Continent,
in the words of his famous speech to the Reichstag during the second
Moroccan crisis.[79] Throughout the pre-war period, he continued to
talk almost exclusively of the alignment of European powers, the
maintenance of European peace, and the possibility of a European
- rather than world - war. His principal policy - reconciliation with
Britain - was designed to 'decisively strengthen our position in the
European concert in material and moral terms', and his 'main goal'
arguably continued to be the 'loosening of the entente'.[80] As he tried
to extricate himself from the most extreme versions of naval policy
in the years between 1911 and 1914, Bethmann was more conscious
than ever that the European Continent constituted the basis of
German power.

Many historians have commented on the support in government
and sections of the public for a Central European customs union and
power bloc (*Mitteleuropa*), often misinterpreted as part of a 'return'
to *Kontinentalpolitik*. Such support has usually been seen as a sign
of despair, most recently by Neitzel, as other opportunities of gaining
world power status seemed to have been exhausted.[81] Yet how grave,
in the opinion of the majority of Wilhelmine observers, had the
Reich's position in the world become? Some on the right - especially
the far right - were convinced that the German Empire had more
or less run out of time to achieve its ambitions of world power. The
Pan-German author of *Berlin–Bagdad*, Albert Ritter, for example,
proposed that the states of *Mitteleuropa* were in the same position
in 1914 as those of the German Confederation before 1866; that is,
they were weak and in danger of annihilation, unless they could unite
and become an independent and fearsome federation.[82] Most onlookers, however, were more sanguine, which was one reason that
plans for either an economic or political *Mitteleuropa* were relatively
rare, much less common than in the 1890s, and nearly always
hypothetical. Even some who, like the liberal industrialist Walther
Rathenau, believed that most of the world had already been parti-
tioned irreversibly by the other powers were confident that a Central

European customs union offered a realistic prospect of preserving peace and reducing nationalist hatred.[83] In December 1913, he wrote:

> There remains one last possibility: the striving for a Central European customs union which, for good or ill, over the long or short term, the western states will join . . . The task of creating economic freedom for the countries of our European zone is a difficult one; but it is not insoluble . . . the goal would be to create an economic unit, which would be at least equal, perhaps superior to the American one, and within the group there would no longer be backward, stagnating and unproductive areas . . . But at the same time the sting will be taken out of the nationalistic hatred of nations . . . What prevents nations from trusting each other, from supporting each other, sharing and enjoying each other's property and strengths is only indirectly a question of power, imperialism and expansion: at its core these are economic questions. Once the economy of Europe is merged within a community, and this will happen more quickly than we think, then politics also merges.[84]

The majority of left liberals, Catholics and socialists shared Rathenau's underlying optimism. Some, like the right-wing Centre Party academic Martin Spahn, contended that 'everything that was within reach of German influence must be united – from Hamburg to Trieste' – in order 'to compete with England', which was 'Germany's only serious rival.[85] Most were less interested in *Mitteleuropa*, but still believed that the German economy would continue to expand, either by maintaining access to the markets of other states or, in Rohrbach's words, by 'a rational treatment' of 'the most important spheres of interest and future areas of German economic life – the Orient, South America, Shantung and its hinterland, colonies in Africa and the South Seas'.[86] Even many National Liberals, such as Gustav Stresemann, agreed with Rohrbach that these strategies offered 'great and good prospects for the material future of Germany'.[87] If the Reich could keep the peace for the next ten to twenty years, partly by the deterrent effect of armaments increases, 'then the hope is justified that the development of our economic forces will give us the leadership of the world', declared the National Liberal deputy and director of the Bund der Industriellen.[88]

Moderate right-wing commentators close to government, such as Delbrück, likewise betrayed few signs of desperation at the Reich's plight. Despite fearing the future rise of Russia – 'a four-hundred-million strong empire' – and the present intentions of Britain, the editor of the *Preussische Jahrbücher* was impressed, like most of his contemporaries, by the rapid economic and military advances made by the German Empire since unification. Whereas 'the English economy is stagnating', 'Germany by contrast experiences a more and more powerful upturn', he wrote in 1904: 'In the iron and steel industry we have caught up with England, the old mistress in this area, and our exports are in the process of a continuing rise.'[89] This economic preeminence, together with naval and army increases, explained why the other continental powers had allied with each other against the Reich – 'the decisive thing is without doubt the fear in which the other powers live beside us' – and why Britain had become such a stubborn enemy.[90] London was aware that, 'with the massive growth of Germany's population and prosperity, its political power had also increased in the same measure: we have been the strongest land power for a long time and we are approaching, with rapid strides, the position of an important sea power'.[91] What was more, this strength could still be used to gain colonies, spheres of influence and open markets, Delbrück asserted in 1912:

Not least those lower classes which are striving upwards and forwards are interested in a large-scale German colonial policy, which makes territories of lower races our subjects and thereby introduces them to higher cultural interests . . . The German Reich is so far advanced in the development of its power that it can bring such thoughts into view and can hope for their realisation . . . But how can this occur? Has the world not been given away? Should we draw the sword in order to take the property of other peoples from them? Not at all. It is not at all true that the world has already been given away. Have the English not in recent years subjugated the Transvaal and extended the borders of India to the East and to the West? Have the Americans not taken Cuba and Panama and the Philippines? In front of our very eyes, the French are taking Morocco and the Italians Tripoli, and the Russians and the English are in the midst of dividing Persia. Who knows, then, what tomorrow will become of Turkey, in particular of Arabia? And of China? Who knows whether Portugal is in a position to keep its great African possessions, Angola and Mozambique? Who knows whether the Kingdom of Belgium will be able to overcome its deep domestic division between clericalism and the Flemish, on the one hand, and socialism and the Walloons, on the other, and retain its rule over the Congo? . . . Our economic relations and our trade are so well developed by now that there is scarcely any place in the world where we don't have interests which would be affected in one way or another by political changes. We are strong enough not to put up with this without in some way, whether by direct sharing or compensation elsewhere, pushing through counter-demands, and we can in this way follow a policy of expansion which, without shying away from war forever and in all circumstances, is very capable, according to the best of our knowledge, of attaining its goal without war.[92]

In common with many other Wilhelmine Germans, Delbrück believed that the Reich was strong enough to win a European war, if it were declared under the right circumstances.[93] Consequently, he continued to advocate building up arms and using the threat of force as an instrument of foreign policy or, in his words, for 'the attainment of positive goals'.[94] However, he also held that military armament would 'keep the peace', allowing the Reich to achieve the status of a world power without the 'truly great danger' of armed conflict.[95]

Like Delbrück, German ministers had not given up hope of attaining colonies or of working with the United Kingdom in order to secure the status of a world power. The attainment of such status continued to appear feasible, but by a variety of means, including the creation of *Mittelafrika*, the construction of a 'land bridge' to the Middle East, the promotion of *Mitteleuropa* and, critically, the maintenance of an 'open door' in areas such as China and South America. It was always apparent, however, that the Reich's main sources of leverage remained on the Continent. Many commentators and virtually all German statesmen believed that the Reich's national security and diplomatic freedom of manoeuvre continued to rest on its military power in Europe. Holstein, Bülow, Kiderlen, Jagow and Bethmann, although differing in their diplomatic strategies, were united in this one respect, as will be shown in the next chapter: they were all prepared to use the threat of force on the European mainland in order to gain diplomatic and territorial concessions on the Continent or overseas.

Notes

1. F.H. Hinsley, *Power and the Pursuit of Peace: Theory and Practice in the History of Relations between States* (Cambridge, 1963), p. 300.
2. G. Schöllgen, *Das Zeitalter des Imperialismus*, 2nd edn (Munich, 1991); G. Schöllgen (ed.), *Escape into War? The Foreign Policy of Imperial Germany* (Oxford, 1990), pp. 121-33.

3. S. Neitzel, *Weltmacht oder Untergang. Die Weltreichslehre im Zeitalter des Imperialismus* (Paderborn, 2000). Also, S. Neitzel, *Kriegsausbruch. Deutschlands Weg in die Katastrophe 1900–1914* (Munich, 2002), pp. 17–68.

4. S. Neitzel (ed.), *1900: Zukunftsvision der Grossmächte* (Paderborn, 2002), p. 56.

5. Ibid.

6. K. Canis, *Von Bismarck zur Weltpolitik: Deutsche Aussempolitik 1890 bis 1902* (Berlin, 1997), pp. 223–56.

7. Bülow cited in M. Fröhlich, *Imperialismus. Deutsche Kolonial- und Weltpolitik 1880–1914*, 2nd edn (Munich, 1997), p. 75.

8. Varnbüler quoted in K.A. Lerman, *The Chancellor as Courtier: Bernhard von Bülow and the Governance of Germany, 1900–1909* (Cambridge, 1990), p. 33.

9. Cited in Canis, *Von Bismarck zur Weltpolitik*, p. 255.

10. Ibid. Wilhelm II to Szögyény, 1898 and 1899, cited in P.M. Kennedy, *The Rise of the Anglo-German Antagonism 1860–1914* (London, 1980), p. 311.

11. Bethmann cited in K. Jarausch, *The Enigmatic Chancellor: Bethmann Hollweg and the Hubris of Imperial Germany* (New Haven, 1973), p. 111.

12. D. Kaiser, 'Germany and the Origins of the First World War', *Journal of Modern History*, 55 (1983), pp. 442–74.

13. Kennedy, *The Rise of the Anglo-German Antagonism*, p. 311.

14. C. Peters, *England and the English* (London, 1904), pp. 376–7.

15. Ibid., pp. 386–7.

16. Ibid., p. 386.

17. Cited in F. Fischer, *War of Illusions* (London, 1975), p. 233. See also Fröhlich, *Imperialismus*, p. 59, who quotes the *Alldeutsche Blätter*: 'We are ready to step into line on the call of our Kaiser, but we can demand in return that we get a price which is worth the sacrifice: to belong to a dominant nation (*Herrenvolk*) that takes its share of the world and does not seek to be reliant on the grace and good will of another nation.'

18. Delbrück cited in Neitzel, *Weltmacht oder Untergang*, p. 183.

19. H. Delbrück, *Vor und nach dem Weltkrieg. Politisch und historische Aufsätze 1902–1925* (Berlin, 1926), p.10.

20. Ibid., 28 November 1905, p. 133.

21. Ibid., December 1913, p. 399.

22. Ibid.

23. For example, *Kreuz-Zeitung*, 14 June 1905, cited in T. Schiemann, *Deutschland und die grosse Politik* (Berlin, 1906), p. 172.

24. *Deutschland und die grosse Politik* (Berlin, 1907), 28 November 1906, pp. 376–7.

25. Schiemann cited in Canis, *Von Bismarck zur Weltpolitik*, p. 228.

26. K. von Westarp, *Konservative Politik im letzten Jahrzehnt des kaiserreiches* (Berlin, 1935), vol. 1, p. 156.

27. Westarp, 5 December 1911, cited ibid., p. 163.

28. *Hilfe*, 3 August 1911, cited in P. Theiner, *Sozialer Liberalismus und deutsche Weltpolitik. Friedrich Naumann im Wilhelminischen Deutschland 1860–1919* (Baden-Baden, 1983), p. 219.

29. W.J. Mommsen, *Max Weber and German Politics, 1890–1920* (Chicago, 1984), p. 69. This line of argument coincides with that of Jost Dülffer, *Im Zeichen der Gewalt. Frieden und krieg im 19. und 20. Jahrhundert* (Cologne, 2003), pp. 58–9.

30. Theiner, *Sozialer Liberalismus und deutsche Weltpolitik*, p. 217.

31. J.J. Sheehan, *The Career of Lujo Brentano: A Study of Liberalism and Social Reform in Germany* (Chicago, 1966), pp. 184–5; Kennedy, *The Rise of the Anglo-German Antagonism*, p. 340.

32. Theiner, *Sozialer Liberalismus und deutsche Weltpolitik*, p. 219.

33. P. Rohrbach, *Deutschland unter den Weltvölkern*, 2nd edn (Berlin, 1908), p. 14.

34. K. Epstein, *Matthias Erzberger und das Dilemma der deutschen Demokratic* (Frankfurt a. M., 1976), pp. 72–3.

35. For Erzberger's views on a national mission, see M. Erzberger, *Politik und Völkerleben* (Paderborn, 1914), pp. 30–41.

36. Epstein, *Matthias Erzberger*, p. 94.

37. Ibid., p. 93.

38. See R. Fletcher, *Revisionism and Empire: Socialist Imperialism in Germany, 1897–1914* (London, 1984), pp. 47–65, for this and many of the following points.

39. Ibid., pp. 81–104.

40. Calwer cited in S. Neitzel, 'Aussenpolitische Zukunftsvorstellungen in Deutschland um 1900', in *1900: Zukunftsvisionen der Grossmächte*, p. 71.

41. Hildebrand in 1911, cited in Fletcher, *Revisionism and Empire*, p. 46.

42. Ibid., pp. 34–43. Also, P. Nettl, *Rosa Luxemburg* (Oxford, 1969), pp. 151–73, and N. Stargardt, *The German Idea of Militarism: Radical and Socialist Critics, 1866–1914* (Cambridge, 1994), p. 83.

43. D.J. Newton, *British Labour, European Socialism and the Struggle for Peace, 1889–1914* (Oxford, 1985), pp. 249–50; *Berliner Tageblatt*, 14 September 1911, reporting Bebel's speech to the Jena party conference; *Vorwärts*, 11 May, 5 and 6 July 1911.

44. V.R. Berghahn, 'Die Mobilisierung der Flottenbewegung', in *Rüstung und Machtpolitik. Zur Anatomie des 'Kalten Krieges' vor 1914* (Düsseldorf, 1973), pp. 36–46.

45. Kennedy, *The Rise of the Anglo-German Antagonism*, p. 422.

46. A. von Tirpitz, *Erinnerungen* (Leipzig, 1919), p. 105.

47. Tirpitz cited in V.R. Berghahn, *Germany and the Approach of War in 1914* (London, 1973), p. 36.

48. Ibid., p. 40.

49. Berghahn, *Rüstung und Machtpolitik*, p. 37.

50. Luxemburg cited in Fröhlich, *Imperialismus*, p. 74.

51. Ibid.

52. A. Kelly, *The Descent of Darwin: The Popularization of Darwinism in Germany, 1860–1914* (Chapel Hill, 1981).

53. W.D. Smith, *The Ideological Origins of Nazi Imperialism* (Oxford, 1986), pp. 83–111.

54. Ratzel cited in Neitzel, *Weltmacht oder Untergang*, p. 85.

55. Sheehan, *The Career of Lujo Brentano*, pp. 178–200; Neitzel, *Weltmacht oder Untergang*, p. 136.

56. H. von Treitschke, *Politik*, 2nd revised edn (Leipzig, 1899) vol. 1, p. 124.

57. Ibid., pp. 120–4.

58. F. von Bernhardi, *Germany and the Next War* (London, 1913), pp. 81–26; Delbrück, *Vor und nach dem Weltkrieg*, p. 209; P. Rohrbach, *Der deutsche Gedanke in der Welt* (Düsseldorf, 1912), pp. 8–9.

59. Ibid.

60. Cited in Neitzel, *Weltmacht oder Untergang*, p. 84.

61. Rohrbach, *Deutschland unter den Weltvölkern*, p. 319.

62. Ibid., p. 22.

63. Even the anglophile left-liberal press courted such views; for example, *Berliner Tageblatt*, 8 November 1905.

64. O. Hintze, 'Die Hohenzollern und ihr Werk' (1915), cited in Frölich, *Imperialismus*, p. 76. On Hintze's conservatism in the area of foreign policy, when compared with Max Weber, see Jürgen Kocka's contribution to W.J. Mommsen and J.G. Osterhammel (eds), *Max Weber and his Contemporaries* (London, 1987), pp. 284–95.

65. O. Hintze, 'Imperialismus und Weltpolitik' (1907), in G. Oestreich (ed.), *Otto Hintze. Staat und Verfassung*, 2nd revised edn (Göttingen, 1962), pp. 467–8.

66. Ibid., p. 469.

67. Ibid.

68. Schiemann, *Deutschland und die grosse Politik* (Berlin, 1906), 14 June 1905, p. 172.

69. Ibid.

70. Ibid. (Berlin, 1907), 23 May 1906, p. 190.

71. Accordingly, Schiemann remained optimistic in 1911–12; ibid. (Berlin, 1912), 13 and 27 September, 18 October 1911, pp. 247, 265, 298.

72. Delbrück, *Vor und nach dem Weltkrieg*, 28 November 1905, 26 July 1908, October 1909, 24 July 1912, December 1913, pp. 132–5, 205–212, 309–10, 368–78, 397–401.

73. Ibid., 26 June 1908, p. 207.

74. For more on this subject, see L. Cecil, *The German Diplomatic Service, 1871–1914* (Princeton, 1976).

75. Ibid., p. 72.

76. Bülow to Rath, 12 February 1912, cited in K.A. Lerman, 'Bismarck's Heir: Chancellor Bernhard von Bülow and the National Idea, 1890–1918', in J. Breuilly (ed.), *The State of Germany: The National Idea in the Making, Unmaking and Remaking of a Modern Nation-State* (London, 1992), p. 113.

77. B. von Bülow, *Imperial Germany*, 6th edn (London, 1914), pp. 10–11.

78. Ibid., p. 11.

79. Cited in Fischer, *War of Illusions*, p. 90.

80. Bethmann cited in Jarausch, *The Enigmatic Chancellor*, pp. 113, 126.

81. Neitzel, *Weltmacht oder Untergang*, pp. 117–88, 198–209.

82. Ibid., pp. 206–7.

83. Rathenau cited in H. James, *A German Identity, 1770–1990* (London, 1989), p. 109. See also P. Theiner, '"Mitteleuropa"-Pläne im Wilhelminischen Deutschland', in H. Berding (ed.), *Wirtschaftliche und politische Integration in Europa im 19. und 20. Jahrhundert* (Göttingen, 1984), pp. 135–6.

84. Rathenau, writing in December 1913, cited in W.J. Mommsen, 'Die Mitteleuropaidee und die Mitteleuropaplanungen im Deutschen Reich vor und während des Ersten Weltkriegs', in R.G. Plaschka (ed.), *Mitteleuropa-Konzeptionen in der ersten Hälfte des 20. Jahrhunderts* (Vienna, 1995), p. 12.

85. Spahn, 20 December 1912, cited in Fischer, *War of Illusions*, p. 242.

86. Rohrbach, *Deutschland unter den Weltvölkern*, p. 344.

87. Ibid.

88. Stresemann, July 1913 article in *Panther*, cited in K. Wernecke, *Der Wille zur Weltgeltung. Aussenpolitik und Öffentlichkeit im Kaiserreich am Vorabend des Ersten Weltkrieges* 2nd edn (Düsseldorf, 1970), p. 299.

89. Delbrück, *Vor und nach dem Weltkrieg*, 22 December 1904, p. 51.

90. Ibid., 28 November 1905, 26 July 1908, pp. 133, 208.

91. Ibid.

92. Ibid., 24 July 1912, pp. 370–1.

93. Ibid., 26 July 1908, 24 July 1912, December 1913, pp. 211–12, 376, 399–401.

94. Ibid., December 1913, p. 399. Also, ibid., October 1909, p. 310.

95. Ibid., p. 399.

8

Diplomacy and War: Chancellor, Kaiser and Foreign Office

Policy-makers in the Foreign Office and Chancellery – and in the person of the Kaiser – relied for the conduct of diplomacy on information received from the German military, on opinions in the press, on cases put forward by political parties, economic interests and social groups, and on reports from their own extensive network of ambassadors, consuls, secret advisors and – more occasionally – spies. As a result, German foreign policy was, as historians have rightly pointed out, the product of competing pressures and lobbies. As has been noted, Fritz Fischer and the Hamburg school concentrated on domestic pressures, proposing the existence of a *Primat der Innenpolitik* before 1914, which rested on structural blockages within the 'sham democracy' of the German Empire. Some scholars strongly influenced by Fischer continue to argue that such stalemate and conflict at home created a sense of panic, which in turn pushed statesmen to contemplate a *Flucht nach vorn*, whilst other historians associated with the Hamburg school stress the domestic basis of feelings of self-confidence and superiority, which led to a willingness to risk war.[1] Most recent studies, however, have shifted their focus away from the debate about the primacy of domestic policy and have paid much greater attention to the formulation of foreign policy in its own right. Accordingly, even a scholar such as Wolfgang Mommsen, who gives a prominent role to financial and industrial groups, for instance, and who characterizes the *Kaiserreich* as 'a system of skirted decisions', subordinates these factors to traditions and parameters of policy-making within the Foreign Office itself.[2]

The new emphasis on diplomatic history has been accompanied by two sets of arguments, both of which refute or qualify Fischer's thesis about the aggressive or offensive nature of German policy. First, ministers and officials are assumed to have been motivated by the same sense of despair as army officers, since they were aware of the

Reich's exposed geopolitical and deteriorating military position.[3] Second, the *Reichsleitung* was allegedly trapped by the logic of *Weltpolitik*, where Britain had the upper hand, and of the arms race, in which Russia and France had become increasingly dominant. From this perspective, with the Rubicon – in Hildebrand's phrase – already crossed, the notorious unsteadiness of the Reich's foreign policy appears to have been caused by the contortions of a power attempting – almost inevitably in vain, at least in peacetime – both to become a world power and to escape encirclement within Europe.[4] A hardening of two opposing blocs of allies – Germany, Austria–Hungary and Italy in the Triple Alliance, and France, Russia and Britain in the Triple Entente, together with a number of half-aligned powers in the Balkans – is seen to be the product of the two sets of circumstances.

In both series of arguments, historians have raised doubts about the government's freedom of manoeuvre. As for the army, however, the evidence in support of such a case is highly contentious, given the obvious temptation for those in power subsequently to maintain that they had had little responsibility for, or no alternative to, the course of action which led to the catastrophes of the First World War. Thus, although diplomatic correspondence, unlike military documents, has survived the Second World War largely intact, there is, as Konrad Jarausch points out, a lack of reflection and explanation in the hurried, ad hoc dispatches of the pre-war era, which is held to obscure 'the power-political logic of [Bethmann's] apparently self-contradictory foreign policy'.[5] In order to compensate for such a deficit, Jarausch continues, historians have relied heavily on the diary and work of Bethmann's secretary Kurt Riezler, yet they have rightly been challenged by those who doubt whether Riezler's strategic writings are representative of Bethmann's own views – since the secretary was in his twenties and relatively inexperienced – and whether his diary entries, the key pages of which have been inserted separately, constitute a genuine contemporaneous record.[6] As a result, scholars have been obliged to use the memoirs and retrospective correspondence of the main protagonists, but these, too, have long been open to question, with Fischer publishing proof in 1969 – taken from holdings of Jagow's correspondence in the *Auswärtiges Amt* – that important facts had been covered up or distorted. Accordingly, the Political Director of the Foreign Office, Wilhelm von Stumm, wrote to Jagow in 1919, warning him of a possible contradiction between an instruction on 21 July to localize the war and the official story that German diplomats had not been forewarned of the Austrian ultimatum to Serbia on 23 July. 'What will also cause offence', he went on, 'is Heinrich [von Tschirschky]'s information that the u[ltimatum] was to be phrased in such a way that S[erbia] could not accept it and also that Tsch[irschky] has said that he had advised in favour of war, naturally against S[erbia].'[7] In the light of these and other contradictions, Schöllgen's recent injunction to take 'the protagonists at their word' should be treated with caution.[8]

With hindsight, German diplomats and statesmen emphasized the constraints under which they had worked before 1914. Questioned by the left liberal Conrad Haussmann in 1917, for instance, Bethmann pointed to the influence of the military – 'Yes, the generals', he sighed – and to the widespread sense of doom which pervaded ruling elites as they were confronted by the supposedly worsening international position of the *Kaiserreich*: 'Lord, yes, in a certain sense it was a preventive war. But only if war was hanging over our heads, if it had to come two years later much more dangerously and inevitably, and if the military said today war is still possible without defeat, but no longer in two years.'[9] The Chancellor's memoir, *Betrachtungen zum Weltkrieg*, contained similar doom-laden musings about 'our struggle for life'.[10] 'Austria–Hungary made war on Serbia in order to ensure its own survival, and Germany covered its ally for the same reason', he contended. 'Both were acting under the force of self-preservation.'[11] Notwithstanding the popularity of Darwinian metaphors and the Chancellor's well-documented horror of war, it appears highly probable that Bethmann overstated any feelings of despair before 1914 as a consequence of Germany's defeat in 1918 and with a view to exonerating German policy-makers of the unexpected suffering of the First World War. Although it is true that there are some pre-war references to 'self-defence' and 'the act of a man fighting for his life', such utterances are limited in number and almost always designed to convince a domestic or British audience of the rectitude of the Reich government's actions.[12] The Chancellor's request to the German ambassador in London on 3 August 1914 to 'please state to Sir Edward Grey that, if we should take the step of violating Belgian neutrality, we would do so compelled by the duty of self-preservation' was typical.[13] Most such mitigating pleas came during the July crisis or – like this one – after the actual declaration of war.

Despite occasional instrumental Darwinian rhetoric, German statesmen were confident before 1914 that the Reich would be victorious in a European war. The official reports of the General Staff and the War Ministry had, after all, been optimistic. This fact was eagerly taken up by those like Stumm, who argued in February 1915 that 'nobody could have foreseen that militarily everything would not work out as one had believed', and by those such as Riezler, who claimed in May of the same year that Moltke 'did say yes! we would succeed' at the beginning of July 1914.[14] More significantly, the Under-Secretary of State at the Foreign Office, Arthur Zimmermann, told the Austrian envoy, Alexander Graf von Hoyos, on 3 July that the German army 'was strong enough to conduct the war on both fronts alone', if Austro-Hungarian forces had to be deployed exclusively in the Balkans.[15] This assurance was confirmed by Zimmermann's immediate superior, Jagow, who stated on 18 July that Germany would back Austria if it failed to achieve a localization of the conflict and Russia became involved. Although he did not want a preventive war, he went on, if war were to break out, the Reich could not stand by and 'throw over' Vienna.[16] In other words, the Reich had the potential to wage a preventive war, even though the Secretary of State was opposed to the idea. He repeated the assurance on 30 July, as did Bethmann.[17]

The notion of a successfully prosecuted European war had underpinned German foreign policy throughout the Wilhelmine era. Policy-makers argued in their defence that they had been pushed by circumstances into an increasingly desperate policy of risk, as the Reich was encircled by the Entente powers and as its political position in Europe and the world worsened. Diplomatic historians have tended to concentrate on such shifting 'political' circumstances and the correspondingly erratic nature of German policy-making. Thus, Friedrich von Holstein, who had come to dominate the Foreign Office during the 1890s, continued to concentrate more on Europe than the rest of the world, avoiding – through his policy of a 'free hand' – alliance commitments to Russia or Britain, since he was convinced that the imperial ambitions of the other powers would clash, allowing the Reich to make gains as an onlooker or mediator. By contrast, Bülow pursued 'the Kaiser's policies' of *Weltpolitik* and *Flottenpolitik* in order to acquire territory and influence on a world stage, not least because he had been promoted to Secretary of State at the Foreign Office in 1897 and Chancellor in 1900 as part of an attempt by a clique of courtiers to change the nature of Wilhelmine politics. As a consequence, Bülow was more willing to distance Germany from Britain and to attempt a rapprochement with Russia. Under his successor, Bethmann Hollweg, this policy was reversed, as the Chancellor sought a détente with London and an agreement to limit German ship-building in return for British neutrality in any future conflict. To an extent, such initiatives were undermined, as in the Bülow era, by the *Auswärtiges Amt* and, especially, the Secretary of State, Kiderlen-Wächter, who sought in 1911 to force Britain and France into concessions or to break up the Entente, as either London, Paris or St Petersburg decided that its alliance commitments were not worth the risk of war. The Reich, according to this reading of policy-making, lacked any fixity of purpose, oscillating between pourparlers and acts of coercion, between Britain, Russia and, even, France, and between world and continental politics. The result seemed to be a growing mistrust of Germany on the part of the other European powers.

According to Schöllgen, a succession of German chancellors and secretaries of state had followed a zig-zag course in the formulation and conduct of foreign policy after 1890, partly because of their need to achieve world power against the wishes of 'older' European states, at the same time as avoiding isolation on the Continent. From this plausible set of premises, he reaches the erroneous conclusion that Wilhelmine policy-making lacked any consistency, and that *Weltpolitik* and continental politics were mutually exclusive alternatives to each other. Guided by the apparent preoccupations of diplomats themselves, both the Hamburg school and its critics have devoted a disproportionate amount of attention to Germany's policy towards Britain, positing that the Wilhelmstrasse abandoned the aim of creating a Central European bloc (*Mitteleuropa*), which had been predominant under Caprivi, in favour of a policy of navalism and *Weltpolitik* after 1897.[18] The priority throughout the period between 1897 and 1913 was, therefore, focused on Britain and the acquisition of territory and markets overseas, with policy-makers only redirecting their gaze definitively towards the European mainland on the eve of the First World War, after the failure of the Haldane talks. This understanding of Wilhelmine policy-making explains the amount of weight given in most narratives to Sir Edward Grey and the British Foreign Office as a factor in Bethmann's calculations during the July crisis.

Such interpretations overlook the continental premises of German diplomacy throughout the Bismarckian and Wilhelmine eras. From this point of view, *Weltpolitik* rested on the continental foundations of the Reich's Great Power status. Accordingly, discussions in Germany about the formation of world powers or world empires tended to assume a German domination of *Mitteleuropa* or of Europe as a whole.[19] Thus, as policy-makers encountered opposition to their plans to gain the colonies, navy, markets, and political influence of a world power, they not only flitted from one policy to another, intervening in diverse areas from China and Venezuela to Baghdad and Bucharest, but also returned repeatedly to the continental basis of German power. This logic can be seen within the two principal phases of the Reich's policy towards Britain: navalism and the notion of a 'danger zone' under Bülow; and rapprochement and the quest for an Anglo-German agreement under Bethmann. The former, which envisaged the construction of a German navy strong enough to deter Britain from entering a war against the Reich, was underwritten by Holstein's so-called 'hostage theory' (*Geiseltheorie*), which foresaw an attack against France as a means of influencing British policy and of compensating for the confiscation of German colonies and shipping by Britain in the event of an Anglo-German war. During the first Moroccan crisis, even Tirpitz accepted the argument that Berlin could only affect decisions in London by putting pressure on France: 'In reality, the desired "pression" can be put on France *only through* Germany's threat of war.'[20]

The latter phase of the Reich's policy towards Britain – rapprochement – was founded on the idea of a naval agreement and neutrality pact. Article 3 of Bethmann's draft of a such a pact, passed on to Haldane in February 1912, stated that if either power became entangled in a war, the other would try to localize the conflict and would at least observe 'a benevolent neutrality'.[21] In other words, the Chancellor made any naval agreement conditional on British abstention from a continental war. 'As regards the political aspect of the question', he told the German ambassador in London, 'the degree of our unwillingness to be accommodating over the naval building issue will depend on the extent of the political agreement.'[22] Although Bethmann subsequently watered down his proposals, he refused to accept Grey's vague assurance that Britain would not 'join in any unprovoked attack', since it left too much scope for British intervention in a conflict.[23] The Chancellor's priority was further to strengthen the Reich's continental political and military position so that the German government could enter a European war with the best possible chance of British neutrality. This was in keeping with Kiderlen's response to Bethmann's original draft, when it was first sent to him in 1909: it 'probably covers everything in the event of war that we can wish for', he wrote.[24]

By the turn of the century, Wilhelmine statesmen seemed to have good grounds, supported by regular diplomatic and military reports, to believe in the superiority of German forces on the European mainland. As a result, the task of the Chancellor and Foreign Office, wrote Bülow in 1912, was to preserve 'German dignity and our position on the Continent', as well as to make the transition to *Weltpolitik* and build the navy.[25] Bethmann agreed. 'Germany can only pursue a strong policy in the sense of world policy if it remains strong on the Continent', he reminded the Reichstag in November 1911. 'Only the authority which we exert as a continental power makes it possible for us to engage in world trade and colonial policy – both collapse if we do not keep our strength at home.'[26] The assumption, of course, was that the Reich had already attained a position of strength on the Continent. Indeed, Bülow was so confident of Germany's power-base by the turn of the century that he was willing to tell the Reichstag in 1902 that the Triple Alliance was 'no longer an absolute necessity'.[27] Germany did not need to commit itself to compromising alliances but could afford to retain a 'free hand', Holstein asserted two years later during hostilities prior to the Russo-Japanese war, since it was 'the strongest military power in the world'.[28] By the time of Bethmann's chancellorship, the 'unreliability' of Italy as an ally had become an accepted fact, yet officials continued to trust in the military leverage available to the Reich, even though its 'political' position had worsened.[29] In 1912, Bethmann remained optimistic that Germany could 'drive forward quietly and patiently on all fronts'.[30] He later admitted, during the First World War, that 'we have not been able to avoid the mistake of underestimating the forces of our enemies . . . We inherited this failing from peacetime.'[31] The basis of this optimism was the supposed military security of the *Kaiserreich* on the European mainland.

Such security was affected by the deterioration of Germany's diplomatic position from the turn of the century onwards, with the signing of the Entente cordiale in 1904 and the Anglo-Russian Entente in 1907, reinforced by an Anglo-French naval agreement in 1912 and Russian support for Serbia and other 'Slav' states during the Bosnian crisis of 1908–9 and the Balkan wars of 1912–13. For their part, the Reich's leaders counted on the backing of Austria–Hungary alone, effectively discounting the possibility of Italian intervention, despite the renewal of the Triple Alliance in 1907 and 1913. There is little indication that this worsening diplomatic constellation provoked a fundamental shift in the conduct of German foreign policy, however, in part because that policy had long since been founded on the idea of military 'independence'. In conjunction with Schlieffen's and

Moltke's strategy of dealing with one power at a time in a two-front war, the details of which were disclosed to Bethmann in 1912, the civilian government was confident that Germany could defeat its principal enemies on its own, as Zimmermann and others revealed during the July crisis itself.[32] Like military planners, diplomats tended to pay a disproportionate amount of attention to the Great Powers in their evaluation of European politics, especially in the assessment of threats to national security. In *Deutsche Politik*, Bülow included one short section on Turkey, whose 'collapse' he lamented but about whose 'limits' he had 'never had any illusions', and devoted the rest of the book's analysis of foreign policy to Britain, France, Russia and Italy, usually examined in isolation.[33] Other memoirs, written during or after the war, tended to do the same.

The structure of alliances in Europe, which was later held partly responsible for the outbreak of the First World War, seemed to most German diplomats before 1914 to be temporary and negotiable. In particular, the loyalties and inclinations of Russia and Britain, whose failings had been exposed in the Boer and Russo-Japanese wars, were open to a wide variety of interpretations. This confusion about the true nature of either power encouraged the continuation of diplomatic negotiations, since there was always a chance that such talks might achieve Bethmann's 'main goal' of 'loosening the Entente'.[34] Thus, to Moltke's chagrin, the Chancellor believed, 'from the first day on', that it was both possible and necessary to reach an understanding with London.[35] As late as February 1914, he continued to be optimistic that 'we are making quiet progress with England'.[36] Only France's warnings, he added, stood in the way of further agreement. Similarly, Bethmann kept on working towards an improvement in Berlin's relationship with St Petersburg. In 1905, Wilhelm II had actually signed the draft of a defensive alliance with Russia at Björkö and, in 1910, he and Nicholas II came to an understanding at Potsdam which, according to Bethmann, prevented either power entering into any coalition with 'an aggressive edge (*Spitze*) vis-à-vis the other'.[37] Arguably, official German attitudes to Russia only began to change significantly in 1914, after a series of war scares and in the context of Russian armament. Until then, although he did not expect 'a fundamental revision of Russian policy', Bethmann did anticipate 'the re-establishment of close and trusting [Russo-German] relations'.[38] 'In the amelioration of our ties with Russia', he continued, 'I see, above all, a springboard for an agreement with Britain.'[39] In other words, the Chancellor believed, possibly until 1914, in the fluidity of Germany's relationship with London and St Petersburg. The Reich's relationship with France was less flexible, given the latter's refusal to accept the Treaty of Frankfurt and the annexation of Alsace-Lorraine, but even here diplomats optimistically predicted the establishment of cordial ties during and after the Moroccan crises of 1905 and 1911.[40]

When policy-makers assessed the Reich's opponents individually, they seemed to have good grounds for optimism. As has been seen, between the turn of the century and 1913, France constituted the single most significant threat to German national security. Yet diplomatic correspondence, in common with military and press reportage, emphasized French decline.[41] The motif of decline, although dating back to 1870 and beyond, appeared consistently only after the public dénouement of the Dreyfus Affair between 1898 and 1900.[42] Consequently, Georg Herbert von Münster-Derneburg, the German ambassador in Paris at the time, was sure that, in France, 'everything was going downhill', whereas in Germany 'we can talk of a turn for the better'.[43] Decline, in turn, was seen to quell revanchism and promote conciliation. 'France', he wrote in November 1898, 'does not feel as strong as it believed itself to be', pushing it 'to seek feelers with Germany in order to achieve, if not a direct alliance, then at least better relations'.[44] These and other similar reports set the tone for diplomatic dispatches for the next decade and a half. Thus, the next ambassador, Hugo Fürst von Radolin, repeated the same argument 'that France was going backwards, militarily, politically, and socially', and his secretary at the embassy confirmed that 'it does not want, as a result of foreign entanglements, to be disturbed in its tranquil enjoyment of life, its quiet occupation, and its pronounced habit of saving'.[45] Finally, Wilhelm von Schoen, Radolin's successor after 1910, was arguably most emphatic of all, repeatedly expressing his conviction that France had been weakened externally, by the duplicity and unreliability of its allies, and internally, by the republicanization of its institutions.

Many French commentators, Schoen observed in April 1914, did not believe that the Third Republic, which 'wastes its energy in bitter party struggles', was strong enough to confront the Reich.[46] Both the ambassador and military attaché in Paris wrote repeatedly to Berlin throughout the period between 1912 and 1914 that any temptation in France to underestimate German strength was overridden by an acute consciousness of French weakness at home and abroad:

The events of last summer showed that Russia had no inclination to support France unreservedly for the sake of Morocco, that the Russo-French alliance now is of less practical worth, therefore, than at the time of Algeciras. Its friendship with England, too, only proved to be temporarily helpful and only, as always, when it served England's own interests . . . . Further, there has been a sharpening of tension with Spain . . . [and] its friendship with Italy has undergone a deep and apparently lasting shock . . . . In addition, internal conditions in France give much cause for concern. The instability of governments, the unproductive nature of an exaggeratedly parliamentary regime, the confusion of the parties, increasing lack of order, discipline and public safety threaten the reputation or even, in the opinion of many, the existence of republican institutions . . . the nation does not want a war.[47]

All such reporting appears to have confirmed Bülow in his long-held belief that France was an 'after-civilisation', and that 'time is running in our favour'.[48] Similar judgements were made by Bethmann, resurfacing during the July crisis. 'We have reason for doubting, and sincerely trust that France, burdened at the present time with all sorts of troubles, will do everything she can to prevent Russia from intervening', he wrote to the Secretary of State for Alsace-Lorraine on 16 July 1914.[49] Jagow and Zimmermann, too, were convinced that the French government would not want to go to war.[50] This assumption rested on an established view in diplomatic circles – and elsewhere – that France was a declining and inferior military force.

Despite their perception of French weakness, few diplomats challenged the idea that France remained the principal threat to national security. Russia, despite seeming to rival its ally in terms of military might around the turn of the century, did not become the Reich's main enemy, in the opinion of the German government, until the very eve of the First World War. Contrary to the claims of some historians, who see the 'Russian menace' as an ever-present and increasing concern in the calculations of Wilhelmine policy-makers, there is little indication in the diplomatic sources that such stereotypes dictated the formulation of German foreign policy, notwithstanding admiration of Russian resources on the part of Bülow, who had served in the embassy at St Petersburg in the 1880s, and of Bethmann, who visited Russia in 1912.[51] During the 1900s and 1910s, the relationship between Berlin and St Petersburg was characterized by two sets of assumptions, both of which limited enmity and helped to prevent conflict. The first was more significant around the turn of the century, when Russian policy was directed towards the Far

East, although it persisted until the outbreak of the First World War: Germany and Russia, it was claimed, had few conflicts of interest, unlike Britain, France, and Russia, which were held to be ideologically and strategically incompatible. Russia and Prussia, and subsequently Germany, had traditionally enjoyed cordial and close relations, not least because of dynastic ties between the cousins Wilhelm II and Nicholas II.

Bülow's policy towards Russia in the early 1900s, which involved German neutrality during the Russo-Japanese war and the signature of the draft of a defensive treaty by Wilhelm II and Nicholas II in 1905, cultivated the idea of this historical friendship, as he spelled out to the ambassador in St Petersburg in 1902, encouraging him to suggest, as if it were self-evident, '1. that, with the increase in Russian power, the number of Russia's enemies also increases, 2. that Germany does not belong to these, because it does not lie in the way of Russian zones of expansion, 3. that France only remains Russia's ally out of hatred and fear of Germany'.[52] The fact that German officials accepted such claims was demonstrated, amongst other things, by their certainty that Russia and Britain would always be enemies and by their subsequent interpretation of the Anglo-Russian Entente in 1907 as, at least in part, a sign of Russian 'weakness' after defeat in the Russo-Japanese war and near-collapse during the 1905 revolution.[53] Three years later, the Foreign Office counsellor Wilhelm von Stumm continued to maintain, in opposition to the speculation of Germany's military attaché in St Petersburg but in support of the ambassador, that 'there is no substance at all in the claim that the Russian–English treaty has had the threatening of Germany by Russia as a prerequisite'. If there were a war between Germany, Russia and France, then it was likely that Britain would join the Reich's enemies, 'but Russia and Germany have no real conflicts of interest', and were, therefore, less likely to go to war against each other.[54] Bethmann concurred with his counsellor and ambassador: 'Against the probability of Russia's active entry [into a war] in support of Britain, without the compulsion of the Franco-Russian alliance, speaks the fact that no immediate conflicts of interest exist between Russia and ourselves.'[55] The ambassador could still be found arguing this case in the summer of 1912.[56] For his part, the Chancellor was said by Riezler to have raised the possibility of 'a lasting agreement with Russia' during the July crisis itself.[57]

The main reason for persisting hopes of reconciliation with St Petersburg – and policy-makers' second set of assumptions about

Russia – was the belief that the country's weaknesses had been exposed and aggravated during the Russo-Japanese war and 1905 revolution. Even before the events of 1904–6, Holstein had predicted that Russia's finances 'would scarcely stand a war'.[58] Others, however, such as Bülow had asserted that 'time is on Russia's side' and had backed St Petersburg in the war with Japan, expecting a Russian victory.[59] Defeat and revolution, therefore, caused a fundamental reassessment, especially by former supporters of Russia. This was why, explained Bülow, he had agreed to Wilhelm II's limitation of the Björkö draft treaty to Europe, against the wishes of Moltke, who wanted Russia to threaten India in order to deter Britain. The neighbouring state would be 'fully incapable' of waging such a war 'within a generation', since it 'is now and for a long time extremely weakened in terms of troops and resources, and in addition will lose thousands of millions in war costs and will need just as much for reorganisation and reconstruction after the peace treaty'.[60] In another memorandum in 1906, the Chancellor relayed without comment the Austrian Foreign Minister's opinion that it would take a long time before Russia recovered its inner health, for all that was 'genuinely Russian' – church, bureaucracy and court – had completely failed.[61] With such failure in mind, German policy-makers assumed from this point onwards that the Russian government would try, where possible, to avoid a continental war.

At all major junctures between 1904 and 1914, diplomats assured the Chancellery that St Petersburg would advise against war. Thus, during the first Moroccan crisis, it was anticipated that Russian reluctance to get involved would prevent a Franco-German conflict; during Austria's annexation of Bosnia, the Russian government was said to have renounced 'all bellicose policies', in the knowledge 'that a war could mean the financial ruin of Russia and the reignition of revolution, with unforeseeable consequences'; during the second Moroccan crisis, St Petersburg was said to have been aloof vis-à-vis Paris, holding 'a long period of quiet to be necessary in order to let the wounds heal which the Japanese war and revolution have inflicted'; and during the Balkan wars, there was said to be 'relatively little enthusiasm for joining the Balkan states', because of 'the feeling that Russia was not yet adequately prepared for a big European war'.[62] It is true that, by 1913, the German ambassador in Russia had begun to voice doubts about the capacity of the tsarist government to resist 'the well-known witch-hunts of the Pan-Slavists, backed by several Grand Dukes and Duchesses as well as individual military men', yet he was insistent that a majority of the country's ruling elites did not desire war.[63] 'I do not believe', wrote the ambassador during the 1914 Russo-German 'war scare' in the press, 'that the government and people in Russia want such a war and that they hold it to be unavoidable, much less do I believe that any decisive groups at all are pursuing a political programme with the aim of a conflict with us.'[64] Only 'a relatively small circle of chauvinists, who are not to be taken seriously, and perhaps one or two military men' contemplated a war with Germany.[65] Despite strong criticism from the Kaiser, the ambassador continued to emphasize the defensive character of Russian armaments, explaining them as a 'striving to raise the war-readiness of the army, which had shown itself inadequate during the Japanese war and which had suffered as a result of this [Balkan] war, the wish of the military not to remain too far behind its western neighbour after the last army increases in Germany, pressure from France, nationalist influences and, not least, the ubiquitous, undiminished, dominant and deep mistrust of Austria–Hungary here'.[66] Despite the alarums of the German military and the right-wing press, then, diplomats do not seem to have thought that Russia was planning to attack the *Kaiserreich*. As late as 26 July 1914, Bethmann repeated the same argument: it should not be assumed that St Petersburg would unleash a European war.[67]

The Reich, by contrast, was believed to be in a position to mount a successful war throughout the period from the mid-1890s to 1914, drawing on the precedents of the wars of unification in the 1860s, the 'War-in-Sight' crisis in 1875, and the Boulanger crisis in 1887. 'We are a young people and perhaps still have too much faith in violence', counselled the Chancellor in 1913, at once describing the proclivity of public debate in the past and prescribing a new, more peaceful trajectory for the immediate future, while he attempted to reach an agreement with London.[68] Even at such conciliatory moments, however, after German and British leaders had mediated between Russia and Austria–Hungary in the two Balkan wars in 1912–13, there is little sign that the Wilhelmstrasse had given up the threat of a continental conflict as part of a longer-term diplomatic strategy. After the turn of the century, in particular, the possibility of war was arguably always present in statesmen's minds. 'The greatest task of diplomacy', wrote Bülow in his memoirs, was 'to run the state in such a way that it [could] eventually enter a war under the most favourable conditions possible'.[69] Such aims were borne out in the German government's precipitate rejection of most of the proposals of the

1899 and 1907 Hague Peace Conferences.[70] After 1909, despite attempting to come to terms with Britain, Bethmann continued the same tradition, contemplating the prospect of an armed conflict – in writing – in all of the years before the outbreak of the First World War.[71] 'Its unity achieved, Germany sees its population increase disproportionately each day, its navy, its industry, its commerce assume a development without equal and . . . it is somehow condemned to expand beyond its borders [au dehors]', the Chancellor lamented to the French ambassador in January 1914, in an outpouring which hardly seemed designed to win over his interlocutor. 'If you refuse that which is the legitimate share of every growing being, you will not stop its growth . . . . Believe me, let's take account of facts and get rid of what divides us. It would be dangerous not to.'[72] Bethmann, it is true, would have preferred to keep the peace, but his policy was founded on the ability of the Reich to force the submission of the other powers by threatening to start a continental war. It can be argued that such military potential formed the basis of both Bülow's and his successor's attempts at peaceful 'political' cooperation, as well as their use of brinkmanship.

Attempts to use the threat of force in order to extract concessions from the Entente powers came at regular intervals throughout the 1900s and early 1910s. In 1905, at the time of the first Moroccan crisis, the evidence – although not absolutely conclusive – strongly suggests that German policy-makers accepted the risk of war in order to oblige France to take account of the Reich, both in Morocco and in Europe. 'French Moroccan policy was an obvious attempt to set Germany aside in an important decision on foreign affairs, an attempt to adjust the balance of power in Europe in favour of France', reported Bülow in 1914. 'A precedent would have been established which must of necessity have tempted to repetition. We could not risk that.'[73] Only by exercising power, declared Holstein, would Germany 'be loved on its own account', just as 'France's *rapprochement* with England began immediately after Fashoda, when the French saw that they could accomplish nothing *against* England.'[74] In order to achieve such goals, the Foreign Office counsellor, who dominated the formulation of policy until July 1905 and who combined with Bülow to convince Wilhelm II to make the visit to Tangiers, was prepared privately to consider war. 'I became convinced', he told the diplomat Oscar von der Lancken-Wakenitz in 1909, 'that, before we were strangled by the circle of the other Great Powers, we must use all our energy to break this circle and in so doing must not shrink back even from the ultimate step.'[75] A more reliable witness, Alfred Graf von Monts, who was ambassador in Rome and a close friend of Holstein, asked shortly before the former counsellor died whether this 'ultimate step' had been contemplated, only to be met by what he understood to be a silent admission.[76] Both Bülow and Holstein were encouraged by Schlieffen at various junctures in 1904 that the time was 'advantageous' for a European war.[77] Even in September 1905, reported the Saxon military attaché in Berlin, 'a war against the allies France and Britain continues to be regarded as a possibility at the highest level here'.[78] By this time, Bülow had switched to a conciliatory policy towards France, initially in the hope of drawing the Quai d'Orsay into a continental alliance, after Wilhelm II and Nicholas II had signed the draft of a defensive alliance at Björkö in July 1905. Before that date, the Chancellor had, according to his own later testimony, not shied away 'from confronting France with the question of war'.[79] Certainly, when Bethmann looked back on the previous decade, from the standpoint of early June 1914, it was the Kaiser whom he thought had resisted a preventive war, not Bülow or the Foreign Office.[80]

In 1908, during the Bosnian annexation crisis, German leaders again risked war, in the knowledge of Germany and Austria–Hungary's military superiority. Bülow himself had helped to bring together the German and Austrian Chiefs of Staff after more than fifteen years of latent hostility under Schlieffen. The reports which Moltke produced in conjunction with Conrad von Hötzendorf consequently carried even greater authority than usual. 'We can take on the fight against [the French army] with a prospect of complete success', declared Moltke in January 1909, whilst the Russian army 'had still not overcome the repercussions of the years of war and revolution.'[81] Such reports, combined with diplomats' assessments of Russian and French passivity, informed Bülow's aggressive policy:

> Also in the event that difficulties and complications should arise, our ally will be able to count on us. Still, I find it hard to believe in the occurrence of serious complications. On the part of Russia, an inimical or even bellicose stance is not to be feared, since it has been directed towards tranquil and peaceful developments, after the serious upheavals which it has undergone. England might be little inclined to fire off a cannonshot because of eastern questions. On the part of France, I felt certain that it did not want a war at all, least of all one because of eastern matters.[82]

Even a year before the Bosnian crisis, Germany's ambassador in Vienna had told Friedrich von Bernhardi that 'war was unavoidable, and that he, Tschirschky, was completely prepared to wage it. Therefore, he always worked hand in hand with the Chief of the General Staff v. Moltke.'[83] A year after the crisis, the Chancellor, although more moderate than his ambassador, confirmed that the policy of brinkmanship had been deliberate: 'From the first moment I was convinced that Germany was isolated and even at the risk of war had to stand at Austria's side. I considered it highly probable that we would preserve peace if we remained firm, and that we would break the net of encirclement which existed more in imagination than in fact.'[84] Thus, Bülow was ready to risk conflict in 1908-9, even though encirclement was largely a question of 'imagination'.

In 1911, Bülow's successor continued the policy of brinkmanship, in spite of his stated intention on coming to office of avoiding a policy of bluster and reaching a diplomatic agreement with Britain. As on previous occasions, military advice was unambiguous. 'On our side – even among the higher ranks – it is emphasized that we should use the situation, which is relatively favourable for us, to strike', recorded the Bavarian military attaché in September 1911.[85] This degree of optimism created the conditions for another attempt to force concessions and retain - in Kiderlen's words - 'political influence in the world' by publicly mooting the possibility of a continental war.[86] 'The French', wrote the Secretary of State at the Foreign Office, 'must get the impression "*that we are prepared for the ultimate step*".'[87] In a revealing speech to the Reichstag in November 1911, Bethmann made the same point: 'Belatedly, unfortunately very belatedly, Germany has joined the ranks of the colonial peoples; let them not then blame us if on this occasion we try to gain whatever we can . . . If necessary [Germany] will draw its sword. Only on this basis can there be any foreign policy.'[88] Historians have claimed that such declarations were designed primarily to appeal to a nationalist domestic audience and to trick the French government into giving way, at a time when the German army and navy were not technically prepared for war.[89] Yet the private statements of Kiderlen and other diplomats suggest that the threat of an armed conflict was intended seriously. 'We can only achieve a satisfactory settlement if we are prepared to draw the ultimate consequences', the Secretary of State had warned in his first resignation letter - the full contents of which were kept secret - to a wavering Wilhelm II, before continuing in a second letter, likewise not fully disclosed to the monarch, that 'it could happen in the course of the negotiations, if they are pursued seriously on our part, that such tension was created that we must say positively to the French that we are determined to take the ultimate step. And if this is to be effective we must be mentally prepared for it.'[90] Bethmann was initially convinced, after plying the Secretary of State with drink in order to find out, as Riezler put it, 'what he ultimately wants', that 'Kiderlen not only considers the possibility of war but wants it.'[91] Subsequently, he was persuaded by the head of the Press Section, Otto Hammann, 'that Kiderlen was not out to make war', since, according to Riezler, he 'believes in [diplomatic] success'.[92] Nevertheless, concluded the Chancellor's secretary, Bethmann 'has conceded to Kiderlen that we must hold out and accept the risk of war'.[93] After the perceived failure of the 'Panther's leap', the Chancellor was anxious to caution those who had irresponsibly called for an armed conflict in 1911 and to emphasize that he could not have gone to war over Morocco. Throughout the critical early part of the crisis, however, he had been willing to support Kiderlen's policy of *force majeure* and brinkmanship. As Hammann later recalled: 'Just as we didn't seek war, we didn't fear it either.'[94]

German policy-making in the decade before the First World War was characterized by a willingness to contemplate the necessity of an armed conflict on the European mainland. In 1905–6, 1908–9 and 1911–12, different governments used the threat of war, in the belief – as in July 1914 – that the crises would be resolved diplomatically, in order to gain concessions overseas and in the Near East, or to maintain the Reich's political influence and prestige within the European states system. Thus, despite trying to prove that war in 1914 was defensive and unavoidable, Bethmann postulated, looking back from the vantage point of 1915, that the isolation of Germany and decline of Austria–Hungary 'forced us to adopt a policy of utmost risk, a risk that grew with each repetition, first in the Moroccan crisis of 1905, then in the Bosnian quarrel, and once again in the Moroccan confrontation'.[95] Beyond these points of actual brinkmanship, there is convincing evidence that the prospect of war was constantly present in diplomats' and statesmen's minds as they formulated foreign policy, even though they were confident that the Reich would not be attacked, at least over the short or medium term. The Balkan wars of 1912–13 arguably constituted the most indicative test of such warlike intentions, since the German government wished to keep the peace and maintain its policy of rapprochement with Britain. However, on this occasion, too, policy-makers made it clear in private and in public that they were not, in Kiderlen's phrase, 'afraid of war'.[96] In the Reichstag on 2 December 1912, Bethmann went so far as to spell out the conditions in which he would go to war: if Austria were attacked by a third party, 'and if their existence was thereby threatened, we would, faithful to our treaty obligation, step firmly on to their side and would fight to preserve our own position in Europe, and to defend our own future and security'.[97] Throughout the pre-war period, German statesmen admitted that they were ready to pursue a policy of 'utmost risk'.

To Bethmann and the civilian leaders of the Reich, who retained control of foreign policy until mobilization on 31 July, war was not an end in itself, but rather a necessary, if undesirable, element in a strategy of brinkmanship. This policy of risking war to attain diplomatic goals constituted a point of intersection between the brooding social Darwinism of the Chief of the General Staff and the early-nineteenth-century, 'old-fashioned humanitarianism' of the Chancellor.[98] By 1914, the prospects of success for a policy of brinkmanship appeared to be good. Abroad, France was believed by Bethmann and the Foreign Office to have 'all sorts of troubles', which would encourage it to 'admonish' Russia 'to keep the peace' and refrain from intervening in an Austro-Serbian conflict.[99] More importantly, at home, the swing of public attention in 1914 from France to Russia, which was now perceived to be the main enemy of the Reich, had reconciled liberals and many socialists to the idea of a 'defensive' war against tsarist autocracy and 'the Asiatic spirit', as *Vorwärts* put it.[100] Whereas most left-wing politicians and journalists thought that France was militarily inferior and pacific, they were convinced that Russia was aggressive, unpredictable and powerful. In effect, such anti-Russian sentiment on the left removed the barrier, which had existed in 1905 and 1911, between brinkmanship and military conflict. Bethmann knew that a war of defence against Russia constituted 'the cause', which Bülow had sought in vain in 1906, to 'inspire the German people'.[101] He realized that he could risk conflict in 1914, without losing public support, as long as he avoided 'creating the incontrovertible suspicion that we wanted war'.[102] The necessity of rendering military conflict acceptable to left-wing Catholics, left liberals and socialists explains the Chancellor's frenzied efforts after the Austrian ultimatum to depict Russia as the 'aggressor'.[103] This endeavour, of course, did not imply that Bethmann wanted war. It does suggest, though, that he had considered and accepted the eventuality of conflict as an integral part of brinkmanship.

In other words, many of Bethmann's critical decisions during the July crisis, which will be examined in the next chapter, can be traced back to a policy of continental domination, which had been devised in the years between 1904 and 1913 with reference to France. The premises of that policy, despite Bethmann's protestations of self-defence in his memoirs, were offensive. Germany was, he put it to the French ambassador in Berlin in January 1914, 'forced to expand'.[104] Such admissions militate against the proclivity of recent historiography, which has tended to understate the seriousness with which threats of war were made in the years before July 1914.

Notes

1. For an example of the former, see H. James, *A German Identity, 1770–1990* (London, 1989), p. 110; for the latter, see I. Geiss, *Der lange Weg in die Katastrophe: Die Vorgeschichte des Ersten Weltkrieges, 1815–1914* (Munich, 1990), pp. 54, 116, 123.

2. W.J. Mommsen, *Imperial Germany* (London, 1995), pp. 1-19, 75-100; W.J. Mommsen, *Grossmachtstellung und Weltpolitik, 1870–1914: Die Aussenpolitik des Deutschen Reiches* (Frankfurt a. M., 1993), pp. 139-321.

3. See Chapter 6, especially D. Stevenson, *Armaments and the Coming of War: Europe, 1904–1914* (Oxford, 1996); D.G. Herrmann, *The Arming of Europe and the Making of the First World War* (Princeton, 1996).

4. K. Hildebrand, *Das vergangene Reich: Deutsche Aussenpolitik von Bismarck bis Hitler 1871–1945* (Stuttgart, 1995), p. 220. Also, G. Schöllgen (ed.), *Escape into War? The Foreign Policy of Imperial Germany* (Oxford, 1990), pp. 121-34.

5. K. Jarausch, *The Enigmatic Chancellor: Bethmann Hollweg and the Hubris of Imperial Germany* (New Haven, 1973), p. 143.

6. B. Sösemann, 'Die Tagebücher Kurt Riezlers: Untersuchungen zu ihrer Echtheit und Edition', *Historische Zeitschrift*, 236 (1983), pp. 327-69; J.W. Langdon, *July 1914: The Long Debate, 1918–1990* (Oxford, 1991), pp. 109-17.

7. Stumm to Jagow, 21 March 1919, cited in F. Fischer, *War of Illusions* (London, 1975), p. 467.

8. G. Schöllgen, 'Kriegsgefahr und Krisenmanagement vor 1914: Zur Aussenpolitik des kaiserlichen Deutschlands', *Historische Zeitschrift*, 267 (1998), pp. 411-12.

9. Note by Haussmann, 24 February 1918, cited in Jarausch, *The Enigmatic Chancellor*, p. 149.

10. T.T.F.A. v. Bethmann Hollweg, *Reflections on the World War* (London, 1920), p. 150.

11. Ibid., p. 124.

12. Bethmann to K.M. v. Lichnowsky, 3 August 1914, cited in I. Geiss (ed.), *July 1914: The Outbreak of the First World War* (London, 1967), pp. 354-5.

13. Ibid.

14. Cited in A. Mombauer, 'A Reluctant Military Leader? Helmuth von Moltke and the July Crisis of 1914', *War in History*, 6 (1999), pp. 417-18.

15. Ibid.

16. Jagow to Lichnowsky, 18 July 1914, in Geiss, *July 1914*, p. 123.

17. Ibid., pp. 307, 293.

18. On the Hamburg school, see Fischer, *War of Illusions*, pp. 44-68; V.R. Berghahn, *Germany and the Approach of War in 1914* (London, 1973), pp. 43-64, 125-44, and P.M. Kennedy, *The Rise of the Anglo-German Antagonism 1860-1914* (London, 1980). For critics, see works by Schöllgen, Canis, and Hildebrand, listed above.

19. Fischer, *War of Illusions*, pp. 137, 139.

20. Tirpitz, cited in H. Raulff, *Zwischen Machtpolitik und Imperialismus. Die deutsche Frankreichpolitik 1904-1905* (Düsseldorf, 1976), p. 77.

21. Cited in Fischer, *War of Illusions*, p. 124.

22. Bethmann to P. v. Metternich, cited ibid., p. 125.

23. Ibid., p. 130.

24. Kiderlen to Bethmann, cited ibid., p. 124.

25. Bülow, 12 February 1912, cited in K.A. Lerman, 'Bismarck's Heir: Chancellor Bernhard von Bülow and the National Idea, 1890-1918', in J. Breuilly (ed.), *The State of Germany. The National Idea in the Making, Unmaking and Remaking of a Modern Nation-State* (London, 1992), p. 113.

26. Bethmann, 9 November 1911, cited in Fischer, *War of Illusions*, p. 90.

27. Bülow, 8 January 1902, cited in Hildebrand, *Das vergangene Reich*, p. 259.

28. Holstein memorandum, 23 December 1903, *Grosse Politik*, vol. 19, p. 73.

29. Jarausch, *The Enigmatic Chancellor*, p. 131.

30. Bethmann to K.J.G. Eisendecher, 22 July 1912, cited ibid., p. 110.

31. Bethmann, cited in G. Krumeich, 'Le déclin de la France dans la pensée politique et militaire allemande avant la première guerre mondiale', in J.-C. Allain (ed.), *La Moyenne puissance au XXe siècle* (Paris, 1988), p. 105.

32. See next chapter.

33. B. v. Bülow, *Imperial Germany*, 6th edn (London, 1914) p. 61.

34. Jarausch, *The Enigmatic Chancellor*, p. 126.

35. Ibid., p. 113.

36. Ibid., p. 142.

37. Cited in Mommsen, *Grossmachtstellung und Weltpolitik*, p. 210.

38. Cited in Jarausch, *The Enigmatic Chancellor*, p. 117.

39. Cited in Mommsen, *Grossmachtstellung und Weltpolitik*, p. 211.

40. For more detail, see M. Hewitson, 'Germany and France before the First World War: A Reassessment of Wilhelmine Foreign Policy', *English Historical Review*, 115 (2000), pp. 570–606.

41. Ibid.

42. G. Krumeich, 'La puissance militaire française vue de l'Allemagne autour de 1900', in P. Milza and R. Poidevin (eds), *La Puissance française à la belle époque* (Brussels, 1992), pp. 207–8; M. Hewitson, *National Identity and Political Thought in Germany: Wilhelmine Depictions of the French Third Republic, 1890–1914*, pp. 159–220.

43. Münster-Derneburg to C. zu Hohenlohe-Schillingsfürst, 5 January 1899, *Auswärtiges Amt*, R7056, A259.

44. Münster-Derneburg to Hohenlohe-Schillingsfürst, 24 November 1898, *Grosse Politik*, vol. 13, p. 244.

45. H. Rogge (ed.), *Friedrich von Holstein* (Berlin, 1932), p. 285; H. v. Flotow to B. v. Bülow, 23 April 1906, *Grosse Politik*, vol. 21, pp. 348–9.

46. Schoen, 4 April 1914, AA R7042, A6753.

47. Schoen to Bethmann, 22 March 1912, *Grosse Politik*, vol. 31, pp. 396–401.

48. Rogge, *Friedrich von Holstein*, p. 289; Bülow to Wilhelm II, 27 June 1907, *Grosse Politik*, vol. 21, p. 576. See also Bülow to Metternich, 6 November 1905, *Grosse Politik*, vol. 19, p. 673: the French 'have no wish at all to pick a quarrel with us'.

49. Bethmann to S. v. Roedern, 16 July 1914, in Geiss, *July 1914*, p. 118.

50. Jagow, cited in Krumeich, 'Le déclin de la France', p. 104; Zimmermann, reported by others in Geiss, *July 1914*, pp. 120–1, 130.

51. See, particularly, A. Hillgruber, 'Deutsche Russland-Politik 1871–1918', *Saeculum*, 27 (1976), pp. 94–108, and T.R.E. Paddock, 'Still Stuck at Sevastopol: The Depiction of Russia during the Russo-Japanese War and at the Beginning of the First World War in the German Press', *German History*, 16 (1998), pp. 358–76.

52. Bülow to F.J. v. Alvensleben, 23 March 1902, *Grosse Politik*, vol. 18, pp. 542–3. On the seriousness of the Björkö negotiations, see B. Vogel, *Deutsche Russlandpolitik: Das Scheitern der deutschen Weltpolitik unter Bülow, 1900–1906* (Düsseldorf, 1973). See also J. Dülffer, 'Deutsch-russische Beziehungen 1870–1914', in I. Mieck and P. Guillen (eds), *Deutschland – Frankreich – Russland: Begegnungen und Konfrontationen* (Munich, 2000), p. 102, on Marschall's and Hohenlohe's view that St Petersburg aimed over the longer term for a Russo-German alliance alone.

53. H. v. Miquel to Bülow, 5 September 1907, *Grosse Politik*, vol. 25, p. 41.

54. Stumm, 16 April 1910, ibid., pp. 533–4.

55. Bethmann to F. v. Pourtalès, 19 April 1910, ibid., p. 534.

56. Pourtalès to Bethmann, 19 July 1912, ibid., vol. 31, p. 453.

57. Cited in Jarausch, *The Enigmatic Chancellor*, pp. 163-4.

58. Holstein memorandum, 24 March 1902, *Grosse Politik*, vol. 19, p. 3.

59. Bülow to H. v. Preussen, 30 March 1905, ibid., p. 417.

60. Bülow memorandum, 30 July 1905, ibid., p. 478.

61. Bülow memorandum, 16 November 1906, ibid., vol. 22, pp. 50-1.

62. Respectively, Dr v. Mühlberg to Bülow, 10 August 1905, ibid., p. 493; Pourtalès to Bülow, 13 November 1908, ibid., vol. 26, p. 270; Metternich to Bethmann Hollweg, 25 September 1911, in E.T.S. Dugdale (ed.), *German Diplomatic Documents, 1871-1914* (London, 1928), vol. 9, p. 17; Pourtalès to Bethmann, 19 July 1912, *Grosse Politik*, vol. 31, p. 451; Pourtalès to Bethmann, 9 October 1912, *Grosse Politik*, vol. 33, p. 196.

63. Pourtalès to Jagow, 6 February 1913, ibid., vol. 34, p. 330.

64. Pourtalès to Bethmann, 11 March 1914, ibid., vol. 39, pp. 550-1.

65. Pourtalès to Bethmann, 21 March 1914, ibid., p. 571.

66. Pourtalès to Bethmann, 11 March 1914, ibid., pp. 550-1

67. Bethmann to Pourtalès, 26 July 1914, in K. Kautsky et al. (eds.), *Outbreak of the First World War* (Oxford, 1924), p. 222.

68. Cited in Jarausch, *The Enigmatic Chancellor*, p. 145.

69. B. v. Bülow, *Denkwürdigkeiten* (Berlin, 1930-1), vol. 3, p. 207.

70. J. Dülffer, *Im Zeichen der Gewalt. Frieden und Krieg im 19. und 20. Jahrhundert* (Cologne, 2003), pp. 66-76.

71. See, for instance, testimony in Fischer, *War of Illusions*, pp. 64-6, 86, 90, 129, 16, 166, 270.

72. J. Cambon to G. Doumergue, 28 January 1914, cited ibid., p. 445.

73. Bülow, *Imperial Germany*, pp. 80-1.

74. Holstein memorandum, 22 February 1906, *Grosse Politik*, vol. 21, pp. 207-8.

75. Lancken-Wakenitz, cited in Fischer, *War of Illusions*, p. 56.

76. Monts, cited in N. Rich, *Friedrich von Holstein: Politics and Diplomacy in the Era of Bismarck and Wilhelm II* (Cambridge, 1965), ii. p. 699.

77. Ibid., p. 698; A. Mombauer, *Helmuth von Moltke and the Origins of the First World War* (Cambridge, 2001), p. 44.

78. Freiherr von Salza und Lichtenau, cited in Fischer, *War of Illusions*, p. 55.

79. Bülow, cited in Raulff, *Zwischen Machtpolitik und Imperialismus*, p. 134.

80. Bethmann, cited in Jarausch, *The Enigmatic Chancellor*, p. 151.

81. Moltke the Younger, cited in Mombauer, *Helmuth von Moltke*, p. 112.

82. Bülow to Tschirschky, 13 October 1908, *Grosse Politik*, vol. 26, no. 9033, p. 161.

83. Tschirschky, cited in Mombauer, *Helmuth von Moltke*, p. 114.

84. Bülow, cited in Jarausch, *The Enigmatic Chancellor*, p. 62.

85. Gebsattel, cited in Mombauer, *Helmuth von Moltke*, p. 122.

86. Kiderlen-Wächter to Zimmermann, 16 June 1911, cited in Fischer, *War of Illusions*, p. 73.

87. Cited ibid., p. 77.

88. Bethmann, 9 November 1911, cited ibid., p. 90.

89. See the recent work of R. Forsbach, *Alfred von Kiderlen-Wächter 1852–1912. Ein Diplomatenleben im kaiserreich* (Göttingen, 1997), ii. pp. 539–40. On the absence of preparations for war, see E. Oncken, *Panthersprung nach Agadir: Die deutsche Politik während der Zweiten Marokkokrise* (Düsseldorf, 1981), pp. 291–5.

90. Kiderlen-Wächter, July 1911, cited in Fischer, *War of Illusions*, p. 77.

91. K. Riezler, 30 July 1911, cited in Jarausch, *The Enigmatic Chancellor*, p. 123.

92. Ibid.

93. Ibid.

94. Hammann, cited in Mombauer, *Helmuth von Moltke*, p. 122.

95. Bethmann to Bülow, 10 June 1915, cited ibid., p. 148.

96. Kiderlen-Wächter, 26 November 1912, cited in Fischer, *War of Illusions*, p. 158.

97. Bethmann, 2 December 1912, cited ibid., p. 159.

98. Riezler, cited in Jarausch, *The Enigmatic Chancellor*, p. 149, on Bethmann; A. Bucholz, *Moltke, Schlieffen and Prussian War Planning* (Oxford, 1991), pp. 214–22, on Moltke.

99. Bethmann and Zimmermann, cited in Geiss, *July 1914*, pp. 118, 121, 130.

100. Cited in Paddock, 'Still Stuck at Sevastopol', p. 358. Also, N. Stargardt, *The German Idea of Militarism: Radical and Socialist Critics, 1866–1914* (Cambridge, 1994), pp. 54–67, 142–6.

101. N. Ferguson, *The Pity of War* (London, 1998), p. 25.

102. Bethmann to Tschirschky, 30 July 1914, in Geiss, *July 1914*, p. 305.

103. Jarausch, *The Enigmatic Chancellor*, p. 169.

104. Bethmann to J. Cambon, January 1914, cited in F. Fischer, 'The Foreign Policy of Imperial Germany and the Outbreak of the First World War', in Schöllgen, *Escape into War*, p. 26. For Bethmann's argument about self-defence, see his *Reflections on the World War*, p. 163.

9

The July Crisis: Brinkmanship and War

Few events have been scrutinized as closely as those leading to the outbreak of the First World War in 1914. During the war itself, the various powers published their respective 'coloured books', including the *Deutsches Weissbuch* on 3 August 1914, followed by much more extensive collections of documents during the 1920s and 30s. Most notably, *Die Grosse Politik der Europäischen Kabinette* was sponsored by the German Foreign Office in order to answer the charge of the Versailles Peace Treaty (1919) that the Reich had been 'guilty' of starting the war (Article 231). Its forty volumes became a template for other similar series, such as *The British Documents on the Origins of the War*.[1] Since the Fischer controversy in the 1960s, historians have expended much time and effort uncovering further documents, including the private diaries and correspondence of personal assistants such as Kurt Riezler, military men such as Erich von Falkenhayn, courtiers such as Georg Alexander von Müller and journalists such as Theodor Wolff, which have been used to 'correct' the self-justificatory biases of the official account of the *Auswärtiges Amt*.[2] The new documents, the majority of which relate directly to the July crisis, seem to have established consensus amongst historians that German leaders self-consciously risked war in 1914. Scholars still fail to agree on how 'desperate' or 'defensive' particular actions were, whose actions – those of diplomats, the Chancellor, the military, or the Kaiser – were decisive, and to what extent such actions were affected by public opinion and political parties.[3]

Most historians would concur that sections of public opinion or German political parties played only a secondary part in pushing the government to war during the July crisis itself. Thus, when the critical decisions were made in the week after the assassination at Sarajevo, many politicians were away from Berlin on holiday, and most of the press was optimistic about the prospects of peace. On the Baltic island of Rügen, Friedrich Ebert, the leader of the SPD, was typical of the majority of deputies in refusing to believe in the seriousness of events, despite his likely arrest, if war were to break out.[4] Similarly, the press played down the gravity of the crisis. Liberal newspapers such as the *Vossische Zeitung* and the *Frankfurter Zeitung* claimed that the 'Serbian government had no part in the crime', even though they criticized Belgrade for allowing that crime to occur.[5] Likewise, National Liberal publications such as the *National-Zeitung* and *Magdeburgische Zeitung* did not think that the available evidence justified 'the stamping of Serbian officials as murderers'.[6] Proof of Serbia's guilt had been alleged to exist, but had never been supplied, wrote Maximilian Harden, the editor of *Die Zukunft*, on 18 July: 'And if it could be proved that a couple of fools, tramps, or criminals from Belgrade were involved in the conspiracy, would even that certainty justify the indictment of an entire nation?'[7] Even right-wing papers which had previously been strongly in favour of war, such as the *Berliner Neueste Nachrichten*, were cautious about pulling Austria's chestnuts out of the fire when the Reich's own interests were not directly involved. 'We can rightly claim a position in the background. Some evidence *from the Danube* of the *Nibelungentreue* is our due', the nationalist organ complained on 17 July.[8] By this time, with little inkling of official intentions and actions, most journalists had again begun to concentrate on other news stories, having discounted the possibility of conflict much more quickly than in the Balkan wars or the two Moroccan crises. Thus, for readers of the press, avidly following the twists and turns of the trial of Joseph Caillaux's wife for the murder of the editor of *Le Figaro*, or speculating about an attempt on Rasputin's life in Russia, there was no sign of a crisis at all until the official *Norddeutsche Allgemeine Zeitung* referred to the likelihood of a localized conflict on 19 July.[9] This revelation, which transformed the attitude of many right-wing and liberal newspapers, was made deliberately after the German and Austrian governments had already taken the key decisions. The press seemed to be following rather than making events in July 1914.

Arguably, Bethmann's retrospective claim that 'the war did not arise out of single diplomatic actions, but rather is a result of public passion', referred not to the events of the July crisis, but to a broader culmination of 'Pan-German' criticism over the previous decade and a half, which made the government anxious to avoid another 'national humiliation' at all costs in 1914.[10] Thus, when it became evident after Austria's ultimatum to Serbia on 23 July that significant sections of the press and populace were in favour of war, the government supposedly felt powerless to oppose them.[11] From both private and official records, however, there is no indication that Bethmann Hollweg, Jagow, Zimmermann, the Kaiser or Moltke believed, even in late July, that they had been pushed into war by a bellicose and critical public. Accordingly, in the early part of the crisis, German leaders talked of the need to bolster Austria's position and control Serbia, not avoid another humiliation. The Chancellor's priority at this point was to prevent information leaking to the press – via the impetuous and nationalistic Crown Prince, for example – 'which our enemies would consider as a planned provocation after all that has transpired'.[12] Consequently, on 23 July, Bethmann's Vice-Chancellor and Secretary of State for the Interior, Clemens von Delbrück, who had been informed a week beforehand about the Austrian ultimatum at his Thuringian spa resort, recorded with satisfaction in his diary that 'we have not spoken about foreign policy at all, the daily press was completely calm, and no one amongst the visitors present suspected the slightest thing about the imminent danger of war'.[13]

In the latter part of the crisis, as press and public became more agitated, the Chancellor and other German leaders gave no hint that they were being borne along on a tide of pro-war sentiment in right-wing newspapers and amongst nationalist demonstrators in major German cities. Instead, the Chancellor continued to worry about popular opposition and divisions in the Reichstag, which threatened to delay the passage of war credits.[14] No doubt aware of widespread popular apprehension at the prospect of an armed conflict, notwithstanding an escalation of calls for war in the nationalist press and public, Bethmann was fearful that an army clampdown on the SPD 'might have fatal effects on the uniformity, depth and strength of patriotic feeling'.[15] Throughout the last days of peace, the Chancellor and those around him remained preoccupied by the necessity of creating the impression that the Reich had been 'attacked' by Russia, 'because otherwise we shall not have public opinion on our side'.[16] Subsequent elation in official, military and court circles that, in the words of the Chief of Wilhelm II's Naval Cabinet on 1 August, 'the mood is brilliant' was so pronounced precisely because such a mood had not been anticipated.[17] It was recognized that the support of a majority of the public and press was based on the myth of a 'defensive' war: 'The government has managed brilliantly to make us appear the attacked.'[18] Ruling elites were conscious that they had had to orchestrate support for the war. They were not pushed into it.

The question, then, becomes: which sections of Germany's ruling elites were responsible for the decisions leading to war? In theory, the Kaiser should have played a dominant role.[19] He was formally responsible for coordinating foreign policy, declaring war and appointing ministers, in accordance with Articles 11 and 18 of the constitution, as well as being Commander-in-Chief of the German army. According to the Treaty of Versailles, he was a 'war criminal'. At virtually every juncture in the years before 1914, Wilhelm II had acted as though he was in charge, issuing commands and calling for war. 'The perpetual emphasis on peace at every opportunity – suitable and unsuitable – has, in the last 43 years of peace, produced an altogether eunuch-like attitude amongst the statesmen and diplomats of Europe', he declared at the start of the first Balkan war, as Bethmann attempted to cooperate with Britain in a policy of détente.[20] The monarch overrode ministers and berated diplomats, warning the German ambassador in St Petersburg, Friedrich von Pourtalès – 'dear Pourzel' – that he 'would do better to leave unwritten' reports about Russia's lack of bellicosity: 'He makes those who are ignorant of Russia and weak, suspect characters amongst his readers, totally confused! Also, he is not in the least convincing.'[21] On another occasion, in 1912, after the Foreign Office had tried to resist increases in Tirpitz's ship-building programme, Wilhelm declared forthrightly and dismissively: 'I'll tell you something, you diplomats have filled your pants, the entire Wilhelmstrasse stinks of –.'[22] Courtiers like Philipp zu Eulenburg-Hertefeld believed that such utterances resounded throughout diplomatic circles and helped to shape policy in both Berlin and Vienna. Even the Kaiser's marginal comments could, he said, be found 'fluttering remarkable distances and in astonishing places'.[23]

Psychologically, however, the markedly belligerent, aggressive character of the Kaiser's marginalia, the reflection of which appears in the Vienna Cabinet meeting of 7 July, does not mean that he necessarily had belligerent *intentions*. One needs to know Kaiser Wilhelm as well as I do to be able to explain this contradiction. The explanation is that the Kaiser's hyper-vivacious nature in fact knows *only the superlative*. To him something is either magnificent, splendid, incomparable – or atrocious, infamous, intolerable. The intermediate notes desert him *entirely* (I mean, if he is expressing his feelings), whenever he chooses his words. That is why his speeches always impressed *strongly* – and offended strongly. That is why, too, his marginalia are so dangerous, for they all, without exception, have the character of exclamation marks . . . Neither Count Berchtold nor Count Stürgkh (Austria's two leading ministers) is therefore to be censured for reading a belligerent *intention* into Kaiser Wilhelm's stance.[24]

Beyond the shuttered world of courtiers, however, relatively few of those in power believed that Wilhelm II's stance was decisive. Although he did occasionally succeed in removing envoys and statesmen, he was too inconsistent to create a 'personal regime', even at the turn of the century, when his powers were least restricted. After a series of court scandals, one of which discredited Eulenburg himself, and numerous ill-advised interventions in foreign policy, such as the *Daily Telegraph* affair in 1908, the Kaiser's sphere of action became more and more limited during the decade before the First World War. Not only did he find himself surrounded in 1914 by 'eunuch-like' diplomats such as Pourtalès, Karl Max von Lichnowsky in London and Wilhelm von Schoen in Paris; he was also actively opposed by the Wilhelmstrasse itself, with counsellors and secretaries of state, often in conjunction with the Chancellor, nullifying and pre-empting his arbitrary and extreme impulses. Thus, Holstein and Bülow pushed Wilhelm to go to Tangiers against his will in 1905; Kiderlen sent a gunboat to Agadir and threatened war in 1911, in spite of imperial opposition; and Bethmann collaborated with London in bringing peace to the Balkans in 1912–13, notwithstanding the 'War Council' convened by the Kaiser against Britain on 8 December 1912.

Even at his most impulsive, such as when the Austrian envoy, Alexander von Hoyos asked for Germany's support on 5 July 1914, after the assassination of the Habsburg Crown Prince in Sarajevo on 28 June, Wilhelm II gave his immediate backing to Ladislaus Szögyény-Marich, the Austrian ambassador in Berlin, but added that he must 'first hear what the Imperial Chancellor has to say': 'The first thing he assured me was that he had expected some serious step on our part towards Serbia, but that at the same time he must confess that the detailed statement of His Majesty [Franz Josef] made him regard a serious European complication possible and that he could give no definite answer before having taken counsel with the Imperial Chancellor.'[25] When the Austrian ambassador returned after lunch to press his case again, the Kaiser stated 'that we might in this case, as in all others, rely upon Germany's full support', but reaffirmed his need to consult Bethmann: 'He must, as he said before, first hear what the Imperial Chancellor has to say, but he did not doubt in the least that Herr von Bethmann Hollweg would agree with him.'[26] As Luigi Albertini correctly indicates, these royal assurances were – by Wilhelm II's standards – so carefully worded because he recognized that the Chancellor had successfully opposed him in the past.[27] Given such qualifications, Bethmann had the chance to modify the government's reply to Vienna, but, as the Kaiser anticipated, saw no need to do so.

For most of the July crisis, the monarch was kept out of Berlin on his yearly 'Nordlandreise' off the Norwegian coast, from where he made strident calls for war, before returning to the capital and calling for peace, having read the Serbian reply to Austria's ultimatum on 28 July. Although the most important members of the military – Moltke, Falkenhayn, Waldersee, Tirpitz – had returned from their holidays to Berlin by 24 July, the Kaiser only came back on the 27th, against the wishes of the Chancellor and Foreign Office. He was not shown the content of the Serbian reply to the Austrian ultimatum until the next day, even though it had been sent to the Reich government three days earlier, on 25 July. His relieved reaction – 'that every reason for war drops away' and that Vienna should be conciliatory – was not passed on by Bethmann until after Austria's declaration of war against Serbia, one hour later, and in a greatly distorted form, without reference to the monarch's hope of peace.[28]

Having been engaged by the Foreign Office to write a string of letters to Tsar Nicholas II, which failed to deter Russia from mobilizing for war, Wilhelm made one final intervention on 1 August, when he attempted to call off German mobilization in the West in order to allow Britain – and possibly France – to declare their neutrality, in response to unreliable information from Lichnowsky, the Reich's anglophile ambassador in London. On each occasion except the last one, whether counselling war or peace, the Kaiser's demands were overridden. In response to Wilhelm's request to stop Germany's western mobilization, which had been issued at 5 p.m. on 1 August, Moltke had been prepared to put forward an opposing point of view, stating forcefully that: 'We cannot do that; if that were to happen, we would disrupt the whole army and would give up any chance of success.'[29] Despite suffering, according to his wife, a slight stroke, the Chief of the General Staff had not actually given the written order to stop the 16th Division entering Luxembourg, as the Kaiser had commanded.[30] If Falkenhayn's diary is to be believed, something of a stand-off had ensued, with Moltke informing the Division by telephone that it was not to march 'for the moment'.[31] Since further telegrams from Lichnowsky shortly afterwards immediately cast doubt on earlier optimism about British neutrality, it is difficult to say how the dispute would have been resolved. It seems likely, however, that Wilhelm II's rapid acceptance of the need to continue western mobilization, just after 11 p.m. on the same day, was caused in part by the opposition of his Chief of the General Staff.[32] Like Bethmann only days beforehand, Moltke had been prepared to oppose the will of his monarch.

Such actions beg the question, however, whether the army – the other main rival of the Chancellor and Foreign Office – had not gained the upper hand during the latter part of the crisis. Unlike the Kaiser, the generals did not try to escape conflict. Indeed, some historians argue that the General Staff and War Ministry succeeded in 1914, after disappointment at inaction during previous international crises, in circumventing civilian government and forcing a declaration of war.[33] Thus, although most of the highest echelons of the General Staff and War Ministry were away from Berlin throughout much of July, they were informed regularly of what was going on there. Waldersee, despite later denials to a parliamentary commission in 1919, was recalled three times to the German capital, and he was repeatedly in contact with his Austrian counterparts, making enquiries about the precise nature of their military plans.[34] Moltke, who had arrived in Karlsbad on 28 June for a one-month cure, returned almost a week early, since he knew that the period after the delivery of the Austrian ultimatum would be 'critical'. 'I am sorry not to be able to stay here another week, but I have to return to Berlin', he wrote to his wife on 22 July. 'Tomorrow, the 23rd, is the critical day! I am eager to find out what will happen.'[35] Back in the capital, the generals, whose 'renewed pressure . . . for allowing things to drift towards war' had been noted by the Saxon envoy as early as 2 July, allegedly mounted a 'military take-over' during the last days before war.[36] In particular, they are said to have crossed the line between military and political affairs, interfering in the conduct of foreign policy and using privileged information to accelerate the pace of events. The threshold was supposedly crossed by Moltke's submission to Bethmann on 29 July of a 'Summary of the Political Situation', before being made completely irrelevant by the army's imposition of mobilization over the following three days.

Against this case, it can be argued that military leaders were wary of interfering in political matters. Thus, Falkenhayn, who was considerably more bellicose than Moltke throughout most of the July crisis, refused to oppose the Chancellor's resistance to the idea of putting Germany on a war footing, 'for it is his task to determine policy, and he is not to be disturbed in this by military advisors'.[37] Understandably, Bethmann, too, was aware of the extent of his political responsibilities and seems to have treated the Chief of Staff's 'Summary' in the same way as other military assessments, ignoring its naïve and belated 'political' analysis of Serbian 'mischief-making', and heeding its warnings about Russian mobilization, which would, he wrote to the ambassador in St Petersburg, 'force us to mobilise'.[38] The Chancellor had known since 1912 that the imperative of speed in Moltke's military strategy would allow very little time for negotiation, once Russia and France had begun preparations for war. Nevertheless, he ignored Falkenhayn's call for a declaration of 'a situation of imminent danger of war' on 29 July and the Chief of the General Staff's explicit demand for a general mobilization on 30 July. Instead, he adhered to his policy of encouraging Britain to localize the conflict and, failing this, of allowing Russia to assume the role of aggressor by mobilizing first.

Although he was certainly hastened into war, with Falkenhayn reporting an 'argument' (*Auseinandersetzung*) between the Chancellor and Moltke on the evening of 30 July, Bethmann gave every indication of accepting the timetable of military preparations.[39] 'We have accepted the role of a mediator', he told the ambassadors of the German states on the same day, 'and it must quickly be brought to a result, because the more time passes, the more Russia and France will gain advantages in their military preparations.'[40] Moreover, the Chancellor also seemed to concede the need for war, after his eleventh-hour call for a 'halt in Belgrade' had failed to convince Vienna and looked unlikely to dissuade St Petersburg. Falkenhayn's diary entry for the important meeting on 30 July, when the first stage of German mobilization was decided for noon the next day, suggests that he and Moltke had 'finally got the decision over a declaration of imminent danger of war accepted', implying that Bethmann had come to admit the necessity of a European conflict.[41] Such an admission was implied by the Chancellor's instruction to the ambassador in Vienna at 11.00 p.m. on the same evening – as soon as news of Russia's general mobilization began to arrive in Berlin – that all mediation attempts should be stopped.[42] If Bethmann had not accepted the need for war, he would have had good reason for continuing to put pressure on Berchtold in order to limit the scope of Austria's campaign against Serbia and to halt Russian mobilization. In other words, the Chancellor chose to enter war at the same time as giving up hope of 'localizing' the conflict to Serbia and Austria alone. He was not forced into a declaration of war by the army.

It is, of course, true that Bethmann and the Wilhelmstrasse founded their policy on army assurances of the Reich's military superiority. Correspondingly, at the very start of the First World War, even later sceptics such as Bülow and Wilhelm von Schoen, the former ambassador in Paris, were confident that the conflict would be short, and they retained, in the former's words, 'the utmost trust in Chief of the General Staff v. Moltke'.[43] As the war turned to attrition, slaughter and a possible defeat, those most closely implicated in the events of the July crisis began to blame the pre-war assessments of the military, as Bethmann did to Conrad Haussmann in 1917.[44] Such evidence, though, had also been corroborated earlier in the war by more minor officials such as Botho von Wedel, a *Vortragender Rat* in the Foreign Office, who had less need to defend himself against charges of recklessness. When Wolff accused the 'Staatsleitung' of underestimating the land forces of France, Belgium and Russia, and overestimating those of Austria–Hungary and Britain, the counsellor objected that 'the false estimates stemmed from the military' and that 'the For[eign] Off[ice] were able to base a strong policy on it'.[45] The point, however, as Wedel hinted, was that Bethmann, Jagow, Zimmermann and other diplomats, together with their predecessors, had chosen to pursue a strong policy on the basis of over-optimistic army evaluations. They had not been forced to do so. 'Certainly, Bethmann quite self-evidently did not want it [a war against Russia]', Wolff declared to Bülow in 1915. 'He and others were pushed into it, but they still told themselves in the unconscious of the soul: "and if it does come to a war with Russia – then we shall wage it." . . . And Jagow and Stumm, too, saw, still only in their unconscious, the possibility of war.'[46]

This tacitly offensive strategy during the July crisis, which derived from more than a decade of diplomatic brinkmanship, can be traced in seven overlapping policy initiatives: namely, the issuing of the so-called 'blank cheque' to Austria on 5 July; the formulation of a deliberately harsh ultimatum to Serbia by 23 July; attempts to 'localize' the conflict throughout most of July; the refusal of mediation after Serbia's response to the ultimatum on 25 July; the conditional nature of Bethmann Hollweg's eleventh-hour policy of conciliation between 29 and 31 July; persistent efforts to achieve British neutrality, particularly after the failure of 'localization'; and the tactical imperative before Germany's declaration of war against Russia on 1 August to cast the tsarist state as the aggressor.

During the July crisis, Bethmann pursued a well-established policy of brinkmanship. In the critical early part of the crisis until 6 July, after he had confirmed Wilhelm II's 'blank cheque' to Vienna's ambassador in Berlin and had proceeded to urge a quick Austrian intervention in Serbia, the Chancellor oversaw Germany's policy with a clear view of the possible consequences. According to reports from St Petersburg over the preceding year and a half, the chances of Russia intervening in a war between Austria and Serbia were significant, notwithstanding British and French pressure for a localization of the conflict. During the second Balkan war in 1913, which served as a portent for events a year later, the German ambassador had warned the Foreign Office that the warmongers in Russia would come to dictate policy if Austria invaded Serbia, irrespective of the disastrous domestic consequences which this might have for the tsarist regime.[47] A few days later, Bethmann confirmed the conclusions of the report in a dispatch to the Austrian Foreign Minister:

> As far as I can judge the situation in Russia, on the basis of information which I have cause to believe is reliable, we can reckon with certainty that the forces, which stand behind the Pan-Slavist agitation, will win the upper hand if Austria–Hungary should get involved in a conflict with Serbia . . . One must also arrive at the conclusion, after objective enquiry, that it is almost impossible for Russia, without an enormous loss of prestige, given its traditional relations with the Balkan states, to look on without acting during a military advance against Serbia by Austria–Hungary. The consequences of Russian involvement, however, are plain for all to see. It would turn into an armed conflict of the Triple Alliance – predictably not supported by Italy with great enthusiasm – against the powers of the Triple Entente, in which Germany would have to bear the entire heavy burden of a French and English attack.[48]

At the start of the July crisis, Bethmann remained 'pessimistic', in the words of the German ambassador in London, who had just returned from Berlin.[49] Germany, warned Lichnowsky, was in an awkward position, since it would be accused of holding Austria back, if it told the Austrians 'nothing must be done . . . ; on the other hand, if it let events take their course there was the possibility of very serious trouble'.[50] On 2 July, a contact in the Wilhelmstrasse had told the Saxon minister in Berlin that 'Russia would mobilise and world war could no longer be prevented', if Austria-Hungary declared war on Serbia, although this was still unlikely.[51] Yet Bethmann authorized his ambassador in Vienna to give assurances that 'the Empire would certainly stand by Austria-Hungary' as early as 4 July, and he confirmed this blank cheque, even after Hoyos had told Zimmermann on 5 July that Austria intended to attack Serbia and reduce the size of its territory.[52] On the next day, the Chancellor went on to advise 'immediate action' as the best solution to Vienna's difficulties in the Balkans.[53] 'From an international point of view, he considers the present moment as more favourable than some later time', wrote the Austrian ambassador in Berlin, making it clear that Bethmann had sanctioned a war with Serbia, with all the dangers which this entailed.[54] Although some historians have rightly pointed out that the German ambassador in Vienna, Heinrich von Tschirschky, sometimes went, in fits of bellicosity, beyond his brief, and that Berchtold's reports of German support to the Austrian Common Ministerial Council could have been exaggerated in order to convince opponents of strong action like the Hungarian Premier, István Tisza, it is worth recalling that Tschirschky was known at the time for his early caution, which provoked a very public rebuke from Wilhelm II. Moreover, Berchtold's claim that Berlin had advised Austria-Hungary to 'act first' was backed up by the confidential reports of the Austrian ambassador, who – after a meeting with Bethmann and Zimmermann on 6 July – had 'ascertained that the Imperial Chancellor, like his imperial master, considers immediate action on our part as the best solution of our difficulties in the Balkans'.[55] Finally, these witnesses were corroborated by others outside the Foreign Office, such as the Kaiser's adjutant, Hans von Plessen, who noted the prevalent opinion of the Potsdam meeting on 5 July, at which Wilhelm II, Bethmann, Jagow, Falkenhayn and Moriz von Lyncker, the Chief of the Military Cabinet, were present: 'the sooner the Austrians make their move against Serbia the better'.[56] Even at the beginning of the July crisis, it could be contended, the Chancellor and the Foreign Office pushed for immediate action against Serbia in the knowledge that a European war was a possible outcome.

The uncompromising nature of the Austrian ultimatum to Serbia on 23 July, whose demands included Austrian-led judicial proceedings against those involved in the assassination plot and in the anti-Austrian movement generally, helped to ensure that a war came about. As Bülow pointed out, no country would have been able to accept the terms, not even San Marino, given contemporary views of state sovereignty and national honour.[57] Bethmann himself predicted on 21 July, without further comment, that the ultimatum would be 'refused'.[58] Assured of German support – in Hoyos's words – 'in whatever circumstances', Vienna rejected Belgrade's response on the grounds that the latter, despite promising to collaborate with Habsburg officials, had refused Austrian participation in domestic judicial proceedings as 'unconstitutional'.[59] Both Bethmann and Jagow, at the time and subsequently, maintained that they were ignorant of the ultimatum's contents and that they merely reacted to decisions taken in Vienna. As the former put it in 1915: 'We did not even know of the note.'[60] The ultimatum 'seemed to me to be pretty stiff and going beyond its purpose', wrote Jagow in his book on the causes and outbreak of the war.[61] Such claims were patently false, as Luigi Albertini established during the 1950s.[62] Thus, Tschirschky had telegraphed Berchtold as early as 10 July to find out what Austria would demand of Serbia. On the next day, Jagow made the explicit suggestion of an 'ultimatum' in his reply to Vienna.

Thereafter, so many communications passed between Berlin and Vienna that even the Bavarian Legation was fully aware of the main terms of the Austrian note by 18 July.[63] On the previous day, the Saxon Chargé d'Affaires had reported that he did not yet know the precise content of the demands, 'but it is not to be ruled out that they will be "hard for Serbia to swallow"'.[64] Certainly, Szögyény, the Austrian ambassador, was never in any doubt about the German position, as he spelled out on 12 July:

Both H. M. Kaiser Wilhelm and all other responsible personages here not only stand firmly in allied loyalty behind the Monarchy but invite us most emphatically not to let the present moment pass but to take vigorous measures against Serbia and make a clean sweep of the revolutionary conspirators' nest once and for all, leaving it entirely to us what means we think right to select . . . I think a certain explanation is necessary why authoritative German circles and not least H. M. Kaiser himself – one might almost say – press us to undertake possibly even military measures against Serbia. It is evident that after the deplorable events that have taken place the Monarchy must proceed with the utmost vigour against Serbia. But that the German government also from its own standpoint should regard the present moment as politically the most suitable needs further elucidation. The choice of the present moment is in the German view, which I altogether share, prompted by general political considerations and by special considerations arising out of the Sarajevo murder. Germany has recently been strengthened in her conviction that Russia is arming for war against her western neighbours . . . but is not at the present moment sufficiently forward with her preparations. Therefore it is by no means certain that, if Serbia becomes involved in a war with us, Russia would resort to arms in her support. And if she did so, she is far from being so militarily prepared and powerful as she will probably be some years hence. The German government further believes it has sure indications that England would not join in a war over a Balkan country even should this lead to a passage of arms with Russia and eventually even of France.[65]

From the start, Bethmann and the Foreign Office knew of the existence and contents of the Austrian ultimatum, and they realized that it might bring about a European war, although they hoped that such a conflict could be avoided.[66] Their priority in this period was, according to Jagow on 16 July, to avoid 'giving the impression that we had any wish to stand as a hindrance in the way of Austrian action or to prescribe definite limits or aims for it'.[67] By 21 July, the German Secretary of State at the Foreign Office had come to assume that Vienna's *'ultima ratio'* was either 'a provisional occupation of Serbian territory' or 'a partition of Serbia', but he nevertheless continued to tell Szögyény 'that Germany will unquestionably back [Austria] unconditionally and with her whole strength'.[68] In the view of the Wilhelmstrasse, the ultimatum was likely to lead to a war between Austria and Serbia, followed by occupation and, possibly, partition.

The Reich government's stated policy throughout most of July was for a 'localization' of the conflict. In their memoirs, retrospective interviews and in the diplomatic correspondence of the time, Bethmann, Jagow, Zimmermann and Stumm contended, in the words of Stumm on 25 July 1914, that 'whenever one shows firmness, all sorts of friendships come to light, on which one would not have counted any longer'.[69] The fullest statement of this policy of localization, the realization of which was believed to depend on speed and resolution, was Jagow's private letter to Lichnowsky on 18 July, since the Secretary of State had to convince his sceptical ambassador in London to persuade Britain to constrain Russia and France. 'We must attempt to localise the conflict between Austria and Serbia', he asserted. 'Whether we shall succeed in this will depend first on Russia, and secondly, on the moderating influence of Russia's allies. The more determined Austria shows herself, the more energetically we support her, so much the more quiet will Russia remain.'[70] Yet, localization was not only founded on the possibility of presenting the unprepared Entente powers with a *fait accompli*, it was also based on the assumption of German military superiority, at least over the short term. Thus, although Jagow went on to warn Lichnowsky of Russia's army and navy increases, probably in a much exaggerated form in order to overcome the latter's deep reservations, he admitted that 'Russia is not ready to strike at present. Nor will France and England be anxious for war at the present time.'[71]

In private discussions with other officials, the secretaries of state and Foreign Office counsellors were much less guarded. Consequently, the Bavarian, Badenese and Saxon representatives in Berlin reported back to their governments in mid-July that 'England is altogether peaceably minded and neither France nor Russia appears to feel any inclination for war.'[72] The residue of such optimism was still apparent as late as 29 July, the day after Austria's declaration of war on Serbia, as the Badenese envoy, after talks with his Bavarian counterpart, Stumm and Clemens von Delbrück, demonstrated:

> Favourable to the prospects of peace is the fact that the French now really do not desire war in any circumstances, in fact actually fear it on account of their desperate financial position and perhaps also on military grounds; that is why they are setting all levers in motion at St Petersburg to exercise a moderating influence there; but whether the peace-loving ruler and his Foreign Minister will retain the upper hand against the Pan-Slav currents is a thing no one can predict.[73]

In a less reliable retrospective claim, although one considerably more veracious – since less conscious of the need for exculpation – than those of his German counterparts, the former Austrian Foreign Office chief of cabinet Hoyos maintained that Zimmermann had told him that 'we are strong enough to take on France and Russia at the same time, so you will be able to let all the weight of your army gravitate to the Balkans'.[74] Even in conversations with hostile and peace-loving left-liberal journalists, Jagow's confidence in Germany's strength was obvious from his smiling countenance alone, although he again – and for similar reasons as previously with Lichnowsky – added a mantra about the growth of Russia. 'Neither Russia, nor France, nor England wanted war', he told Wolff on 25 July. 'And if it must be (smiling) – one day war will come, if we let things go on as they are, and in two years Russia will be stronger than now.'[75] Russia would 'think twice before letting fly', not least because of the danger of revolution and the lack of adequate *matériel*, and France could 'not want war', given 'the revelations of Senator Humbert about conditions in the army', declared Stumm, as Wolff called in to see him on the way back from his meeting with Jagow.[76] 'Such a good situation will not come about again', he concluded. 'Just see it through and remain firm!'[77] Civilian leaders believed in the possibility of localization because their Russian and French equivalents, they anticipated, would recognize the Reich's military ascendancy.

Mediation failed during the July crisis largely because the German Chancellor and Foreign Office were more willing to risk a European war than to renounce the idea of a 'local' war between Austria–Hungary and Serbia, on which their strategy was predicated. There were, of course, other reasons why the Wilhelmstrasse was wary of submitting Vienna's case to a conference of Great Powers, after Germany's perceived 'humiliation' at the conference of Algeciras during the first Moroccan crisis. Bethmann, in any event, doubted that Austria would accept arbitration in a *de facto* 'European court of justice', since other powers had refused such arbitration when their vital interests were at stake.[78] Yet even Bülow, who had suffered the political consequences of Algeciras, did not believe that such 'historical lessons' were the main explanation for the Reich government's avoidance of mediation: 'Why did Jagow not want the four powers – Germany, Italy, France and England – to meet and seek a way out?'[79] The most convincing answer is that German leaders' priority was to allow – and, at times, prompt – the Ballhausplatz to go to war against Serbia without 'interference' from third parties, partly because they had feared from the start that Austria would not act decisively or forcefully enough. Accordingly, Bethmann removed the assurance of Friedrich von Pourtalès, the Reich's ambassador in St Petersburg, on 26 July that Austria–Hungary did not intend to attack Serbia, before forwarding the telegraph to Tschirschky in Vienna.[80]

The Chancellor and the Foreign Office pushed Berchtold to override Conrad's wish to delay a declaration of war until the Austrian army was ready to fight on 12 August, despite the fact that the Foreign Minister himself had initially envisaged only the breaking off of diplomatic relations and the start of military preparations – not actual operations – when the ultimatum to Serbia was not met on 28 July. As Szögyény reported from Berlin on 25 July: 'Here it is universally taken for granted that an eventual negative reply by Serbia will be followed by a declaration of war from us and military operations. Any delay in commencing military operations is regarded here as a great danger because of the interference of other powers. They urgently advise us to go ahead and confront the world with a *fait accompli.*'[81] In a critical dispatch on 27 July, shortly before the declaration of war, the ambassador assured the Austrian Foreign Office that the German government 'in no way associates itself' with Grey's proposals for mediation – that is, for direct pressure on Vienna to consider Serbia's reply to the ultimatum 'as satisfactory or as a basis for negotiations' – and that it was 'even decidedly against their being considered, and only passes them on in order to conform to the English request', after having 'already declined an English proposal for a conference'.[82] Following the formal commencement of hostilities between Austria and Serbia on the next day, Bethmann continued to reject the idea of a conference and agreed to direct mediation with the Ballhausplatz solely on the understanding that Tschirschky 'carefully avoid giving the impression that we wish to restrain Austria'.[83] Despite the increasing likelihood of a European conflict, the Chancellor was unwilling to try to prevent Austria–Hungary from going to war against Serbia, since this had been the crux of his strategy from early July onwards.

As is well known, between 29 and 31 July, Bethmann did attempt to limit Austrian war aims in a last-minute effort to avert a European conflict. At 3.00 a.m. on 30 July, Bethmann warned Tschirschky that, 'in case Austria refuses all mediation, we stand before a conflagration in which England will be against us; Italy and Romania to all appearances will not go with us, and we two shall be opposed to four Great Powers. On Germany, thanks to England's opposition, the principal burden of the fight will fall.'[84] 'Austria's political prestige, the honour of her arms, as well as her just claims against Serbia, could all be amply satisifed by the occupation of Belgrade or of other places', he went on. 'Under the circumstances, we must urgently and impressively suggest to the consideration of the Vienna cabinet the acceptance of mediation on the above-mentioned honourable conditions. The responsibility for the consequences that would otherwise follow would be an uncommonly heavy one both for Austria and for us.'[85] The confusion that this initiative caused in Vienna, which was also simultaneously receiving instructions from the German military to mobilize against Russia, moved Berchtold to ask sarcastically: 'Who rules: Moltke or Bethmann?'[86] The Chancellor's volte-face itself, carried out against the wishes of most generals, provided an unambiguous answer. It was probably in part a response to news of Russia's partial mobilization, which reached Berlin on 29 July, and in part a reaction to Grey's disclosure that a 'halt in Belgrade' by Austria might be acceptable, but that Britain would intervene in any broader European war.[87] It is unlikely that either event was in itself a sufficient cause of the Chancellor's brief change of course, since each had already been anticipated on various occasions. Rather, it seems that Bethmann, who was said by Tirpitz in his memoirs to have lost his 'composure', was deeply affected by the imminence of a European 'upheaval'.[88]

Nevertheless, the Chancellor – like the rest of the Foreign Office – had always been aware of the possibility that an Austro-Serbian war might escalate into what the Kaiser – on 5 July – had termed 'an international conflict'.[89] Certainly, Bethmann showed no signs of disagreeing with Jagow's confirmation to Lichnowsky on 18 July that, 'if localisation is not attainable and if Russia attacks Austria, then the *casus foederis* will arise, then we cannot sacrifice Austria'.[90] Moreover, throughout the period of 'panic' after 29 July, Bethmann and Jagow continued to give assurances of support to Vienna that 'we are, of course, ready to fulfil the obligations of our alliance', if a European war were to break out.[91] 'Should this conflagration centre be extended, contrary to our hopes, and owing to Russia's interference', wrote the Secretary of State, 'then, true to the obligations of our alliance, we should have to support the neighbouring Monarchy with all the power of the Empire.'[92] Thus, although worried by the approaching vision of a 'conflagration', German leaders had throughout the July crisis – and beforehand – been aware of such a prospect. Indeed, it was an integral part of their long-standing policy of brinkmanship, experience of which led them to believe that the other powers would give way, as long as they themselves maintained a firm stance. As the diplomat Hans von Flotow, an old friend of the Secretary of State, remarked early in the war, Jagow had 'very much reckoned with a belligerent outcome'.[93]

By 31 July, after Bethmann had agreed to mobilization, Germany's quest for mediation came to an end. The Chancellor's policy of limitation, however, continued, as he sought to persuade Britain to remain neutral. Initially, the Wilhelmstrasse had relied on Grey's desire to localize the dispute between Austria and Serbia. Then, when it became evident between 26 and 29 July that the British Foreign Secretary had ceased to believe in the Reich government's will to mediate and that he had proved unable to keep Russia out of an Austro-Serbian war, the Chancellor switched tack and offered the

British ambassador in Berlin a pact just before midnight on 29 July, according to which Germany would guarantee the territorial integrity of France and Belgium in Europe – although not overseas – in return for British neutrality in a European war. After Grey had refused such an offer, Bethmann resorted to pressing Austria–Hungary to halt in Belgrade, partly because this plan to limit hostilities was supported by the British Foreign Secretary. With the advent of German mobilization and subsequent declarations of war against Russia on 1 August and France on the 3rd, the Reich government reverted to its tactic of safeguarding Belgian territory – and respecting Dutch neutrality, if Jagow's dispatch to Lichnowsky on 4 August were to be believed – in the coming war. After all such actions had failed, as Britain's ultimatum to Germany to stop its invasion of Belgium expired at midnight on 4 August, Bethmann and others sought to blame London for the outbreak of a European conflagration. 'Thus we find the Anglo-German conflict to be the ultimate origin of the war', wrote the former Chancellor in his memoirs. 'An action capable of cutting the knot could only have been achieved if the leaders of English political life could have made up their mind to break definitively with that principle of alliances that had stereotyped instead of sterilising the evil.'[94] As a result of its rapid growth, Germany was bound to seek its place in world politics, he went on. German statesmen needed to convince domestic public opinion that 'the great world conflicts in which Germany had become involved could be solved by peaceful negotiation and not by the sword. And the only way to this – I keep on coming back to it – was through an understanding with England.'[95] Since France was 'given up to its ideal of *revanche*, Russia to its historical mission in the Balkans and the Straits, Austria to its internal difficulties', Germany and Britain alone seemed to be 'free' enough gradually to guide the powers away from the spectre of militarist imperialism to the opposite pole of a peaceable and amicable cooperation', but British statesmen refused to accommodate the Reich, preferring 'the supremacy secured by British dreadnoughts and French friendship'.[96] Grey's talent and vision, commented Bethmann in February 1915, were 'limited'.[97]

From the contemporary record, however, it is at least questionable that Britain and British leaders figured so prominently in the Chancellor's calculations. 'England' was important to the Wilhelmstrasse less in its own right than as a means of restraining Russia, especially as it became apparent after 23 July that St Petersburg was contemplating armed intervention in defence of Serbia. Consequently, Bethmann and Jagow were not deflected from their support of an Austrian attack, despite receiving Lichnowsky's reports from 24 July onwards of meetings with Grey, in which the Foreign Secretary expressed the view that an Austro-Serbian war would probably escalate into a European conflict, obliging Britain to intervene.[98] By 27 July, the German ambassador in London wrote that Grey was out of humour for the first time, since he was convinced that 'the key to the situation is Berlin' and that, 'if Berlin seriously means peace, Austria can be restrained from pursuing a foolhardy policy'.[99] It could also be prevented from 'crushing' Serbia.[100] 'Should Austria's intention to use the present occasion to crush Serbia, as Sir E. Grey expressed it, become still more evident, England will, I am convinced, range herself on the side of France and Russia, in order to show that she does not mean to tolerate a moral or still more a military defeat of her group', he warned, later the same day. 'If war comes in these conditions we shall have England against us.'[101] Bethmann's immediate reply later that night indicates that he accepted Lichnowsky's summary of Grey's intentions.[102] All the same, he did nothing to prevent or delay Austria's declaration of war on Serbia the following day. In other words, ensuring Britain's neutrality was subordinate to the achievement of Austria–Hungary's war aims and Germany's diplomatic coup.

Bethmann's primary concern in the period after 28 July was neither the attainment of British neutrality nor the limitation of Austria's war aims, but rather the orchestration of a popular, or at least plausible, war of national 'defence'. Many of Bethmann's references to Russian strength and aggression in late July and early August probably derived from this endeavour. 'It is imperative that the responsibility for the eventual extension of the war among those nations not originally immediately concerned should, under all circumstances, fall on Russia', he warned Tschirschky on 28 July, half a day before he became preoccupied – following a report from Moltke – by Russian and French preparations for war.[103] At this stage, he was, on the contrary, more concerned about how to avoid British, French and Russian calls for mediation, not war, and retain his position as the defensive, injured party:

> According to the Austrian General Staff, an active military movement against Serbia will not be possible before 12 August. As a result, the [German] Imperial Government is placed in the extraordinarily difficult position of being exposed in the meantime to the mediation and conference proposals of the other Cabinets, and if it continues to maintain its

previous aloofness in the face of such proposals, it will incur the odium of having been responsible for a world war, even, finally, amongst the German people themselves. A successful war on three fronts cannot be commenced and carried on on any such basis.[104]

The only way out of this dilemma, which also offered a remote chance of avoiding a world war, was to accept mediation, with the primary intention of 'ruthlessly' putting Russia 'in the wrong'.[105] Britain had promised on 30 July to work to stop French and Russian preparations for war. 'If England's efforts succeed, while Vienna declines everything, Vienna will be giving documentary evidence that it absolutely wants a war, into which we shall be drawn, while Russia remains free of responsibility', Bethmann informed Tschirschky. 'That would place us, in the eyes of our own people, in an untenable situation.'[106] The Chancellor concluded by reiterating that he only urged such mediation proposals on Vienna because they included the occupation of Belgrade 'or other places' and 'guarantees for the future', preserving Austria–Hungary's 'status for her in every way'.[107] When Berchtold delayed and then refused, Bethmann and Jagow continued to pledge military backing.[108] News of Russia's general mobilization during the night of 30 July had already created the illusion of a defensive war. German attempts to restrict Austrian actions were immediately curtailed, suggesting – as has already been noted – that Bethmann was not primarily interested in averting war at this stage.[109] Berlin could have continued to put pressure on Vienna to specify and circumscribe its war aims in order to convince Russia to halt its moblization. Such an action, however, would have militated against the direction of Germany's policy of brinkmanship, which had been formulated during the decade or so before 1914 and which was reactivated after the assassination in Sarajevo on 28 June.

During the July crisis, Bethmann and the Foreign Office remained fully in control of policy-making and deliberately risked the outbreak of a European war. In his correspondence and, particularly, in his memoirs, the Chancellor gave the impression that he was fearful of Russia and overwhelmed by an 'avalanche' which 'could no longer be avoided'.[110] However, his correspondence with the German ambassador in Vienna, to whom he was most candid, shows that Bethmann was not forced into a conflict by circumstances beyond his control, but chose to go to war rather than risk a loss of prestige or a renunciation of Austria's new-found position of strength vis-à-vis Serbia. At the very least, the Chancellor had argued as early as

28 July that a temporary occupation of Belgrade and other parts of Serbia was required, on the model of Germany's occupation of France after 1871, in order to force Serbian compliance with Austrian demands and to guarantee future 'good behaviour'.[111] 'As soon as the Austrian demands should be complied with', and here he alluded to the full demands of Vienna's ultimatum of 23 July, 'evacuation would follow.'[112] Bethmann knew that such 'minimum' terms would probably not be acceptable to Russia, which had rejected the possibility of Serbia's full compliance with the original ultimatum, but the political gains from making the gesture would be considerable: 'Should the Russian government fail to recognise the justice of this point of view, it would have against it the public opinion of all Europe, which is now in the process of turning away from Austria. As a further result, the general diplomatic, and probably the military, situation would undergo material alteration in favour of Austria–Hungary and her allies.'[113] If an escalation of the war was necessary to achieve such minimum demands, 'cutting the vital cord of the Greater Serbia propaganda', the Chancellor and Foreign Office were ready to take responsibility for it, as is borne out by their repeated assurances that they would support the neighbouring monarchy, if a European or world war were to break out.[114] Bethmann did not want 'to be drawn wantonly into a world conflagration by Vienna', but he never threatened to withdraw his support for a war on behalf of Austria–Hungary.[115] It is probable that the Chancellor realized that Vienna's supposed territorial disinterestedness, which he had sought – but failed – to establish to the satisfaction of Russia and the Entente between 29 and 31 July, would prove illusory once an Austro-Serbian war had begun. Certainly, earlier German enquiries of the Ballhausplatz had suggested that Serbia would be divided between friendly neighbouring powers or partially annexed by Austria.[116] This goal of strengthening Austria–Hungary, the Reich's only dependable ally, in the critical area of the Balkans, and at the same time gaining a German diplomatic victory over the Entente, made the privately acknowledged risk of a European war seem worthwhile.

In July 1914, and especially after Austria's declaration of war on Serbia on 28 July, Bethmann and the Foreign Office demonstrated unambiguously that civilian leaders – like their military counterparts – were willing to countenance a conflagration. This does not mean that they actually worked to provoke war. Most of their efforts in the remaining days of peace were directed at localizing the conflict which they had helped to orchestrate. The main component of their strategy was to convince Britain to put pressure on Russia and France – in part, by maintaining its own neutrality – not to intervene in a war between Austria–Hungary and Serbia. 'It should be perfectly obvious to [Grey] that this balance of power would be utterly destroyed if we should desert Austria and she should be demolished by Russia', wrote Jagow on 18 July to Lichnowsky. 'Therefore, if he is honest and logical, he must stand by us in attempting to localize the conflict.'[117] By 29 July, after Grey had declared that Britain would back the Entente in a continental war, Bethmann recognized that his previous policy of localization – that is, using Britain to keep Russia out of a Balkan war, at the same time as refusing to convene a conference of the powers – had failed. He now tried to press Austria–Hungary directly, in contradistinction to his previous policy, to 'halt in Belgrade' and to accept mediation.[118] He seems to have acted partly out of fear of world war, after the failure of his policy of localization.

There were distinct limits, however, to Bethmann's desire for peace. The Chancellor's switch from a policy of localization, through which Austria was to be given a free hand in a conflict with Serbia, to an acceptance of direct mediation, whereby Berlin encouraged Vienna to define and limit its war aims, did not constitute a complete turn-around, motivated by horror at the prospect of a European or world war. Rather, it was accompanied by a series of conditions and reservations. The most obvious of the latter concerned the tardiness of the change in policy itself, which came more than two days after the German ambassador in London had complained on 27 July that the Reich's adherence to localization lacked credibility, since the stand-off between Austria and Russia could only be resolved by German 'pressure on Vienna'.[119] Despite such warnings, with tension between the powers mounting and military preparations increasing, Bethmann rejected a policy of direct and open mediation until 29 July. Even then, mediation was founded on important conditions, which the German government refused to compromise for the sake of peace. These conditions included ruling out the notion of a European conference or recourse to international law; refusing to reverse Austria's declaration of war against Serbia, even after it had become clear that this would lead to the intervention of Russia and, consequently, France and Britain; and defending Austria's right to bolster its own position and status as a Great Power by controlling Serbia and suppressing Greater Serbian nationalism. Such conditions were not primarily the result of premonitions of German weakness vis-à-vis a future Russian threat, which was usually referred to strategically at the time to convince sceptics like Lichnowsky, nor were they the inevitable corollary of the Austrian monarchy's fight for its 'existence', as Jagow subsequently maintained.[120] Rather, they were the consequence of the Reich's long-established policy of brinkmanship. Bethmann, Jagow, Zimmermann, Stumm and others genuinely did not believe that the Entente powers, given their perceived military inferiority, would be drawn into a European war. Nonetheless, if they were embroiled in such a conflict, German leaders were confident that the Reich and its allies would win.

Notes

1. For more on this topic, see A. Mombauer, *The Origins of the First World War: Controversies and Consensus* (London, 2002), pp. 21–77.

2. See, in particular, K.D. Erdmann (ed.), *Kurt Riezler. Tagebücher, Aufsätze, Dokumente* (Göttingen, 1972); E. v. Falkenhayn, extract from 'Tagebuch', in the Bundesarchiv, Berlin; W. Görlitz (ed.), *Der Kaiser ... Aufzeichnungen des Chefs des Marinekabinetts Admiral Georg Alexander von Müller über die Ära Wilhelm II.* (Göttingen, 1965); B. Sösemann (ed.), *Theodor Wolff, Tagebücher 1914–1919. Der Erste Weltkrieg und die Entstehung der Weimarer Republik in Tagebüchern, Leitartikeln und Briefen des Chefredakteurs am 'Berliner Tageblatt' und Mitbegründers der 'Deutschen Demokratischen Partei'*, 2 vols (Boppard am Rhein, 1984).

3. For a recent statement of the 'defensive' case, which also accepts the notion of 'risk', see K. Hildebrand, 'Saturiertheit und Prestige: Das Deutsche Reich als Staat im Staatensystem 1871–1918', *Geschichte in Wissenschaft und Unterricht*, 4 (1989), pp. 193–202; K. Hildebrand, 'Reich-Grossmacht-Nation: Betrachtungen zur Geschichte der deutschen Aussenpolitik 1871–1918', *Historische Zeitschrift*, 259 (1994), pp. 369–89. For a recent argument in favour of military influence, see A. Mombauer, 'A Reluctant Military Leader? Helmuth von Moltke and the July Crisis of 1914', *War in History*, 6 (1999), pp. 417–46, and for the case in favour of Wilhelm II's influence, J.C.G. Röhl, *The Kaiser and his Court* (London, 1995).

4. P. Scheidemann, *Memoirs of a Social Democrat* (London, 1929), pp. 191–2.

5. *Vossische Zeitung*, 29 June 1914, and *Frankfurter Zeitung*, 1 July 1914, cited in E.M. Carroll, *Germany and the Great Powers, 1860–1914: A Study in Public Opinion and Foreign Policy* (New York, 1938), p. 773.

6. *Magdeburgische Zeitung*, 2 July 1914, and *National Zeitung*, 7 July 1914, cited in Carroll, *Germany and the Great Powers*, pp. 773–4.

7. Harden, 'Falsche Mäuler', *Zukunft*, 18 July 1914, cited in Carroll, *Germany and the Great Powers*, p. 783.

8. *Berliner Neueste Nachrichten*, 17 July 1914, cited in Carroll, *Germany and the Great Powers*.

9. *Norddeutsche Allgemeine Zeitung*, 19 July 1914, cited in Carroll, *Germany and the Great Powers*.

10. Bethmann to T. Wolff, 5 February 1915, cited in K. Jarausch, 'The Illusion of Limited War: Chancellor Bethmann Hollweg's Calculated Risk, July 1914', *Central European History*, 2 (1969), p. 76.

11. This is the implication of various articles by Wolfgang Mommsen; for instance, 'The Causes and Objectives of German Imperialism before 1914' and 'Public Opinion and Foreign Policy in Germany, 1897-1914', in *Imperial Germany* (London, 1995), pp. 75-100, 189-204.

12. Bethmann to Wilhelm II, 20 July 1914, cited in Jarausch, 'The Illusion of Limited War', p. 62.

13. Delbrück, 23 July 1914, cited in C. Geinitz, *Kriegsfurcht und Kampfbereitschaft. Das Augusterlebnis in Freilburg* (Essen, 1998), pp. 51-2.

14. Bethmann voiced such worries, for instance, at a meeting of Prussian ministers and Reich secretaries of state on 18 July 1914; see F. Fischer, *War of Illusions* (London, 1975), p. 483.

15. Cited ibid.

16. Bethmann, 29 July 1914, cited ibid., p. 494.

17. G.A. v. Müller, diary entry, 1 August 1914, ibid., p. 505.

18. Ibid.

19. For a sustained, but ultimately unconvincing, attempt to prove this point, see R.R. McLean, *Royalty and Diplomacy in Europe, 1890-1914* (Cambridge, 2001).

20. Wilhelm II, 4 October 1912, cited in W.J. Mommsen, *Grossmachtstellung und Weltpolitik, 1870-1914: Die Aussenpolitik des Deutschen Reiches* (Frankfurt a. M., 1993), p. 244-5.

21. Wilhelm marginalia, 11 March 1914, *Grosse Politik*, p. 554.

22. Wilhelm II to W. v. Stumm, 15 January 1912, cited in J.C.G. Röhl, 'Admiral von Müller and the Approach of War, 1911-1914', *Historical Journal*, 12 (1969), p. 657.

23. Eulenburg-Hertefeld to K. Breysig, September 1919, in J.C.G. Röhl (ed.), *1914: Delusion or Design?* (London, 1973), p. 125.

24. Eulenburg to Breysig, 22 September 1919, ibid., pp. 131-2.

25. Szögyény-Marich to Berchtold, 5 July 1914, cited in S.R. Williamson and R. Van Wyk (eds), *July 1914: Soldiers, Statesmen and the Coming of the Great War* (Boston, 2003), p. 97.

26. Cited in I. Geiss (ed.), *July 1914: The Outbreak of the First World War* (London, 1967), pp. 76-77. Geiss unjustifiably contends that 'Wilhelm II had changed his mind' after lunch, issuing the so-called 'blank cheque' before consulting Bethmann (p. 70).

27. L. Albertini, *The Origins of the War of 1914* (Oxford, 1953) vol. 2, pp. 138–42, gives a much more balanced account of the available documents about the Hoyas mission than does Geiss.

28. Geiss, *July 1914*, pp. 222–3.

29. G.A. v. Müller, *Diary*, cited in A. Mombauer, *Helmuth von Moltke and the Origins of the First World War* (Cambridge, 2001), p. 220.

30. Ibid., p. 222, on Moltke's wife's recollection; see H. Afflerbach *Falkenhayn: Politisches Denken und Handeln in Kaiserreich*, 2nd edn (Munich, 1996), p. 167, on the Chief of Staff's failure. to give the order halting the operations of the 16th Division.

31. Cited in R.F. Hamilton and H.H. Herwig (eds), *The Origins of World War I* (Cambridge, 2003), pp. 182–3.

32. The best account of the incident is in Afflerbach, *Falkenhayn*, pp. 163–7. Falkenhayn seems to have been convinced that Grey was bluffing. He was therefore prepared to wait until this became apparent.

33. Mombauer, 'A Reluctant Military Leader?', p. 420–1.

34. Ibid., pp. 427–9.

35. Moltke to his wife, 22 July 1914, quoted ibid., pp. 428–9.

36. Cited ibid., p. 421. The term 'military take-over' is used by Mombauer, ibid., p. 433.

37. Falkenhayn diary, 29 July 1914, cited in Afflerbach, *Falkenhayn*, p. 157.

38. Moltke to Bethmann, 29 July 1914, cited in Afflerbach, *Falkenhayn*, pp. 282–4; Bethmann to F. v. Pourtalès, 29 July 1914, in Geiss, *July 1914*, p. 285.

39. Falkenhayn diary, 29 July 1914, cited in Afflerbach, *Falkenhayn*, p. 158–9.

40. Bethmann, 30 July 1914, cited in K. Jarausch, *The Enigmatic Chancellor: Bethmann Hollweg and the Hubris of Imperial Germany* (New Haven, 1973), p. 172.

41. Ibid., pp. 158–9.

42. Fischer, *War of Illusions*, p. 498.

43. Bülow, reported by Theodor Wolff in his diary on 12 August 1914, cited in Sösemann, *Theodor Wolff, Tagebücher*, vol. 1, p. 72. Wolff recorded Schoen's prediction on 10 August that the war would last four months, ibid., p. 71.

44. Cited in Fischer, *War of Illusions*, p. 468.

45. Wolff's diary, 29 October 1914, in Sösemann, *Theodor Wolff, Tagebücher*, vol. 1, p. 114.

46. Wolff's diary, 12 June 1915, in Sösemann, *Theodor Wolff, Tagebücher*, vol. 1, pp. 233–4.

47. Pourtalès to Jagow, 6 February 1913, *Grosse Politik*, vol. 34, pp. 330–1.

48. Bethmann to Berchtold, 10 February 1913, ibid., p. 347.

49. Sir E. Grey, cited in Fischer, *War of Illusions*, p. 473.

50. Ibid., p. 472.

51. Freiherr von Salza und Lichtenau to C. Vitzthum von Eckstädt, 2 July 1914, in Geiss, *July 1914*, pp. 67–8.

52. Note by section chief in the Austrian Foreign Ministry, cited in Fischer, *War of Illusions*, p. 476; A. v. Hoyos's conversation with A. Zimmermann, ibid., pp. 477–8.

53. Szögyény-Ladislaus to Berchtold, 6 July 1914, in Geiss, *July 1914*, p. 79.

54. Ibid.

55. On Tschirschky's role, see especially Albertini, *The Origins of the War*, vol. 2, pp. 131–40, 150–55, which includes Lichnowsky's recollection, after he had called at the Wilhelmstrasse on 5 July, 'that Tschirschky had been reprimanded because he reported that he had counselled moderation in Vienna towards Serbia'. L. Szögyény to L. v. Berchtold, 6 July 1914, cited in Geiss, *July 1914*, p. 79.

56. Plessen, diary, cited in Albertini, *The Origins of the War*, vol. 2, p. 142.

57. Wolff's diary, 31 January 1916, cited in Sösemann, *Theodor Wolff, Tagebücher*, vol. 1, p. 342.

58. Bethmann to Wilhelm II, 21 July 1914, in M. Montgelas and W. Schücking (eds), *Outbreak of the World War: German Documents Collected by Karl Kautsky* (New York, 1924), p. 150.

59. Hoyos, cited in Albertini, *The Origins of the War*, vol. 2, p. 145.

60. Wolff's diary, 9 February 1915, Sösemann, *Theodor Wolff, Tagebücher*, vol. 1, p. 156.

61. G. v. Jagow, *Ursachen und Ausbruch des Weltkrieges* (Berlin, 1919), p. 110.

62. Albertini, *The Origins of the War of 1914*.

63. Cited in Albertini, *The Origins of the War*, vol. 2, p. 269.

64. Ibid., p. 261.

65. Szögyény-Ladislaus to Berchtold, 12 July 1914, ibid., pp. 156–7.

66. The Chancellor, for example, referred to the ultimatum on 20 July, even in his correspondence with Wilhelm II. See Bethmann to Wilhelm II, 20 July 1914, in Montgelas and Schücking (eds.), *Outbreak of the World War*, p. 139.

67. Jagow to Tschirschky, 16 July 1914, in Albertini, *The Origins of the War*, vol. 2, p. 262.

68. Jagow to Szögyény-Ladislaus, 21 July 1914, in Albertini, *The Origins of the War*, vol. 2, pp. 262–3.

69. Wolff diary, 25 July 1914, in Sösemann, *Theodor Wolff, Tagebücher*, vol. 1, p. 64.

70. Jagow to Lichnowsky, 18 July 1914, Geiss, *July 1914*, p. 123.

71. Ibid.

72. Saxon Chargé d'Affaires to Saxon Minister of Foreign Affairs, 17 July 1914, cited in Albertini, *The Origins of the War*, vol. 2, p. 159. For the Bavarian and Badenese reports, ibid.

73. Ibid., p. 161.

74. Hoyos to Albertini, 21 November 1933, ibid., p. 147.

75. Wolff diary, 25 July 1914, Sösemann, *Theodor Wolff, Tagebücher*, vol. 1, p. 64.

76. Ibid.

77. Ibid., p. 65.

78. Bethmann, 27 July 1914, Geiss, *July 1914*, pp. 237-8.

79. Wolff diary, 11 December 1914, Sösemann, *Theodor Wolff, Tagebücher*, vol. 1, p. 135.

80. Albertini, *The Origins of the War*, vol. 2, p. 430.

81. L. v. Szögyény-Ladislaus to the Austrian Foreign Office, 25 July 1914, cited ibid., p. 453.

82. L. v. Szögyény-Ladislaus to the Austrian Foreign Office, 27 July 1914, ibid., p. 445. The reference to Serbia's reply as 'a basis for negotiations' and to the fact that Germany had already rejected the idea of conference was contained in a despatch from the German Foreign Office to Tschirschky on 27 July, ibid., p. 448.

83. Bethmann to Tschirschky, 28 July 1914, in Albertini, *The Origins of the War*, vol. 2, p. 478.

84. Bethmann to Tschirschky, 29 July 1914, Geiss, *July 1914*, pp. 291-2.

85. Ibid., p. 292.

86. Cited in Williamson and Van Wyk (eds), *July 1914*, p. 70.

87. N. Rich, *Great Power Diplomacy, 1814-1914* (New York, 1992), p. 452.

88. A. v. Tirpitz, *Erinnerungen* (Leipzig, 1919), pp. 239-41. Bethmann's reference to an upheaval (*Umwälzung*) comes from Riezler's diary entry for 7 July 1914, in Erdmann, *Kurt Riezler*, p. 183.

89. T.T.F.A. v. Bethmann Hollweg, *Betrachtungen zum Weltkrieg* (Berlin, 1919), vol. 1, p. 135.

90. Jagow to Lichnowsky, 18 July 1914, cited in Albertini, *The Origins of the War*, vol. 2, p. 158.

91. Bethmann to Tschirschky, 30 July 1914, in Geiss, *July 1914*, p. 293.

92. Jagow to various missions, 30 July 1914, ibid., p. 307.

93. Wolff diary, 5 April 1915, in Sösemann, *Theodor Wolff, Tagebücher*, vol. 1, p. 196.

94. T.T.F.A. v. Bethmann Hollweg, *Reflections on the World War* (London, 1920), pp. 166-7.

95. Ibid., p. 115.

96. Ibid.

97. Bethmann to Wolff, diary, 9 February 1915, in Sösemann, *Theodor Wolff, Tagebücher*, vol. 1, p. 156.

98. Lichnowsky to Jagow, 24 July 1914, in Geiss, *July 1914*, p. 183.

99. Cited in Albertini, *The Origins of the War*, vol. 2, p. 442.

100. Lichnowsky to the German Foreign Office, 27 July 1914, cited ibid.

101. Ibid.

102. Bethmann to Lichnowsky, 28 July 1914, in Geiss, *July 1914*, p. 243.

103. Bethmann to Tschirschky, 28 July 1914, in Geiss, *July 1914*, p. 259. For Bethmann's response to Russian and French war preparations, see ibid., pp. 284-5.

104. Ibid., p. 259.

105. Bethmann, cited in Jarausch, *The Enigmatic Chancellor*, p. 169.

106. Bethmann to Tschirschky, 30 July 1914, in Geiss, *July 1914*, p. 305.

107. Ibid. The conditions were first mentioned by Lichnowsky to Jagow, 29 July 1914, ibid., pp. 288-90.

108. See, for instance, Jagow to various missions, 30 July 1914, ibid., p. 307.

109. Fischer, *War of Illusions*, p. 498.

110. Bethmann Hollweg, *Reflections on the World War*, p. 161.

111. Bethmann to Tschirschky, 28 July 1914, in Geiss, *July 1914*, p. 260.

112. Ibid.

113. Ibid.

114. Ibid.; Jagow to various missions, 30 July 1914, ibid., 307; also, Bethmann to Tschirschky, 30 July 1914, ibid., p. 293.

115. Ibid.

116. For example, Jagow to Tschirschky, 17 July 1914, cited in Albertini, *The Origins of the War*, vol. 2, p. 476.

117. Jagow to Lichnowsky, 18 July 1914, in Geiss, *July 1914*, p. 124.

118. Bethmann to Tschirschky, 30 July 1914, ibid., p. 292.

119. Lichnowsky to Jagow, 27 July 1914, ibid., pp. 239-40.

120. For references to a Russian menace, see Lichnowsky to Jagow, 18 July 1914, ibid., p. 123. For a retrospective allusion to Germany's defence of Austria-Hungary's 'existence', see Jagow, *Ursachen und Ausbruch des Weltkrieges*.

10

Conclusion: Germany and the Question of Guilt

Since August 1914, the debate about the causes of the First World War has included the ascription of moral responsibility for the events leading to what contemporaries like the satirist Karl Kraus perceived to be 'the last days of humanity'.[1] The question of guilt was posed most starkly at the Versailles Peace Conference in 1919. The Allied powers' answer in Article 231 of the Treaty – 'that Germany and its allies are responsible for all losses and damages' – was rejected by the German government and most German political parties at the time, and has been debated by historians ever since.[2] The Allied Commission on the Responsibility of the Authors of the War and on Enforcements of Penalties, which reported to the conference, concluded that Germany and Austria–Hungary had consciously and successfully caused the outbreak of a catastrophic conflagration: '1. The war was premeditated by the Central Powers together with their allies, Turkey and Bulgaria, and was the result of acts deliberately committed in order to make it unavoidable. 2. Germany, in agreement with Austria–Hungary, deliberately worked to defeat all the many conciliatory proposals made by the Entente Powers and their repeated efforts to avoid war.'[3] By singling out Germany and referring to Austria–Hungary, Turkey and Bulgaria collectively, the peace-makers implied that the Reich had been primarily responsible for the outbreak of war.

Between the 1920s and 1960s, such allegations were widely and summarily dismissed, especially by German historians. Fritz Fischer's criticism of Gerhard Ritter and of post-war historiographical ortho-doxy in the Federal Republic re-established the idea that Germany had been largely responsible for the First World War, as part of a more general case about a German *Sonderweg* during the nineteenth and twentieth centuries. Expansionism in the 1930s under the Nazis, argued Fischerites, was closely linked to that of the Wilhelmine era.

The First World War and the question of guilt, Ritter declared, was 'particularly stirring for us Germans, because if it was caused solely or primarily by the excessive political ambition of our nation and our government, as our war-opponents claimed in 1914, and has recently been affirmed by some German historians, then our national historical consciousness darkens even further than has already been the case through the experiences of the Hitler times!'[4] Policies of *Vergangenheitsbewältigung* after 1968 and the *Historikerstreit* during the mid 1980s, together with the consequences of unification in the 1990s, have ensured that judgements of individuals' moral responsibility for the critical events of 1914 are still deeply felt.

Naturally, such controversy has clouded the investigation of causes, which requires a balanced evaluation of contradictory testimony, a clear view of the unintended consequences of actions and a realistic assessment of human agency within particular historical structures and situations. Partly by studying the policy-makers of other countries, and partly by concentrating on separate sets of causes, such as those relating to the arms race or imperialism, recent historians of the First World War have frequently sought to avoid an overall allocation of blame. Moreover, they have been able, in Mombauer's words, 'to examine German history more dispassionately than historians like Ritter and Fischer, for whom the First and Second World Wars had been part of their personal histories'.[5] Yet they have not removed the question of guilt – that is, an acceptance that certain contemporaries' decisions had horrific consequences for millions of soldiers and civilians. Rather, revisionist scholars' reassessments of the motives of protagonists, their freedom of action and the effects of their decisions have resulted in a substantial mitigation of Wilhelmine statesmen's moral responsibility for the outbreak of war in 1914. According to much recent historiography, German leaders' motives and actions were often defensive, produced by uncontrollable circumstances, leading to unexpected results, and matched by the motives and actions of their counterparts in other states.

This study has raised serious objections to the revisionist case. It has argued – against the thesis of Mommsen and Förster about an agitated and importunate nationalist public – that the largest parties and most popular newspapers had come to harbour reservations about 'offensive' wars, especially those waged against increasingly familiar and allegedly weaker Western European states such as France or, even, Britain. The growing public which such Catholic, left-liberal, socialist and, on occasion, National Liberal and moderate conservative deputies and journalists represented were, by and large, impressed by the scale of Germany's economic progress over the previous forty years and proud of the international position and military power of the new German nation-state. This sense of relative security did not rule out acerbic criticism of the *Kaiserreich*'s institutions and the government's policies, including the erratic conduct of foreign affairs and a comparative failure to gain allies, colonies, and spheres of interest. Noisy debates about 'world empires' and rapid armament, as well as 'war scares' and international crises, appear to have created anxieties amongst many Wilhelmine observers. Few on the left and in the centre, however, were so moved by such fears to contemplate war as a remedy. On the contrary, most seemed to assume – in conjunction with the Reich's industrialists and financiers – that a military conflict would bring about instability and potential disaster. This cautious and sceptical majority, despite occasionally being obscured by the violent posturing of the radical right, provided Bülow and Bethmann with a source of support for moderate foreign policies and the promise of opposition to bellicose ones. Both chancellors, in 1905 and 1911 respectively, acknowledged that they had stopped short of war, in part, because of 'public opinion'. On each occasion, a significant number of politicians and newspapers had made it plain that they could see no grounds for an offensive war against weaker opponents.

The army, which continued to underpin the Foreign Office's strategy of continental brinkmanship even in an era of *Weltpolitik*, constituted the most significant counterweight to the anti-war sentiments of majority public opinion. Both the supposedly conservative War Ministry and the more 'modern' Great General Staff under Schlieffen and Moltke the Younger consistently called for war 'sooner rather than later'. Contrary to the arguments advanced by Stevenson, Herrmann, Mombauer, Förster and Ferguson, however, the generals did not proffer such advice out of despair, fearing that German forces were in the process of being outnumbered in an armaments race which the Reich and its allies, because of demography, financial shortcomings or resistance to expansion within the War Ministry itself, had no prospect of winning. Rather, most military men were convinced not only that the Reich could defend itself, but also that it could successfully prosecute an offensive war of annihilation along the lines first suggested by Schlieffen in the 1890s. Encouraged by Germany's improving military position vis-à-vis its main enemies between the late 1890s and early 1910s, and believing that its military resources and domestic morale would allow it to complete a short offensive campaign against France in the West, the General Staff refused to consider alternative traditions of defensive war or limited offensives, which had been developed under Moltke the Elder during the 1870s and 1880s. Despite being troubled from time to time by Darwinian premonitions of Germany's future extinction, Moltke the Younger maintained Schlieffen's confident predictions of absolute or decisive victory by means of a *Vernichtungskrieg*. Certainly, the impression which he and other high-ranking military officers gave to civilian leaders was that the Reich could win a two-front war.

Bethmann Hollweg, Jagow, Zimmermann and Stumm, who retained control of policy-making until German mobilization on 31 July, managed to pursue their strategy of brinkmanship by negotiating a course between anti-war and pro-war groups. They were not forced into declaring war by the army, but chose to use army predictions of a German victory as the basis of their foreign policy, deploying the threat of a continental conflict in order to gain concessions from the Entente. Despite the fact – in Bülow's words – that 'Wilhelm II did not want war, if only because he did not trust his nerves not to give way under the strain of any really critical situation', the Chancellor and Secretaries of State at the Foreign Office worked on the assumption that they could overcome the monarch's last-minute reluctance to begin hostilities by offering their resignation, as Kiderlen did twice during the second Moroccan crisis, or by withholding diplomatic documents and relying on technical military objections, as they did during the July crisis.[6] The Wilhelmstrasse knew that it could count on right-wing support for war under almost any circumstances and on broader popular backing for repressive measures against 'traitorous' Social Democrats. Thus, noted Riezler on 27 July, 'all Social Democratic leaders are to be arrested on the first day of mobilisation'.[7] All the same, Bethmann had intervened to try to avert such a necessity and the SPD was being 'worked on from all sides' in order to quell resistance to the declaration of war.[8] More importantly for the government, the Centre Party and many liberals were known to have opposed 'aggressive' or 'offensive' wars in the past, in spite of their professed admiration of the army and loyalty to the nation. Such opposition threatened to undermine public morale and to endanger the voting of war credits during the critical early stage of a conflict. By casting Germany as the victim of Russian aggression in 1914, the Chancellor and Foreign Office played on a common fear of 'Slav' barbarity and on left-wing and liberal contempt for 'tsarist autocracy' in order to unite all German parties behind a 'defensive' war. Rather than being 'defensive' on its own account, as has been argued by Hillgruber, Hildebrand and Schöllgen, the Reich government had taken advantage of domestic and international circumstances to continue a policy of brinkmanship or risk, which had been formulated during the decade or so of supposed German ascendancy before 1914.

The 'offensive' foreign policy of the *Kaiserreich* was formulated and conducted, as Holger Herwig has recently pointed out, by 'a small cadre of decision-makers', which was mindful of the opinions of political parties, extra-parliamentary leagues, industrial lobbies, and a wider public, but which viewed them mainly as obstacles to the realization of its own will.[9] Why was this clique in the Foreign Office and the Reich Chancellery prepared to risk war? As a former Secretary of the Interior, rather than a professional diplomat, Bethmann Hollweg, as David Kaiser has indicated, was influenced by right-wing proponents of *Weltpolitik* and was sensitive to the disgruntled agitation of Conservatives and National Liberals, whom he saw as the 'natural' state-supporting parties.[10] Like Jagow, he was also aware, according to Riezler's diary, that Russia was becoming stronger and that the alliance system had come to favour the Entente. Yet even at such a late stage, as he justified his decision to back Austria unconditionally, the Chancellor still seemed to think during the crisis itself that there was a chance of altering the alignment of Great Powers, after the Russian Foreign Minister, Sergei Sazonov, had talked of giving up France, if Germany were to desert Austria–Hungary. 'He seemed to ponder those sorts of possibilities', Riezler wrote of a discussion with Bethmann on 23 July, possibly recorded years after the event. 'It would be better than an agreement with England to come to a lasting settlement with Russia', as long as the 'Serbian thing' passed off well and St Petersburg agreed to safeguard the existence of Austria–Hungary.[11] As Lichnowsky recalled in his 1915 memorandum, answering the charge of the 'influential people' at the Foreign Office, who repeatedly told him that 'Russia would be "ready" in 1916', the counter-argument was always apparent, even if did not suit civilian leaders' attempts to vindicate their 'blank cheque' to Vienna on 5 July: 'Who can prove that we would really have had to fight in 1916?'[12] Right-wing politicians and commentators thought they could prove that the Reich's position would continue to deteriorate, but Bethmann showed himself increasingly willing to criticize them, warning Heydebrand during the second Moroccan crisis that 'the strong man does not always have to strike with the sword' and chastising him for leading 'the Conservatives down demagogic paths'.[13] When they looked back in July 1914, the Chancellor and his colleagues at the Foreign Office were unlikely to have seen merely a catalogue of 'humiliations', listed by the Pan-Germans. Rather, they had continued to pursue imperial and economic interests such as the Baghdad railway and the future partition of Portugal's colonies, they had prevailed on behalf of Austria–Hungary with a show of force in the Bosnian annexation crisis in 1908-9, and they had successfully cooperated with Britain to prevent the Balkan wars from escalating into a European conflagration. This interpretation of events tempers Hildebrand's and Schöllgen's accounts of increasing 'isolation' and mounting pressure inside and outside government for a diplomatic triumph.

German leaders risked military conflict in July 1914 not out of weakness and despair, but from a long-established position of strength. War was an accepted instrument of policy, waged by the United States against Spain in 1898, Britain against the Boers between 1899 and 1902, Japan against Russia in 1904-5, and the Balkan states against Turkey in 1912-13. Threatened use of force – or brinkmanship – was even more common, especially on the part of the most powerful states. A recent study by Jost Dülffer, Martin Kröger and Rolf-Harald Wippich contains analyses of thirty-three international crises which were successfully defused between the Crimean and the First World War.[14] Yet the Reich government, as historians such as Richard Langhorne and L.L. Farrar have rightly pointed out, was more willing than any of its counterparts to contemplate war in the European 'centre' rather than on its 'periphery' in the Near East and overseas.[15] This willingness to initiate a continental war was only tenuously connected to the thwarted imperial ambitions, social Darwinism, defensive nationalism or domestic anxieties of Wilhelmine statesmen, since such feelings were usually mixed with optimism about the Reich's recent economic and demographic growth, its military power and its chances of acquiring further colonies or spheres of interest. Furthermore, it is difficult to distinguish the impact of these sentiments from similar concerns about decadence, imperial decline and national degeneration in other countries. More significant was the combination of a persisting romanticization of military conflict, which was common to most European governments with the exception of Radicals within the Asquith cabinet, and the legitimization of war in German national mythology, as a corollary of the unificatory campaigns of the 1860s. As Bülow, who had served as a volunteer in the Franco-German war, remarked before the outbreak of war in 1914, Bismarck seemed to have 'realised that in Germany the will-power of the nation would not be strengthened, nor national passions roused by friction between the government and the people, but by the clash of German pride and sense of honour with the resistance and demands of foreign nations'.[16] Above all, though, leaders such as Bülow and Bethmann risked a continental war, with the danger of large-scale losses that this entailed, because they believed that Germany was dominant on the European mainland and that this dominance constituted its principal source of leverage to gain diplomatic and territorial concessions. Arguably, their confidence in the Reich's ascendancy was so deeply rooted that they were surprised when Russia and the Entente failed to back down in July 1914, even though they had long been conscious of the potential dangers of an Austrian declaration of war against Serbia.

The readiness of German leaders to use the threat of a European war distinguished them from those in other countries. Austrian statesmen, of course, made the initial declaration of war against Serbia on 28 July, conscious that the conflict could escalate into a continental or world conflagration. Yet, according to the bulk of their correspondence, they were concerned primarily with the eventuality of a third Balkan war, leaving their German counterparts to take care of the 'European' consequences of that conflict. This was the reason that Hoyos's retrospective claim that he had been assured by the Wilhelmstrasse that Vienna could concentrate its army in South Eastern Europe and that Berlin would 'take on France and Russia at the same time' carried such weight.[17] Notwithstanding the case put forward by Günther Kronenbitter, it can still be argued that Austria–Hungary would not have acted without German support, as Tisza spelled out to Tschirschky on 14 July: 'the unconditional manner in which Germany has ranged herself at the side of the monarchy had decidedly been of great influence on the firm attitude of the Emperor'.[18] Such evidence is corroborated by Conrad's discussion with Franz Josef on 5 July:

> I expressed to His Majesty my belief in the unavoidability of war with Serbia.

His Majesty:	'Yes, that is entirely correct, but do we want a war, if everyone is against us, especially Russia?'
I:	'Don't we have our flank covered by Germany?'

His Majesty glanced at me questioningly and said: 'Are you sure about Germany?' He knew that at Konopischt, the heir apparent, Franz Ferdinand, had sought to get the German Kaiser to promise unconditional support for the future. The German Kaiser had evaded the question and left the answer uncertain.

I:	'Your Majesty, we must, however, know where we stand.'
His Majesty:	'Last night a note was sent to Germany in order to get an answer.'
I:	'If the answer says that Germany stands on our side, could we go to war against Serbia?'
His Majesty:	'Then yes. *(After a short pause His Majesty continued):* If Germany does not give the answer, then what?'
I:	'Then we stand, to be sure, alone. We must have the answer soon, for the greatest decision depends on it.'[19]

Germany not only issued the 'blank cheque' on the same day, but also pushed Vienna to act decisively and swiftly against Serbia during mid-July, and overcame Berchtold's and Conrad's reservations about an immediate declaration of war on 28 July. In other words, Berlin had prompted the Ballhausplatz to pursue a policy of brinkmanship similar to its own.

The governments of other states, although they did little to defuse tensions, acted in defence of allies which had been attacked. Thus, despite the Serbian government's suspected complicity in the assassination of Franz Ferdinand, few - if any - contemporaries concluded that such involvement constituted a *de facto* commencement of hostilities justifying Austria–Hungary's declaration of war. Indeed, one of the main reasons for issuing an ultimatum was to give Vienna more defensible grounds for an armed intervention, once the note had been rejected by Belgrade. However, the ultimatum was so harsh, contravening accepted principles of national sovereignty, that even supporters of the German government such as Bülow and Eulenburg saw Serbia as the injured party. 'I was for so many years ambassador in Vienna, in close contact with the statesmen there, that I can assert with confidence that in all the crown lands of Austria *there is not a single statesman* who could have written a note with that content, form and manner of expression', wrote the latter in 1919. '[T]hey are one and all too soft - quite apart from the fact that there would have been immense difficulties in gaining the aged Emperor Franz Josef's assent, had he not already been convinced of the necessity of war after firm agreements with Kaiser Wilhelm and the murdered Archduke Franz Ferdinand. The note was Prussian to the marrow.'[20] What was more, the courtier went on in the same correspondence, German statesmen must have realized that St Petersburg would be drawn into defending Serbia, if Austria attacked:

> The Serbian question, with the Great Pan-Slav movement behind it, finally amounts to nothing other than a raw, *direct* area of friction *with Russia* – and the danger of a world war, *as soon as* Austria *took military action* against Serbia – (i.e. against Russia!) – would grow beyond all bounds . . . Serbia is Russia. If Austria marches against Serbia, and *if Berlin does not prevent* Austria's *belligerent action*, then the great breaking wave of world war rolls irresistibly towards us. I repeat: Berlin *must* know that, otherwise *idiots* live in the Wilhelmstrasse. Kaiser Wilhelm *must* know that'[21]

In fact, the relationship between Belgrade and St Petersburg was not as close as Eulenburg thought, for there is no evidence that Russian statesmen either knew of the Sarajevo plot or encouraged Serbia to resist Austria–Hungary's demands.[22] Sazonov's backing of Serbia, especially after Belgrade's reply to the Austrian note on 25 July, his agreement to partial mobilization, which spurred on the German General Staff to advise greater haste, and his refusal to back down, even after Germany had signalled its intention to join Austria–Hungary in the case of Russian intervention, all served to worsen the tension during the July crisis. The Russian Foreign Minister's decisions, though, were largely reactive, since German leaders had effectively sanctioned a war against Serbia before 28 July and had decided to mobilize against Russia by 29 July, irrespective of St Petersburg's future actions.[23] Bethmann, Jagow, Zimmermann, Stumm and other diplomats were therefore heavily implicated in acts of aggression, to which Sasonov – however misguided some of his decisions – was responding.

Similar pleas could be entered on behalf of France and Britain, in spite of Niall Ferguson's ingenious but implausible argument that British planners had 'set the course for a military confrontation' at the Committee of Imperial Defence meeting on 23 August 1911, when it was decided that the United Kingdom would join France in a war with Germany.[24] Britain had not, after all, pledged its support in the event of an 'offensive' or 'aggressive' war. However, such a rebuttal of the case about British 'aggression' does not answer the broader charge brought by Paul Schroeder and David Calleo in the 1970s that the Entente should have made greater efforts to accommodate a recently unified and expanding German nation-state.[25] In particular, Britain, which had more freedom of manoeuvre than the other powers, actively opposed German *Weltpolitik* and enforced a restrictive European balance of power, purportedly pushing Wilhelmine statesmen to consider a continental war as the only way out of a diplomatic *impasse*. By contrast, this study has cast doubt on the idea that pre-war leaders in Germany felt trapped by the contradictory logic of European and world politics. Instead, a policy of brinkmanship was formulated – and attempted – during a period of German ascendancy between the turn of the century and the eve of the war, when reports from ambassadors, counsellors, generals and military attachés were, on the whole, optimistic. By 1914, although they were worried about the re-emergence of Russia and were troubled by diplomatic 'defeats' over Algeciras and Agadir, German ministers still had little reason to despair: the *Kaiserreich* had acquired a significant number of colonies, which Bethmann and his advisors hoped to supplement with further acquisitions or spheres of interest in *Mittelafrika*, China, South America and the Near East; its fleet, having successfully traversed the 'danger zone', posed a credible threat to that of Britain, according to the terms of Tirpitz's theory of deterrence; its population and economy continued to grow; and its army remained dominant in Europe, or so it was believed. Against this background, in which it had become almost routine for German statesmen – in 1905, 1908, 1911 and 1914 – to risk war, it is unlikely that concessions by the Entente would have led to a rapid alteration of policy, which would have been necessary to avert conflict.

The threat of a continental war had become an instrument of policy in the *Kaiserreich* in the decade or so before 1914, restricted more by domestic criticism than by fear of defeat. Bethmann's premonition of 'a revolution of all that exists', despite appearing portentous after the First World War, was far less representative, even of his own actions, than Bülow's admission that warfare was still the cornerstone of politics:

> I can only give the necessary emphasis to the policy which I have to pursue as responsible director of the Reich's affairs, if I am fully convinced that we are ready at any time, with weapons in our hands, to defend our well-earned rights and protect the honour of the German name.[26]

Conclusion

In 1914, as in the mid-nineteenth century, a European war remained an acceptable risk to those policy-makers who were confident of success.

Notes

1. This was the title of Kraus's 792-page reportage-drama and critique of the First World War, published in Vienna and Leipzig in 1922.
2. K. Dederke, *Reich und Republik. Deutschland 1917–1933* (Stuttgart, 1969), p. 40.
3. Cited in A. Mombauer, *The Origins of the First World War: Controversies and Consensus* (London, 2002), p. 41.
4. Gerhard Ritter's publication for the Bundeszentrale für politische Bildung, *Der erste Weltkrieg* (Bonn, 1964), cited ibid., p. 138.
5. Mombauer, *The Origins of the First World War*, p. 175.
6. B. v. Bülow, *Memoirs* (London, 1931), vol. 3, p. 149.
7. K.D. Erdmann (ed.), *Kurt Riezler. Tagebücher, Aufsätze, Dokumente* (Göttingen, 1972), p. 193.
8. Ibid.
9. R.F. Hamilton and H.H. Herwig (eds), *The Origins of World War I* (Cambridge, 2003), p. 156.
10. D. Kaiser, 'Germany and the Origins of the First World War', *Journal of Modern History*, 55 (1983), especially pp. 462–74.
11. Erdmann, *Kurt Riezler*, p. 189.
12. Lichnowsky, memorandum, January 1915, cited in J.C.G. Röhl (ed.), *1914: Delusion or Design?* (London, 1973), p. 104.
13. Cited in K. Jarausch, *The Enigmatic Chancellor: Bethmann Hollweg and the Hubris of Imperial Germany* (New Haven, 1973), p. 125.
14. J. Dülffer, M. Kröger and R.-H. Wippich (eds), *Vermiedene Kriege. Deeskalation von Konflikten der Grossmächte zwischen Krimkrieg und Erstem Weltkrieg 1856–1914* (Munich, 1997).
15. R. Langhorne, *The Collapse of the Concert of Europe: International Politics, 1890–1914* (London, 1981); L. L. Farrar, *Arrogance and Anxiety: The Ambivalence of German Power, 1848–1914* (Iowa City, 1981).
16. B. v. Bülow, *Imperial Germany*, 6th edn (London, 1914) pp. 7–8.
17. Hoyos to L. Albertini, 21 November 1933, in L. Albertini, *The Origins of the War of 1914* (Oxford, 1952–57), vol. 2, p. 147.
18. Cited ibid., p. 176. G. Kronenbitter, *'Krieg im Frieden': Die Führung der K.u.K. Armee und die Grossmachtpolitik Österreich-Ugarns 1906–1914* (Munich, 2003).

19. F. Conrad v. Hötzendorf, Notes on His Audience with Emperor Franz Joseph, 5 July 1914, cited in S.R. Williamson and R. Van Wyk (eds), *July 1914: Soldiers, Statesmen and the Coming of the Great War* (Boston, 2003), p. 59.

20. Eulenburg to K. Breysig, 9 September 1919, in Röhl (ed.), *1914: Delusion or Design?*, p. 116.

21. Eulenburg to Breysig, 22 September 1919, ibid., p. 134.

22. S.R. Williamson, 'The Origins of World War I', *Journal of Interdisciplinary History*, 18 (1988), pp. 795–818; D. Lieven, *Russia and the Origins of the First World War* (London, 1983).

23. A. Mombauer, *Helmuth von Moltke and the Origins of the First World War* (Cambridge, 2001), pp. 199–201; Mombauer, *The Origins of the First World War*, p. 204.

24. N. Ferguson, *The Pity of War* (London, 1998), p. 65.

25. P.W. Schroeder, 'World War I as Galloping Gertie: A Reply to Joachim Remak', in H.W. Koch (ed.), *The Origins of the First World War Great Power Rivalry and German War Aims* (London, 1972), pp. 101–27. See also D. Calleo, *The German Problem Reconsidered: Germany and the World Order, 1870 to the Present* (Cambridge, 1978), pp. 9–84.

26. Bethmann's statement was recorded by Riezler in his diary entry for 7 July 1914, in Erdmann, *Kurt Riezler*, p. 183. Bülow is cited in P. Winzen, 'Der Krieg in Bülows Kalkül', in J. Dülffer and K. Holl (eds), *Bereit zum Krieg: Kriegsmentalität im Wilhelminischen Deutschland, 1890–1914* (Göttingen, 1986), p. 167.

Select Bibliography

Afflerbach, H., *Falkenhayn: Politisches Denken und Handeln im Kaiserreich*, 2nd edn (Munich, 1994)

——, *Der Dreibund. Europäische Grossmacht- und Allianzpolitik vor dem Ersten Weltkrieg* (Vienna, 2002)

Albertini, L., *The Origins of the War of 1914*, 3 vols (Oxford, 1952–57)

Alf, W., (ed.), *Deutschlands Sonderung von Europa, 1862–1945* (Frankfurt a. M., 1984)

Allain, J.-C., *Agadir 1911: Une Crise impérialiste en Europe pour la conquête du Maroc* (Paris, 1976)

Altrichter, H., *Konstitutionalismus und Imperialismus. Der Reichstag und die deutsch-russischen Beziehungen 1890–1914* (Frankfurt a. M., 1977)

Anderson, E.N., *The First Moroccan Crisis, 1904–1906* (Hamden, 1966)

Anderson, P.R., *The Background of Anti-English Feeling in Germany, 1890–1902* (Washington, 1939)

Angelow, J., 'Vom "Bündnis" zum "Block". Struktur, Forschungsstand und Problemlage einer Geschichte des Zweibundes 1879–1914', *Militärgeschichtliche Mitteilungen*, 54 (1995)

——, *Kalkül und Prestige. Der Zweibund am Vorabend des Ersten Weltkrieges* (Cologne, 2000)

Aretin, K.O. von and W. Conze (eds), *Deutschland und Russland im Zeitalter des Kapitalismus 1861–1914* (Wiesbaden, 1977)

Baglione, F.M., 'Mysticism and Domination: Theories of Self-Preservation, Expansion and Racial Superiority in German Imperialist Ideology' (Diss., Cambridge, Mass., 1981)

Bald, D., *Der deutsche Generalstab 1859–1939. Reform und Restauration in Ausbildung und Bildung* (Munich, 1977)

Barclay, D.E. and E. Glaser-Schmidt (eds), *Transatlantic Images and Perceptions: Germany and America since 1776* (Cambridge, 1997)

Bariéty, J. and R. Poidevin, *Les Relations franco-allemandes, 1815–1975* (Paris, 1977)

Barlow, I.C., *The Agadir Crisis* (Durham, NC, 1940)

Barraclough, G., 'Europa, Amerika und Russland in der Vorstellung und Denken des 19. Jahrhunderts', *Historische Zeitschrift, 203* (1966)

——, *From Agadir to Armageddon: Anatomy of a Crisis* (London, 1982)

Becker, F., *Bilder vom Krieg und Nation. Die Einigungskriege in der bürgerlichen Öffentlichkeit Deutschlands 1864–1913* (Munich, 2001)

Becker, J. et al. (eds), *Lange und kurze Wege in den Ersten Weltkrieg. Vier Beiträge zur Kriegsursachenforschung* (Munich, 1996)

Becker, P.E., *Sozialdarwinismus, Rassismus, Antisemitismus und Völkischer Gedanke. Wege ins Dritte Reich*, 2 vols. (Stuttgart, 1990)

Bendick, R., *Kriegserwartung und Kriegserfahrung. Der Erste Weltkrieg in deutschen und französischen Schulgeschichtsbüchern, 1900–1945* (Pfaffenweiler, 1999)

Benz, W. and H. Graml (eds), *Aspekte deutscher Aussenpolitik im 20. Jahrhundert* (Stuttgart, 1976)

Berghahn, V.R., *Der Tirpitz-Plan. Genesis und Verfall einer innenpolitischen Krisenstrategie unter Wilhelm II* (Düsseldorf, 1971)

——, *Germany and the Approach of War in 1914* (London, 1973)

——, *Rüstung und Machtpolitik. Zur Anatomie des 'Kalten Krieges' vor 1914* (Düsseldorf, 1973)

——, (ed.), *Militarismus* (Gütersloh, 1975)

——, *Militarism: The History of an International Debate 1861–1979* (Leamington Spa, 1981)

——, *Sarajewo, 28. Juni 1914. Der Untergang des alten Europa* (Munich, 1999)

Berghahn, V.R. and W. Deist (eds), *Rüstung im Zeichen der wilhelminischen Weltpolitik* (Düsseldorf, 1988)

Boetticher, F.V., *Schlieffen* (Göttingen, 1973)

Brechtefeld, J., *Mitteleuropa and German Politics, 1848 to the Present* (New York, 1996)

Brose, E.D., *The Kaiser's Army: The Politics of Military Technology during the Machine Age, 1870–1918* (Oxford, 2001)

Bruch, R. vom, *Weltpolitik als Kulturmission. Auswärtige Kulturpolitik und Bildungsbürgertum in Deutschland am Vorabend des Ersten Weltkrieges* (Paderborn, 1982)

Select Bibliography

Bucholz, A., *Hans Delbrück and the German Military Establishment: War Images in Conflict* (Iowa City, 1985)

——, *Moltke, Schlieffen and Prussian War Planning* (Oxford, 1991)

Burchardt, L., *Friedenswirtschaft und Kriegsvorsorge: Deutschlands wirtschaftliche Rüstungsbestrebungen vor 1914* (Boppard, 1968)

Burgelin, H., 'Le mythe de l'ennemi héréditaire dans les relations franco-allemandes', in *Documents: Revues des questions allemandes* (Paris, 1979)

Calleo, D., *The German Problem Reconsidered: Germany and the World Order, 1870 to the Present* (Cambridge, 1978)

Canis, K., *Von Bismarck zur Weltpolitik: Deutsche Aussenpolitik 1890 bis 1902* (Berlin, 1997)

Carroll, E.M., *Germany and the Great Powers, 1860–1914: A Study in Public Opinion and Foreign Policy* (New York, 1938)

Cecil, L., *The German Diplomatic Service, 1871–1914* (Princeton, 1976)

——, *Wilhelm II*, 2 vols. (Chapel Hill, 1996)

Chickering, R., *Imperial Germany and a World without War: The Peace Movement and German Society, 1892–1914* (Princeton, 1975)

——, 'Problems of a German Peace Movement, 1890–1914', in S. Wank (ed.), *Doves and Diplomats* (London, 1978)

——, 'Der "deutsche Wehrverein" und die Reform der deutschen Armee, 1912–1914', *Militärgeschichtliche Mitteilungen*, 15 (1979)

——, 'Patriotic Societies and German Foreign Policy', *International History Review*, 1 (1979)

——, *'We Men Who Feel Most German': A Cultural Study of the Pan-German League, 1886–1914* (London, 1984)

Christadler, M.-L., *Kriegserziehung im Jugendbuch. Literarische Mobilmachung in Deutschland und Frankreich vor 1914* (Frankfurt a. M., 1979)

Clark, C., *Kaiser Wilhelm II* (London, 2000)

Clarke, I. F., *Voices Prophesying War, 1763–1984* (Oxford, 1966)

Clemente, S.E., *For King and Kaiser! The Making of the Prussian Army Officer, 1860–1914* (New York, 1992)

Coetzee, M.S., *The German Army League: Popular Nationalism in Wilhelmine Germany* (Oxford, 1990)

Cole, T.F., 'German Decision-Making on the Eve of the First World War: The Records of the Swiss Embassy in Berlin', in J.C.G. Röhl (ed.), *Der Ort Kaiser Wilhelm II in der deutschen Geschichte* (Munich, 1991)

Craig, G.A., *The Politics of the Prussian Army, 1640–1945* (Oxford, 1955)

—, *From Bismarck to Hitler: Aspects of German Statecraft* (Baltimore, 1958)

Crampton, R.J., *The Hollow Détente: Anglo-German Relations in the Balkans, 1911–1914* (London, 1979)

Dann, O., *Nation und Nationalismus in Deutschland, 1770–1990*, 3rd revised edn (Munich, 1996)

Darby, G., *Origins of the First World War* (London, 1998)

Dehio, L., *Deutschland und die Weltpolitik im 20. Jahrhundert* (Frankfurt a. M., 1961)

Deist, W., 'Die Armee in Staat und Gesellschaft 1890–1914', in M. Stürmer (ed.), *Das kaiserliche Deutschland. Politik und Gesellschaft, 1870–1918* (Düsseldorf, 1970)

—, 'Armee und Arbeiterschaft 1905–1918', *Francia*, 2 (1974)

—, *Flottenpolitik und Flottenpropaganda. Das Nachrichtenbüro des Reichsmarineamtes, 1897–1914* (Stuttgart, 1976)

—, 'Zur Geschichte des preussischen Offizierkorps 1888–1918', in H.H. Hoffmann (ed.), *Das deutsche Offizierkorps 1860–1960* (Boppard, 1980)

—, *The German Military in the Age of Total War* (Leamington Spa, 1985)

—, 'Die Reichswehr und der Krieg der Zukunft', *Militärgeschichtliche Mitteilungen*, 1 (1989)

Demeter, K., *The German Officer Corps in Society and State, 1640–1945* (London, 1965)

Denham, S.D., *Visions of War: Ideologies and Images of War in German Literature before and after the Great War* (Berne, 1992)

Diner, D., *America in the Eyes of the Germans* (Princeton, 1996)

Doderer, H., 'Die vormilitärische Erziehung der deutschen Jugend in der Kaiserzeit', *Geschichte in Wissenschaft und Unterricht*, 49 (1998)

Düding, D. (ed.), *Öffentliche Festkultur. Politische Feste in Deutschland von der Aufklärung bis zum Ersten Weltkrieg* (Reinbek, 1988)

Dukes, J. R., 'Militarism and Arms Policy Revisited: The Origins of the German Army Law of 1913', in J.R. Dukes and J.J. Remak (eds), *Another Germany: A Reconsideration of the Imperial Era* (Boulder, 1988)

Dülffer, J., *Regeln gegen den Krieg? Die Haager Friedenskonferenzen von 1899 und 1907 in der internationalen Politik* (Berlin, 1981)

——, 'Vom europäischen Mächtesystem zum Weltstaatensystem um die Jahrhundertwende', *Historische Mitteilungen der Ranke-Gesellschaft*, 3 (1990)

——, (ed.), *Parlamentarische und öffentliche Kontrolle von Rüstung in Deutschland, 1700–1970. Beiträge zur historischen Friedensforschung* (Düsseldorf, 1992)

——, 'Deutsch-russische Beziehungen 1870–1914', in I. Mieck and P. Guillen (eds), *Deutschland – Frankreich – Russland: Begegnungen und Konfrontationen* (Munich, 2000)

——, *Im Zeichen der Gewalt. Frieden und Krieg im 19. und 20. Jahrhundert* (Cologne, 2003)

Dülffer, J. and K. Holl (eds), *Bereit zum Krieg: Kriegsmentalität im wilhelminischen Deutschland, 1890–1914* (Göttingen, 1986)

Dülffer, J., M. Kröger and R.-H. Wippich (eds), *Vermiedene Kriege. Deeskalation von Konflikten der Grossmächte zwischen Krimkrieg und Erstem Weltkrieg 1856–1914* (Munich, 1997)

Echevarria II, A.J., 'On the Brink of the Abyss: The Warrior Identity and German Military Thought before the Great War', *War and Society*, 13 (1995)

——, 'A Crisis in Warfighting: German Tactical Discussions in the Late Nineteenth Century', *Militärgeschichtlich Mitteilungen*, 55 (1996)

——, 'General Staff Historian Hugo Freiherr von Freytag-Loringhoven and the Dialectics of German Military Thought', *Journal of Modern History*, 60 (1996)

——, *After Clausewitz: German Military Thinkers before the Great War* (Lawrence, Ks, 2000)

Eibicht, R.J., *Schlieffen. Strategie und Politik* (Lünen, 1991)

Eley, G. 'Defining Social Imperialism: Use and Abuse of an Idea', *Social History*, 3 (1976)

——, 'Die Kehrites und das Kaiserreich', *Geschichte und Gesellschaft*, 4 (1978)

——, *Reshaping the German Right: Radical Nationalism and Political Change after Bismarck* (New Haven, 1979)

——, *From Unification to Nazism: Reinterpreting the German Past* (London, 1986)

Elsner, T. von, *Kaisertage. Die Hamburger und das wilhelminische Deutschland im Spiegel öffentlicher Festkultur* (Frankfurt a. M., 1991)

Engel, J., 'Die Wandlung der Bedeutung des Krieges im 19. und 20. Jahrhundert', *Geschichte in Wissenschaft und Unterricht*, 19 (1968)

Epkenhans, M., *Die wilhelminische Flottenrüstung 1908–1914. Weltmachtstreben, industrieller Fortschritt, soziale Integration* (Munich, 1991)

Epstein, F.T., 'Der Komplex "Die russische Gefahr" und sein Einfluss auf die deutsch-russischen Beziehungen im 19. Jahrhundert', in I. Geiss and B.J. Wendt (eds), *Deutschland in der Weltpolitik des 19. und 20. Jahrhunderts* (Düsseldorf, 1974)

Erdmann, K.D., 'Zur Beurteilung Bethmann Hollwegs', *Geschichte in Wissenschaft und Unterricht*, 15 (1964)

—, *Der Erste Weltkrieg* (Munich, 1980)

Evans, R.J.W. and H. Pogge von Strandmann (eds), *The Coming of the First World War* (Oxford, 1988)

Evera, S. Van, 'The Cult of the Offensive and the Origins of the First World War', in S.E. Miller et al (eds), Military Strategy and the Origins of the First World War (Princeton, 1991)

Farrar, L.L., *Arrogance and Anxiety: The Ambivalence of German Power, 1848–1914* (Iowa City, 1981)

—, *The Short War Illusion: German Policy, Strategy and Domestic Affairs, August–December 1914* (Oxford, 1973)

Ferguson, N., 'Germany and the Origins of the First World War: New Perspectives', *Historical Journal*, 35 (1992)

—, 'Public Finance and National Security: The Domestic Origins of the First World War Revisited', *Past and Present*, 142 (1994)

—, *The Pity of War* (London, 1998)

Fesser, R., *Reichskanzler Bernhard Fürst von Bülow. Eine Biographie* (Berlin, 1991)

—, *Der Traum vom Platz an der Sonne. Deutsche 'Weltpolitik' 1897–1914* (Bremen, 1996)

Fischer, F., *Krieg der Illusionen. Die deutsche Politik, 1911–1914* (Düsseldorf, 1969)

—, 'Das Bild Frankreichs in Deutschland in den Jahren vor dem Ersten Weltkrieg', *Revue d'Allemagne*, 4 (1972)

—, *World Power or Decline* (New York, 1974)

—, *Juli 1914: Wir sind nicht hineingeschlittert. Das Staatsgeheimnis um die Riezler Tagebücher* (Reinbek, 1983)

—, *Griff nach der Weltmacht. Die Kriegszielpolitik des kaiserlichen Deutschlands, 1914–1918* (Düsseldorf, 1961)

—, 'Kaiser Wilhelm und die Gestaltung der deutschen Politik von 1914', in J.C.G. Röhl (ed.), *Der Ort Kaiser Wilhelm II in der deutschen Geschichte* (Munich, 1991)

Fischer, J.-U., *Admiral des Kaisers. Georg Alexander von Müller als Chef des Marinekabinetts Wilhelms II* (Frankfurt, 1992)

Fletcher, R., *Revisionism and Empire: Socialist Imperialism in Germany, 1897–1914* (London, 1984)

Foley, R.T., 'Schlieffen's Last *Kriegsspiel*', *War Studies Journal*, 3 (1998) and 4 (1999)

Foerster, R.G., *Die Wehrpflicht. Entstehung, Form und politisch-militärische Wirkung* (Munich, 1994)

—— (ed.), *Generalfeldmarschall von Moltke. Bedeutung und Wirkung* (Munich, 1991)

Forsbach, R., *Alfred von Kiderlen-Wächter 1852–1912. Ein Diplomatenleben im Kaiserreich*, 2 vols. (Göttingen, 1997)

Förster, S., *Der doppelte Militarismus: Die deutsche Heeresrüstungspolitik zwischen Status-quo-Sicherung und Aggression, 1890–1913* (Stuttgart, 1985)

——, 'Facing "People's War": Moltke the Elder and Germany's Military Options after 1871', *Journal of Strategic Studies*, 10 (1987)

——, 'Der deutsche Generalstab und die Illusion des kurzen Krieges, 1871–1914. Metakritik eines Mythos', *Militärgeschichtliche Mitteilungen*, 54 (1995)

——, 'The Armed Forces and Military Planning', in R. Chickering (ed.), *Imperial Germany: A Historiographical Companion* (Westport, 1996)

——, 'Dreams and Nightmares: German Military Leadership and the Images of Future Warfare, 1871–1914', in M.F. Boemeke, R. Chickering and S. Förster (eds), *Anticipating Total War: The German and American Experiences, 1871–1914* (Cambridge, 1999)

——, 'Im Reich des Absurden. Die Ursachen des Ersten Weltkrieges', in B. Wegner (ed.), *Wie Kriege entstehen. Zum historischen Hintergrund von Staatenkonflikten* (Paderborn, 2000)

Franke, H., *Der politisch-militärische Zukunftsroman in Deutschland 1904–1914. Ein populäres Genre in seinem literarischen Umfeld* (Frankfurt, 1985)

Fricke, D., 'Die Sozialistischen Monatshefte und die imperialistische Konzeption eines Kontinentaleuropas', *Zeitschrift für Geschichte*, 23 (1975)

Fröhlich, M., *Imperialismus. Deutsche Kolonial- und Weltpolitik 1880–1914* (Munich, 1994) and 2nd edn (Munich, 1997)

——, *Von Konfrontation zur Koexistenz. Die deutsch–englischen Kolonialbeziehungen zwischen 1884 und 1914* (Bochum, 1990)

Select Bibliography

Gasser, A., *Deutschlands Entschluss zum Präventivkrieg 1913/ 1914* (Basel, 1968)

——, 'Der deutsche Hegemonialkrieg von 1914', in I. Geiss and B.-J. Wendt (eds), *Deutschland in der Weltkrieg des 19. und 20. Jahrhunderts* (Düsseldorf, 1973)

——, *Preussischer Militärgeist und Kriegsentfesselung 1914: Drei Studien zum Ausbruch des Ersten Weltkrieges* (Basel, 1985)

Geinitz, C., *Kriegsfurcht und Kampfbereitschaft. Das Augusterlebnis in Freiburg* (Essen, 1998)

Geiss, I. (ed.), *July 1914: The Outbreak of the First World War* (London, 1967)

——, *German Foreign Policy, 1871-1914* (London, 1976)

——, *Der lange Weg in die Katastrophe. Die Vorgeschichte des Ersten Weltkrieges, 1815-1914* (Munich, 1990)

——, 'Deutschland und Österreich-Ungarn beim Kriegsausbruch 1914. Eine machthistorische Analyse', in M. Gehler et al. (eds), *Ungleiche Partner? Österreich und Deutschland in ihrer gegenseitigen Wahrnehmung* (Stuttgart, 1996)

——, *The Question of German Unification, 1806-1996* (London, 1997)

Geyer, M., *Deutsche Rüstungspolitik 1860-1980* (Frankfurt a. M., 1984)

Gollwitzer, H. *Die Gelbe Gefahr. Geschichte eines Schlagwortes* (Göttingen, 1962)

——, *Die Geschichte des weltpolitischen Denkens*, 2 vols. (Göttingen, 1972-82)

Goltermann, S., *Körper der Nation: Habitusformierung und die Politik des Turnens, 1860-1890* (Göttingen, 1998)

Goodspeed, D.J., *Ludendorff: Soldier, Dictator, Revolutionary* (London, 1966)

Grenville, J.A.S., 'Imperial Germany and Britain: From Cooperation to War', in A. Birke (ed.), *Das gestörte Gleichgewicht. Deutschland als Problem britischer Sicherheit im 19. und 20. Jahrhundert* (Munich, 1990)

Groh, D., '"Je eher desto besser!" Innenpolitische Faktoren für die Präventivkriegsbereitschaft des Deutschen Reiches 1913/14', *Politische Vierteljahresschriften*, 13 (1972)

——, *Russland im Blick Europas*, 2nd edn (Frankfurt a. M., 1988)

Groh, D. and P. Brandt, *'Vaterlandslose Gesellen': Sozialdemokratie und Nation, 1860-1990* (Munich, 1992)

Groote, W. von, 'Historische Vorbilder des Feldzuges 1914 im Westen', *Militärgeschichtlich Mitteilungen*, 1 (1990)

Gründer, H., *Geschichte der deutschen Kolonien* (Paderborn, 2000)

Grunewald, M. (ed.), *Der Europadiskurs in den deutschen Zeitschriften 1871–1914* (Berne, 1996)

Guenane, D. *Les Relations franco-allemandes et les affaires marocaines de 1901 à 1911* (Alger, 1975)

Gutsche, W. *Aufstieg und Fall eines kaiserlichen Reichskanzlers. Theobald von Bethmann Hollweg 1856–1921* (Berlin, 1973)

Hall, R.C., *The Balkan Wars, 1912–1913: Prelude to the First World War* (London, 2000)

Hamilton, R.F. and H.H. Herwig (eds), *The Origins of World War I* (Cambridge, 2003)

Hammer, K., *Deutsche Kriegstheologie 1870–1918* (Munich, 1971)

Hannigan, R.E., 'Continentalism and Mitteleuropa as Points of Departure for a Comparison of American and German Foreign Relations in the Early Twentieth Century', in H. J. Schröder (ed.), *Confrontation and Cooperation: Germany and the United States in the Era of World War I, 1900–1925* (Oxford, 1993)

Hecker, G., *Walther Rathenau und sein Verhältnis zu Militär und Krieg* (Boppard, 1983)

Herrmann, D.G., *The Arming of Europe and the Making of the First World War* (Princeton, 1996)

Herwig, H.H., *The German Naval Officer Corps: A Social and Political History, 1890–1918* (Oxford, 1968)

—, 'Imperial Germany', in E.R. May (ed.), *Knowing One's Enemies: Intelligence Assessment before the Two World Wars* (Princeton, 1984)

—, 'From Tirpitz Plan to Schlieffen Plan: Some Observations on German Military Planning', *Journal of Strategic Studies*, 9 (1986)

—, *'Luxury' Fleet: The Imperial German Navy, 1888–1918* (London, 1991)

—, (ed.), *The Outbreak of World War I: Causes and Responsibilities*, 5th edn (Lexington, Mass., 1991)

—, *The First World War: Germany and Austria–Hungary, 1914–1918* (London, 1997)

Herzfeld, H., *Der erste Weltkrieg* (Munich, 1968)

Hewitson, M., 'German Public Opinion and the Question of Industrial Modernity: Wilhelmine Depictions of the French Economy', *European Review of History*, 7 (2000)

——, 'Germany and France before the First World War: A Reassessment of Wilhelmine Foreign Policy', *English Historical Review*, 115 (2000)

——, 'Nation and Nationalismus: Representation and National Identity in Imperial Germany', in M. Fulbrook and M.W. Swales (eds), *Representing the German Nation: History and Identity in Twentieth-Century Germany* (Manchester, 2000)

——, *National Identity and Political Thought in Germany: Wilhelmine Depictions of the French Third Republic, 1890–1914* (Oxford, 2000)

——, 'Images of the Enemy: German Depictions of the French Military, 1890–1914', *War in History*, 11 (2004)

Hildebrand, K., 'Julikrise 1914: Das europäische Sicherheitsdilemma. Betrachtungen über den Ausbruch des Ersten Weltkrieges', *Geschichte in Wissenschaft und Unterricht*, 7 (1985)

——, *Deutsche Aussenpolitik 1871–1918* (Munich, 1989)

——, 'Saturiertheit und Prestige. Das deutsche Reich als Staat im Staatensystem 1871–1918', *Geschichte in Wissenschaft und Unterricht*, 4 (1989)

——, 'Reich-Grossmacht-Nation: Betrachtungen zur Geschichte der deutschen Aussenpolitik 1871–1945', *Historische Zeitschrift*, 259 (1994)

——, *Das vergangene Reich. Deutsche Aussenpolitik von Bismarck bis Hitler 1871–1945* (Stuttgart, 1995)

Hillgruber, A., 'Kurt Riezlers Theorie des "kalkulierten Risikos" und Bethmann Hollwegs politische Konzeption in der Julikrise 1914', *Historische Zeitschrift*, 202 (1966)

——, 'Deutsche Russland-Politik 1871–1918', *Saeculum*, 27 (1976)

——, *Germany and the Two World Wars* (Cambridge, Mass., 1981)

Hinsley, F.H., *Power and the Pursuit of Peace: Theory and Practice in the History of Relations between States* (Cambridge, 1963)

Hobson, R., *Imperialism at Sea: Naval Strategic Thought, the Ideology of Sea Power and the Tirpitz Plan, 1875–1914* (Boston, 2002)

Hoffmann, S.-L., 'Sakraler Monumentalismus um 1900: Das Leipziger Völkerschlachtdenkmal', in R. Koselleck and M. Jeismann (eds), *Der politische Totenkult. Kriegerdenkmäler in der Moderne* (Munich, 1994)

Holl, J., *Pazifismus in Deutschland* (Frankfurt a. M., 1988)

Holl, J. and G. List (eds), *Liberalismus und imperialistischer Staat* (Göttingen, 1975)

Select Bibliography

Holmes, T.M., 'The Reluctant March on Paris: A Reply to Terence Zuber's "The Schlieffen Plan Reconsidered"', *War in History*, 8 (2001)

Hölzle, E., *Die Selbstentmachtung Europas. Das Experiment des Friedens vor und im Ersten Weltkrieg* (Göttingen, 1975)

Howard, M., 'Men against Fire: Expectations of War in 1914', in S. Miller et al. (eds), *Military Strategy and the Origins of the First World War* (Princeton, 1991)

Hubatsch, W., *Der Admiralstab und die obersten Marinebehörden in Deutschland 1848-1945* (Frankfurt a. M., 1958)

Hughes, M., *Nationalism and Society: Germany, 1800-1945* (London, 1988)

Hünseler, W., 'Die irische Bürgerkriegsgefahr im Kalkül der deutschen Grossbritannienpolitik in der Julikrise 1914', *Militärgeschichtliche Mitteilungen*, 20 (1982)

Ingenlath, M., *Mentale Aufrüstung. Militarisierungstendenzen in Frankreich und Deutschland vor dem Ersten Weltkrieg* (Frankfurt a. M., 1998)

Jäger, W., *Historische Forschung und politische Kultur in Deutschland. Die Debatte 1914-1980 um den Ausbruch des Ersten Weltkrieg* (Göttingen, 1984)

James, H., *A German Identity, 1770-1990* (London, 1989)

Jarausch, K., 'The Illusion of Limited War: Chancellor Bethmann Hollweg's Calculated Risk, July 1914', *Central European History*, 2 (1969)

—, *The Enigmatic Chancellor: Bethmann Hollweg and the Hubris of Imperial Germany* (New Haven, 1973)

Jeismann, M., *Das Vaterland der Feinde* (Stuttgart, 1992)

John, H., *Das Reserveoffizierkorps im Deutschen Kaiserreich, 1890-1914. Ein sozialgeschichtlicher Beitrag zur Untersuchung der gesellschaftlichen Militarisierung im Wilhelminischen Deutschland* (Frankfurt a. M., 1981)

Joll, J., *The Origins of the First World War*, 2nd edn (London, 1992)

Jux, A., *Die Kriegsschrecken des Frühjahrs 1914 in der europäischen Presse* (Berlin, 1929)

Kaelble, H., 'Wahrnehmung der Industrialisierung: Die französische Gesellschaft im Bild der Deutschen zwischen 1891-1914', in W. Süß (ed.), *Übergänge: Zeitgeschichte zwischen Utopie und Machbarkeit* (Berlin, 1989)

Kaiser, D., 'Germany and the Origins of the First World War', *Journal of Modern History*, 55 (1983)

Kelly, A., *The Descent of Darwin: The Popularization of Darwinism in Germany, 1860–1914* (Chapel Hill, 1981)

——, 'The Franco-German War and Unification in German Schoolbooks', in W. Pape (ed.), *1870/71 – 1989/90: German Unifications and the Change of Literary Discourse* (Berlin, 1993)

Kennedy, P.M., (ed.), *The War Plans of the Great Powers, 1880–1914* (London, 1979)

——, *The Rise of the Anglo-German Antagonism 1860–1914* (London, 1980)

—— (ed.), *Grand Strategies in War and Peace* (New Haven, 1991)

Kessel, E., *Moltke* (Stuttgart, 1957)

Kielmannsegg, P. von, *Deutschland und der Erste Weltkrieg*, 2nd edn (Frankfurt a. M., 1980)

Kiessling, F., 'Österreich-Ungarn und die deutsch-englischen Détente-bemühungen 1912–1914', *Historisches Jahrbuch*, 116 (1996)

Kitchen, M., *The German Officer Corps, 1890–1914* (Oxford, 1968)

Koch, H.W., *Der Sozialdarwinismus. Seine Genese und sein Einfluss auf das imperialistische Denken* (Munich, 1973)

—— (ed.), *The Origins of the First World War: Great Power Rivalry and German War Aims* (London, 1972) and 2nd revised edn (London, 1984)

I. Koch, 'Das Russlandbild der deutschen Diplomatie in den Jahren von 1904 bis 1914' (Diss., Bonn, 1953)

Kopolew, L., 'Zunächst zur Waffenbrüderschaft', in M. Keller (ed.), *Russen und Russland aus deutscher Sicht*, vol. 3 (Munich, 1992)

——, 'Am Vorabend des grossen Krieges', in M. Keller (ed.), *Russen und Russland aus deutscher Sicht*, vol. 4 (Munich, 2000)

Kos, F.-J., *Die politischen und wirtschaftlichen Interessen Österreich-Ungarns und Deutschlands in Südosteuropa 1912/13. Die Adriahafen-, die Saloniki- und die Kavallafrage* (Vienna, 1996)

Koselleck, R. and M. Jeismann (eds), *Der politische Totenkult. Kriegerdenkmäle in der Moderne* (Munich, 1994)

Kripper, R., 'Formen literarischer Erinnerung an den Deutsch-Französischen Krieg von 1870/71', in H. Berding, K. Heller and W. Speitkamp (eds), *Krieg und Erinnerung. Fallstudien zum 19. und 20. Jahrhundert* (Göttingen, 2000)

Kronenbitter, G., 'Bundesgenossen? Zur militärpolitischen Kooperation zwischen Berlin und Wien 1912 bis 1914', in W. Bernecker and V. Dotterweich (eds), *Deutschland in den internationalen Beziehungen des 19. und 20. Jahrhunderts* (Munich, 1996)

——, 'Die Macht der Illusionen. Julikrise und Kriseausbruch 1914 aus der Sicht des deutschen Militärattachés in Wien', *Militärgeschichtliche Mitteilungen*, 57 (1998)

——, *'Krieg in Frieden': Die Führung der K.u.K. Armee und die Grossmachtpolitik Österreich-Ungarns 1906–1914* (Munich, 2003)

Krumeich, G., 'Le déclin de la France dans la pensée politique et militaire allemande avant la première guerre mondiale', in J.-C. Allain (ed.), *La Moyenne puissance au XXe siècle* (Paris, 1988)

——, 'La puissance militaire française vue de l'Allemagne autour de 1900', in P. Milza and R. Poidevin (eds), *La Puissance française à la belle époque* (Brussels, 1992)

——, 'Vorstellungen vom Krieg vor 1914', in S. Neitzel (ed.), *1900: Zukunftsvisionen der Grossmächte* (Paderborn, 2002)

Kruse, W., 'Die Kriegsbegeisterung im Deutschen Reich zu Beginn des Ersten Weltkrieges: Entstehungszusammenhänge, Grenzen und ideologische Strukturen', in M. van der Linden und G. Mergner (eds), *Kriegsbegeisterung und mentale Kriegsvorbereitung: Interdisziplinäre Studien* (Berlin, 1991)

——, *Krieg und nationale Integration. Eine Neuinterpretation des sozialdemokratischen Burgfriedenschlusses 1914/1915* (Essen, 1993)

—— (ed.), *Eine Welt von Feinden. Der Grosse Krieg, 1914–1918* (Frankfurt a. M., 1997)

Lahme, F., *Deutsche Aussenpolitik 1890–1894. Von der Gleichgewichtspolitik Bismarcks zur Allianzstrategie Caprivis* (Göttingen, 1990)

Lambi, I.N., *The Navy and German Power Politics, 1862–1914* (Boston, 1984)

Langdon, J., *July 1914: The Long Debate, 1918–1990* (Oxford, 1991)

Langer, W., *Diplomacy of Imperialism* (New York, 1951)

Langewiesche, D., *Nation, Nationalismus, Nationalstaat in Deutschland und Europa* (Munich, 2000)

Langhorne, R., *The Collapse of the Concert of Europe: International Politics, 1890–1914* (London, 1981)

Latzel, K., *Vom Sterben im Krieg. Wandlungen in der Einstellung zum Soldatentod vom Siebenjährigen Krieg bis zum Zweiten Weltkrieg* (Warendorf, 1988)

Lauren, P.G., *Diplomats and Bureaucrats* (Stanford, 1976)

Leed, E.J., *No Man's Land: Combat and Identity in the First World War* (Cambridge, 1979)

Lemmermann, H., *Kriegserziehung im Kaiserreich. Studien zur politischen Funktion von Schule und Schulmusik 1890-1918*, 2 vols. (Bremen, 1984)

Lerman, K.A., *The Chancellor as Courtier: Bernhard von Bülow and the Governance of Germany, 1900-1909* (Cambridge, 1990)

—, 'Bismarck's Heir: Chancellor Bernhard von Bülow and the National Idea, 1890-1918', in J. Breuilly (ed.), *The State of Germany: The National Idea in the Making, Unmaking and Remaking of a Modern Nation-State* (London, 1992)

Linden, M. van der and G. Mergner (eds), *Kriegsbegeisterung und mentale Kriegsvorbereitung. Interdisziplinäre Studien* (Berlin, 1991)

Link, J. and W. Wülfung (eds), *Nationale Mythen und Symbole in der zweiten Hälfte des 19. Jahrhunderts. Strukturen und Funktionen nationaler Identität* (Stuttgart, 1991)

Löhr, H.C. 'Für den König von Preussen arbeiten? Die deutsch-französischen Beziehungen am Vorabend des Ersten Weltkrieges', *Francia*, 23 (1996)

Lowe, J., *The Great Powers, Imperialism and the German Problem, 1865-1925* (London, 1994)

Mai, G., '"Verteidigungskrieg" und "Volksgemeinschaft". Staatliche Selbstbehauptung, nationale Solidarität und soziale Befreiung in Deutschland in der Zeit des Ersten Weltkrieges 1900-1925', in W. Michalka (ed.), *Der Erste Weltkrieg* (Munich, 1994)

Martell, G., *The Origins of the First World War*, 2nd edn (London, 1996)

Maser, W., *Hindenburg. Eine politische Biographie* (Rastatt, 1989)

Massie, R.K., *Dreadnought: Britain, Germany and the Coming of the Great War* (New York, 1991)

Maurer, J.H., *The Outbreak of the First World War: Strategic Planning, Crisis Decision-Making and Deterrence and Failure* (Westport, Conn., 1995)

McClelland, C.E., *The German Historians and England* (Cambridge, 1971)

Meier-Welcker, H. and W. von Groote (eds), *Handbuch zur deutschen Militärgeschichte, 1648-1939*, vol. 5 (Munich, 1979)

Meisner, H.O., *Militärattachés und Militärbevollmächtige in Preussen und im Deutschen Reich* (Berlin, 1957)

Menning, R.R., 'The Collapse of "Global Diplomacy": Germany's Descent into Isolation, 1906-1909' (Diss., Brown University, 1986)

Mertens, L., 'Das Privileg des Einjährig-Freiwilligen Militärdienstes im Kaiserreich und seine gesellschaftliche Bedeutung', *Militärgeschichtliche Mitteilungen*, 39 (1986)

Messerschmidt, M., *Militär und Politik in der Bismarckzeit und im Wilhelminischen Deutschland* (Darmstadt, 1975)

——, *Militärgeschichtliche Aspekte der Entwicklung des deutschen Nationalstaates* (Düsseldorf, 1988)

Meyer, H.C., *Mitteleuropa in German Thought and Action, 1815–1945* (The Hague, 1955)

Meyer, T., *'Endich eine Tat, eine befreiende Tat . . .'. Alfred von Kirderlen-Wächters 'Panthersprung nach Agadir' unter dem Druck der öffentlichen Meinung* (Husum, 1996)

Michalka, W. (ed.), *Der Erste Weltkrieg. Wirkung, Wahrnehmung, Analyse* (Munich, 1994)

Michels, E., *Deutsche in der Fremdenlegion 1870–1945. Mythen und Realitäten* (Paderborn, 1999)

Miller, S. et al. (eds), *Military Strategy and the Origins of the First World War* (Princeton, 1991)

Mogk, W., *Paul Rohrbach und das 'Grössere Deutschland'. Ethischer Imperialismus im Wilhelminischen Zeitalter* (Munich, 1972)

Mombauer, A., 'A Reluctant Military Leader? Helmuth von Moltke and the July Crisis of 1914', *War in History*, 6 (1999)

——, *Helmuth von Moltke and the Origins of the First World War* (Cambridge, 2001)

——, *The Origins of the First World War: Controversies and Consensus* (London, 2002)

Mommsen, W.J., 'The Topos of Inevitable War in Germany in the Decade before 1914', in V.R. Berghahn and M. Kitchen (eds), *Germany in the Age of Total War* (London, 1981)

——, *Grossmachtstellung und Weltpolitik, 1870–1914: Die Aussenpolitik des Deutschen Reiches* (Frankfurt a. M., 1993)

——, 'Die Mitteleuropaidee und die Mitteleuropaplanungen im Deutschen Reich vor und während des Ersten Weltkriegs', in R.G. Plaschka (ed.), *Mitteleuropa-Konzeptionen in der ersten Hälfte des 20. Jahrhunderts* (Vienna, 1995)

——, *Imperial Germany* (London, 1995)

Moncure, J., *Forging the King's Sword: Military Education between Tradition and Modernization, 1871–1918* (New York, 1993)

Moritz, A., *Das Problem des Präventivkrieges in der deutschen Politik während der I. Marokkokrise* (Bern, 1974)

Mosse, G., *Gefallen für das Vaterland. Nationales Heldentum und namenloses Sterben* (Stuttgart, 1993)

Muenkler, H., *Gewalt und Ordnung. Das Bild des Krieges im politischen Denken* (Frankfurt, 1992)

Müller, C., 'Anmerkungen zur Entwicklung von Kriegsbild und operativ-strategischem Szenario im preussisch-deutschen Heer vor dem Ersten Weltkrieg', *Militärgeschichtliche Mitteilungen*, 57 (1998)

Müller, H., 'Die deutsche Arbeiterklasse und die Sedanfeiern', *Zeitschrift für die Geschichtswissenschaft*, 17 (1969)

Neitzel, S., *Weltmacht oder Untergang. Die Weltreichslehre im Zeitalter des Imperialismus* (Paderborn, 2000)

——, *Kriegsausbruch. Deutschlands Weg in die Katastrophe 1900–1914* (Munich, 2002)

—— (ed.), *1900: Zukunftsvisionen der Grossmächte* (Paderborn, 2002)

Nipperdey, T., 'Nationalidee und Nationaldenkmal in Deutschland im 19. Jahrhundert', in *Gesellschaft, Kultur, Theorie* (Göttingen, 1976)

Offer, A., 'Going to War in 1914: A Matter of Honour?', *Politics and Society*, 23 (1995)

Oncken, E., *Panthersprung nach Agadir. Die deutsche Politik während der Zweiten Marokkokrise* (Düsseldorf, 1981)

Ostertag, H., *Bildung, Ausbildung und Erziehung des Offizierkorps im deutschen Kaiserreich 1871 bis 1918: Eliteideal, Anspruch und Wirklichkeit* (Frankfurt a. M., 1990)

Paddock, T.R.E., 'German Perceptions of Russia before the First World War' (Diss., Berkeley, 1994)

——, 'Still Stuck at Sevastopol: The Depiction of Russia during the Russo-Japanese War and the Beginning of the First World War in the German Press', *German History*, 16 (1998)

——, 'Deutsche Historiker als Politiker', in M. Keller (ed.), *Russen und Russland aus deutscher Sicht*, vol. 4 (Munich, 2000)

Paret, P. (ed.), *Makers of Modern Strategy from Machiavelli to the Nuclear Age* (Oxford, 1994)

Peters, M., *Der Alldeutsche Verband am Vorabend des Ersten Weltkrieges, 1908–1914* (Frankfurt a. M., 1992)

Pogge von Strandmann, H., 'Staatsstreichpläne, Alldeutsche und Bethmann Hollweg', in H. Pogge and I. Geiss (eds), *Die Erforderlichkeit des Unmöglichen. Deutschland am Vorabend des Ersten Weltkrieges* (Frankfurt a. M., 1965)

Select Bibliography

—, 'Nationale Verbände zwischen Weltpolitik und Kolonialpolitik', in H. Schottelius and W. Deist (eds), *Marine und Marinepolitik im kaiserlichen Deutschland 1871–1914* (Düsseldorf, 1972)

Poidevin, R., *Les Relations économiques et financières entre la France et l'Allemagne de 1898 à 1914* (Paris, 1969)

Pommerin, R., *Der Kaiser und Amerika. Die USA in der Politik der Reichsleitung 1890–1917* (Cologne, 1986)

Rassow, P., 'Schlieffen und Holstein', *Historische Zeitschrift*, 173 (1952)

Rauh, M., 'Die "Deutsche Frage" vor 1914: Weltmachtstreben und Obrigkeitsstaat?', in J. Becker and A. Hillgruber (eds), *Die Deutsche Frage im 19. und 20. Jahrhundert* (Munich, 1983)

—, 'Die britisch-russische Militärkonvention von 1914 und der Ausbruch des Ersten Weltkrieges', *Militärgeschichtliche Mitteilungen*, 41 (1987)

Raulff, H., *Zwischen Machtpolitik und Imperialismus. Die deutsche Frankreichpolitik 1904–1905* (Düsseldorf, 1976)

Reulecke, J., 'Der Erste Weltkrieg und die Arbeiterschaft im rheinisch-westfälischen Industriegebiet', in *Arbeiterbewegung an Rhein und Ruhr* (Wuppertal, 1974)

Rich, N., *Friedrich von Holstein: Politics and Diplomacy in the Era of Bismarck and Wilhelm II*, 2 vols (Cambridge, 1965)

Riesenberger, D., *Geschichte der Friedensbewegung in Deutschland. Von den Anfängen bis 1933* (Göttingen, 1985)

Ritter, G., *Staatskunst und Kriegshandwerk. Das Problem des 'Militarismus' in Deutschland*, 4 vols, (Munich, 1954–68)

—, 'Die Zusammenarbeit der Generalstäbe Deutschlands und Österreich-Ungarns vor dem ersten Weltkrieg', in W. Berges and C. Hinrichs (eds), *Zur Geschichte der Demokratie* (Berlin, 1958)

—, *The Schlieffen Plan: Critique of a Myth* (London, 1958)

—, 'Der Anteil der Militärs an der Kriegskatastrophe von 1914', *Historische Zeitschrift*, 193 (1961)

Rogge, H., *Holstein und Harden. Politisch-publizistisches Zusammenspiel zweier Aussenseiter des wilhelminischen Reiches* (Munich, 1959)

Röhl, J.C.G., 'Admiral von Müller and the Approach of War, 1911–1914', *Historical Journal*, 12 (1969)

— (ed.), *From Bismarck to Hitler: The Problem of Continuity in German History* (London, 1970)

—, (ed.), *1914: Delusion or Design?* (London, 1973)

——, 'An der Schwelle zum Weltkrieg: Eine Dokumentation über den "Kriegsrat" vom 8. Dezember 1912', *Militärgeschichtliche Mitteilungen*, 21 (1977)

——, 'Die Generalprobe. Zur Geschichte und Bedeutung des "Kriegsrates" vom 8. Dezember 1912', in D. Stegmann, B.-J. Wendt and P.-C. Witt (eds), *Industrielle Gesellschaft und politisches System. Beiträge zur politischen Sozialgeschichte* (Bonn, 1978)

——, 'Vorsätzlicher Krieg? Die Ziele der deutschen Politik im Juli 1914', in W. Michalka (ed.), *Der Erste Weltkrieg* (Munich, 1994)

——, *The Kaiser and his Court* (London, 1995)

Rohrkrämer, T., *Der Militarismus der 'kleinen Leute'. Die Kriegervereine im Deutschen Kaiserreich, 1871–1914* (Munich, 1990)

Rohahn, J., 'Arbeiterbewegung und Kriegsbegeisterung: Die deutsche Sozialdemokratie, 1870–1914', in M. van der Linden and G. Mergner (eds), *Kriegsbegeisterung und mentale Kriegsvorbereitung: Interdisziplinäre Studien* (Berlin, 1991)

Ropponen, R., *Italien als Verbündeter. Die Einstellung der politischen und militärischen Führung Deutschlands und Österreich-Ungarns zu Italien von der Niederlage von Adua 1896 bis zum Ausbruch des Weltkrieges 1914* (Helsinki, 1986)

——, *Die russische Gefahr. Das Verhalten der öffentlichen Meinung Deutschlands und Österreich-Ungarns gegenüber der Aussenpolitik Russlands in der Zeit zwischen dem Frieden von Portsmouth und dem Ausbruch des Ersten Weltkrieges* (Helsinki, 1976)

Rosenberger, B., *Zeitungen als Kriegstreiber? Die Rolle der Presse im Vorfeld des Ersten Weltkrieges* (Cologne, 1998)

Rothenberg, G.E., 'Moltke, Schlieffen and the Doctrine of Strategic Envelopment', in P. Paret (ed.), *Makers of Modern Strategy from Machiavelli to the Nuclear Age* (Oxford, 1986)

Rumschöttel, H., *Das bayerische Offizierkorps 1866–1914* (Berlin, 1973)

Salewski, M., *Tirpitz. Aufstieg, Macht, Scheitern* (Göttingen, 1979)

——, 'Moltke, Schlieffen und die Eisenbahn', in R.G. Foerster (ed.), *Generalfeldmarschall von Moltke* (Munich, 1991)

Samuels, M., 'The Reality of Cannae', *Militärgeschichtliche Mitteilungen*, (1990)

——, *Command or Control? Command, Training and Tactics in the British and German Armies, 1888–1918* (London, 1995)

Saul, K., 'Der Kampf um die Jugend zwischen Volksschule und Kaserne. Ein Beitrag zur "Jugendpflege" im Wilhelminischen Reich 1890–1914', *Militärgeschichtlich Mitteilungen*, 9 (1971)

Select Bibliography

Scheer, F.-K., *Die Deutsche Friedensgesellschaft 1892–1933. Organisation, Ideologie, politische Ziele* (Frankfurt a. M., 1983)

Schenk, W., *Die deutsch–englische Rivalität vor dem Ersten Weltkrieg in der Sicht deutscher Historiker* (Aarau, 1967)

Schieder, T., *Nationalismus und Nationalstaat* (Göttingen, 1991)

Schieder, W. (ed.), *Erster Weltkrieg. Ursachen, Entstehung und Kriegsziele* (Cologne, 1975)

Schmidt, C., 'Ein deutscher Slawophil? August von Haxthausen und die Wiederentdeckung der russischen Bauerngemeinde 1843/44', in M. Keller (ed.), *Russen und Russland*, vol. 3 (Munich, 1992)

Schmidt-Richberg, W., *Die Generalstäbe in Deutschland 1871–1945. Aufgaben in der Armee und Stellung im Staate* (Stuttgart, 1962)

Schneider, U., 'Einheit oder Einigkeit: Der Sedantag im Kaiserreich', in S. Behrenbeck and A. Nützenadel (eds), *Inszenierungen des Nationalstaats. Politische Feiern in Italien und Deutschland seit 1860/71* (Cologne, 2000)

Schöllgen, G. 'Griff nach der Weltmacht? 25 Jahre Fischer-Kontroverse', *Historisches Jahrbuch*, 106 (1986)

——, 'Die Grossmacht als Weltmacht. Idee, Wirklichkeit und Perzeption Deutscher "Weltpolitik" im Zeitalter des Imperialismus', *Historische Zeitschrift*, 248 (1989)

—— (ed.), *Escape into War? The Foreign Policy of Imperial Germany* (Oxford, 1990)

——, *Das Zeitalter des Imperialismus*, 2nd edn (Munich, 1991)

——, 'Kriegsgefahr und Krisenmanagement vor 1914: Zur Aussenpolitik des kaiserlichen Deutschlands', *Historische Zeitschrift*, 267 (1998)

——, *Imperialismus und Gleichgewicht. Deutschland, England udn die orientalische Frage 1871–1914* (Munich, 2000)

Schottelius, H. and W. Deist (eds), *Marine und Marinepolitik im kaiserlichen Deutschland 1871–1914* (Düsseldorf, 1972)

Schröder, H.-C., *Sozialismus und Imperialismus* (Bonn, 1975)

Schroeder, P.W., 'World War I as Galloping Gertie: A Reply to Joachim Remak', in H.W. Koch (ed.), *The Origins of the First World War: Great Power Rivalry and German War Aims* (London, 1972) and 2nd revised edn (London, 1984)

Schubert-Weller, C., 'Kein schöner Tod . . .' *Die Militarisierung der männlichen Jugend und ihr Einsatz im Ersten Weltkrieg 1890–1918* (Munich, 1998)

Schulte, B.-F., *Die deutsche Armee 1900–1914. Zwischen Beharren und Verändern* (Düsseldorf, 1977)

——, 'Zu der Krisenkonferenz vom 8. Dezember 1912 in Berlin', *Historisches Jahrbuch*, 102 (1982)

——, *Europäische Krise und Erster Weltkrieg. Beiträge zur Militärpolitik des Kaiserreichs 1871-1914* (Frankfurt a. M., 1983)

——, *Die Verfälschung der Riezler Tagebücher. Ein Beitrag zur Wissenschaftsgeschichte der 50er und 60er Jahre* (Frankfurt a. M., 1985)

Schüssler, W., *Weltmachtstreben und Flottenbau* (Witten, 1956)

Schwarz, K.-D., *Weltkrieg und Revolution in Nürnberg* (Stuttgart, 1971)

Schwarzmüller, T., *Zwischen Kaiser und 'Führer'. Generalfeldmarschall August von Mackensen* (Paderborn, 1995)

Seligmann, M.S., 'Germany and the Origins of the First World War in the Eyes of the American Diplomatic Establishment', *German History*, 15 (1997)

——, 'A View from Berlin: Colonel Frederick Trench and the Development of British Perceptions of German Aggressive Intent, 1906-1910', *Journal of Strategic Studies*, 23 (2000)

Showalter, D.E., 'The Eastern Front and German Military Planning, 1871-1914: Some Observations', *East European Quarterly*, 15 (1981)

——, 'German Grand Strategy: A Contradiction in Terms?', *Militärgeschichtliche Mitteilungen*, 48 (1990)

Sieburg, H.-O., *Deutschland und Frankreich in der Geschichtsschreibung des neunzehnten Jahrhunderts*, 2 vols. (Wiesbaden, 1954-58)

Smith, H.W., *German Nationalism and Religious Conflict* (Princeton, 1995)

Smith, W.D., *The Ideological Origins of Nazi Imperialism* (Oxford, 1986)

Snyder, J., *The Ideology of the Offensive: Military Decision-Making and the Disasters of 1914* (Ithaca, 1984)

Sösemann, B., 'Die Tagebücher Kurt Riezlers: Untersuchungen zu ihrer Echtheit und Edition', *Historische Zeitschrift*, 236 (1983)

——, 'Die Bereitschaft zum Krieg. Sarajevo 1914', in A. Demandt (ed.), *Das Attentat in der Geschichte* (Cologne, 2000)

Stahl, F.-C., 'Preussische Armee und Reichsheer 1871-1914', in O. Hauser (ed.), *Zur Problematik 'Preussen und das Reich'* (Cologne, 1984)

Stargardt, N., *The German Idea of Militarism: Radical and Socialist Critics, 1866-1914* (Cambridge, 1994)

Steinberg, J., *Yesterday's Deterrent: Tirpitz and the Birth of the German Battle Fleet* (London, 1965)

——, 'The Copenhagen Complex', *Journal of Contemporary History*, 1 (1966)

——, 'Germany and the Russo-Japanese War', *American Historical Review*, 75 (1970)

——, 'Diplomatie als Wille und Vorstellung. Die Berliner Mission Lord Haldanes im Februar 1912', in H. Schottelius and W. Deist (eds), *Marine und Marinepolitik im kaiserlichen Deutschland 1871–1914* (Düsseldorf, 1972)

Stengers, J., 'Guillaume II et le Roi Albert à Potsdam en novembre 1913', *Bulletin de la classe des lettres et des sciences morales et politiques*, 7–12 (1993)

Stern, F., *Bethmann Hollweg und der Krieg. Die Grenzen der Verantwortung* (Tübingen, 1988)

Stevenson, D., *The First World War and International Politics* (Oxford, 1988)

——, *Armaments and the Coming of War: Europe, 1904–1914* (Oxford, 1996)

——, *The Outbreak of the First World War: 1914 in Perspective* (London, 1997)

Stöcker, M., *'Augusterlebnis 1914' in Darmstadt. Legende und Wirklichkeit* (Darmstadt, 1994)

Stolberg-Wernigerode, O. zu, *Die unentschiedene Generation. Deutschlands konservative Führungsschichten am Vorabend des Ersten Weltkrieges* (Munich, 1968)

Stone, N., 'Moltke-Conrad: Relations between the Austro-Hungarian and German General Staffs, 1909–1914', *Historical Journal*, 9 (1966)

Stoncmann, M.R., 'Bürgerliche und adlige Krieger: Zum Verhältnis zwischen Herkunft und Berufskultur im wilhelminischen Armee-Offizierkorps', in H. Reif (ed.), *Bürgertum und Adel im 19. und 20. Jahrhundert* (Berlin, 2000)

Storz, D., *Kriegsbild und Rüstung vor 1914. Europäische Landstreitkräfte vor dem Ersten Weltkrieg* (Berlin, 1992)

Strachan, H., *The First World War*, vol. 1 (Oxford, 2001)

Stromberg, R.N., *Redemption by War: The Intellectuals and 1914* (Lawrence, 1982)

Tannenbaum, E.A., *1900. Die Generation vor dem Grossen Krieg* (Frankfurt, 1978)

Theiner, P., *Sozialer Liberalismus und deutsche Weltpolitik. Friedrich Naumann in Wilhelminischen Deutschland 1860–1919* (Baden-Baden, 1983)

— '"Mitteleuropa"-Pläne im Wilhelminischen Deutschland' in H. Berding (ed.), *Wirtschaftliche und politische Integration in Europa im 19. und 20. Jahrhundert* (Göttingen, 1984)

Trommler, F., 'Inventing the Enemy: German–American Cultural Relations, 1900–1917', in H.-J. Schröder (ed.), *Confrontation and Cooperation: Germany and the United States in the Era of World War I* (Oxford, 1993)

Trumpener, U., 'War Premeditated?', *Central European History*, 9 (1976)

Tunstall, Jr, G.A., 'The Schlieffen Plan: The Diplomacy and Military Strategy of the Central Powers in the East, 1905–1914' (Diss., Rutgers, 1974)

—, *Planning for War against Russia and Serbia: Austro-Hungarian and German Military Strategies, 1871–1914* (New York, 1993)

Turner, L.C.F., 'The Role of the General Staffs in July 1914', *Austrian Journal of Politics and History*, 11 (1965)

—, 'The Significance of the Schlieffen Plan', *Austrian Journal of Politics and History*, 13 (1967)

—, *The Origins of the First World War* (London, 1970)

Uhle-Wettler, F., *Erich Ludendorff in seiner Zeit. Soldat, Stratege, Revolutionär* (Berg, 1995)

—, *Alfred von Tirpitz in seiner Zeit* (Hamburg, 1998)

Ullrich, V., *Die Hamburger Arbeiterbewegung vom Vorabend des Ersten Weltkrieges bis zur Revolution 1918/19*, 2 vols. (Hamburg, 1976)

—, 'Das deutsche Kalkül in der Julikrise 1914 und die Frage der englischen Neutralität', *Geschichte in Wissenschaft und Unterricht*, 334 (1983)

Ulrich, B., J. Vogel and B. Ziemann (eds), *Untertan in Uniform. Militär und Militarismus im Kaiserreich, 1871–1914* (Frankfurt a. M., 2001)

Vagts, A., *Deutschland und die Vereinigten Staaten in der Weltpolitik* (London, 1935)

Veltzke, V., 'Kaiser und Heer 1888–1914', *Forschungen zur Brandenburgisch-Preussischen Geschichte*, 7 (1997)

Venohr, W., *Ludendorff. Legende und Wirklichkeit* (Berlin, 1993)

Select Bibliography

Verhey, J., *The Spirit of 1914: Militarism, Myth and Mobilisation in Germany* (Cambridge, 2000)

Vietsch, E. von, *Bethmann Hollweg. Staatsmann zwischen Macht und Ethos* (Boppard, 1969)

Vogel, B., *Deutsche Russlandpolitik. Das Scheitern der deutschen Weltpolitik unter Bülow, 1900-1906* (Düsseldorf, 1973)

Vogel, J., *Nationen im Gleichschritt. Der Kult der 'Nation im Waffen' in Deutschland und Frankreich 1871-1914* (Göttingen, 1997)

—, 'Der "Folklorenmilitarismus" und seine zeitgenössische Kritik: Deutschland und Frankreich, 1871-1914', in W. Wette (ed.), *Militarismus in Deutschland 1871 bis 1945. Zeitgenössische Analysen und Kritik* (Münster, 1999)

Vogt, A., *Oberst Max Bauer. Generalstabsoffizier im Zwielicht, 1869-1929* (Osnabrück, 1974)

Voigt, G., *Russland in der deutschen Geschichtsschreibung, 1843-1945* (Berlin, 1994)

Vondung, K., *Die Apokalypse in Deutschland* (Munich, 1988)

Wallach, J.L., *Das Dogma der Vernichtungsschlacht: Die Lehren von Clausewitz und Schlieffen und ihre Wirkungen in zwei Weltkriegen* (Frankfurt a. M., 1967)

—, *Kriegstheorien. Ihre Entwicklung im 19. und 20. Jahrhundert* (Frankfurt a. M., 1972)

—, *Anatomie einer Militärhilfe. Die preussisch-deutschen Militärmissionen in der Türkei 1835-1919* (Düsseldorf, 1976)

—, 'Feldmarschall von Schlieffens Interpretation der Kriegslehre Moltkes d. Ä', in R.G. Foerster (ed.), *Generalfeldmarschall von Moltke. Bedentung und Wirkung* (Munich, 1991)

Wehler, H.-U., *Sozialdemokratie und Nationalstaat* (Würzburg, 1962)

—, *Nationalismus* (Munich, 2001)

Weindling, P., *Darwinism and Social Darwinism in Imperial Germany: The Contribution of the Cell Biologist Oscar Hertwig, 1849-1922* (New York, 1991)

Wernecke, K., *Der Wille zur Weltgeltung. Aussenpolitik und Öffentlichkeit im Kaiserreich am Vorabend des Ersten Weltkrieges*, 2nd edn (Düsseldorf, 1970)

Wette, W., *Kriegstheorien deutscher Sozialisten: Marx, Engels, Lassalle, Bernstein, Kautsky, Luxemburg. Ein Beitrag zur Friedensforschung* (Stuttgart, 1971)

— (ed.), *Der Krieg des kleinen Mannes. Eine Militärgeschichte von unten* (Munich, 1992)

— (ed.), *Militarismus in Deutschland 1871 bis 1945. Zeitgenössische Analysen und Kritik* (Münster, 1999)

Williamson, S.R., 'The Origins of World War I', *Journal of Interdisciplinary History*, 18 (1988)

Williamson, S. R. and P. Pastor (eds), *Essays on World War I: Origins and Prisoners of War* (New York, 1983)

Williamson, S. R. and R. Van Wyk (eds), *July 1914: Soldiers, Statesmen and the Coming of the Great War* (Boston, 2003)

Wilson, K., (ed.), *Decisions for War, 1914* (London, 1995)

Winzen, P., *Bülows Weltmachtkonzept. Untersuchungen zur Frühphase seiner Aussenpolitik, 1897–1901* (Boppard, 1977)

Wollstein, G., *Theobald von Bethmann Hollweg. Letzter Erbe Bismarcks, erstes Opfer der Dlochstosslegende* (Göttingen, 1995)

Young, H.F., *Prince Lichnowsky and the Great War* (Athens, Georgia, 1977)

Zechlin, E., *Krieg und Kriegsrisiko. Zur Deutschen Politik im Ersten Weltkrieg* (Düsseldorf, 1979)

Ziemann, B., *Front und Heimat. Ländliche Kriegserfahrungen im südlichen Bayern 1914–1923* (Essen, 1997)

Zmarzlik, H.-G., *Bethmann Hollweg als Reichskanzler 1909–1914. Studien zu Möglichkeiten und Grenzen seiner innerpolitischen Machtstellung* (Düsseldorf, 1957)

Zuber, T., 'The Schlieffen Plan Reconsidered', *War in History*, 6 (1999)

—, 'Terence Holmes Reinvents the Schlieffen Plan', *War in History*, 8 (2001)

—, *Inventing the Schlieffen Plan: German War Planning, 1871–1914* (Oxford, 2002)

Index

Index

Index

Index

Index

Index

Index

Index

Vogel, Jakob 87
Volk, das (nation or people) 45–6, 99
Volkskrieg 96
Völkerschlachtdenkmal 90, 93
Vollmar, Georg von 43, 102
Vorwärts 62, 64, 67, 104, 154, 188
Vossische Zeitung 71, 73, 75–8, 196

Wacht am Rhein 93, 103
Wagner, Adolph 51, 65
Wahre Jakob, Der 62
Waldersee, Georg von 121, 200–1
Walhalla 90
Wallach, Jehuda 123
Walloons 164
Wandel, Franz von 120
War Academy 124
'War Council' of 8 December 1912 4, 115, 119, 199
war literature 92–6,
War Ministry (Prussia) 113, 115–16, 120, 125, 127–9, 135, 137, 173, 201, 225
war scare 225
    of spring 1913 78
    of spring 1914 76
War-in-Sight crisis of 1875 119, 183
Warburg, Max 25–6, 29
'wars of independence' of the 1860s 90, 92
Washington, George 88
Weber, Alfred 151
Weber, Max 53, 150–1
Wedel, Botho von 203
Wehler, Hans-Ulrich 4, 10, 21, 39, 85, 90

Weimar Republic 120
Welcker, Theodor 51
Weltpolitik (world politics; see also imperialism) 12–13, 30, 48, 64, 145–59, 172, 174–5, 225, 227, 232
Wermuth, Adolf 27–8
Werner, Anton von 87–8
West Indies 66, 147
Westarp, Kunow von 99, 149
Westphalia, Treaty of 66
Wilhelm I 87, 90
Wilhelm II 24–5, 46, 56, 61, 88, 90–1, 115–17, 119, 128–9, 135, 146–7, 151, 154–5, 174, 178, 181, 184–6, 197–201, 204–6, 211, 226, 230–1
Wippich, Rolf-Harald 3, 228
Witte, Sergei 146
Württemberg envoy in Berlin 147
Woche, Die 62
Wolff, Theodor 25, 50, 69, 71, 104, 195, 203, 208–9
working classes 41, 103
'world empires' or 'world powers' 48, 63, 145–59 passim, 175, 225

'yellow peril' 146
Yorck von Wartenburg, Paul 86

Zabern incident 89
Zedlitz-Trütschler, Robert von 22
Zimmermann, Arthur 174, 178, 180, 197, 203, 205, 207, 217, 226, 231
Zuber, Terence 123
Zukunft, Die 196